The 1970s and its Legacies in India's Cinemas

This vibrant new collection brings together original research from across the humanities and social sciences that examines the legacies of the 1970s in India's cinemas, offering invaluable insights into this important period. The authors demonstrate that the historical processes underway in the 1970s are important even today, and can be deciphered in the aural and visual medium of Indian cinema. The book explores two central themes: first, popular cinema's role in constructing the decade's public culture; and second, the powerful and under-studied archive of the decade as present in India's popular cinemas even today.

This book is based on a special issue of *South Asian Popular Culture.*

Priya Joshi is Associate Professor of English and Founding Director of the New India Forum at Temple University, USA. She is author of *Bollywood's India: A Public Fantasy* (Columbia, 2014), a sequel to her prize-winning book, *In Another Country: Colonialism, Culture and the English Novel in India* (Columbia, 2002), in which she explored public culture and emerging modernities in South Asia.

Rajinder Dudrah is Senior Lecturer in Screen Studies at the University of Manchester, UK. He has researched and published widely in film, media and cultural studies in international journals. His books include, amongst others, *Bollywood Travels: Culture, Diaspora and Border Crossings in Popular Hindi Cinema* (Routledge, 2012), *Bhangra: Birmingham and Beyond* (2007), *Bollywood: Sociology Goes to the Movies* (2006), *The Bollywood Reader* (with Jigna Desai, 2008), and *Theorising World Cinema* (with Lucia Nagib and Chris Perriam, 2011).

The 1970s and its Legacies in India's Cinemas

Edited by
Priya Joshi and Rajinder Dudrah

Routledge
Taylor & Francis Group
LONDON AND NEW YORK

First published 2014
by Routledge
2 Park Square, Milton Park, Abingdon, Oxfordshire OX14 4RN

and by Routledge
711 Third Avenue, New York, NY 10017, USA

First issued in paperback 2015

Routledge is an imprint of the Taylor & Francis Group, an informa business

British Library Cataloguing in Publication Data
A catalogue record for this book is available from the British Library

ISBN 13: 978-1-138-94832-7 (pbk)
ISBN 13: 978-0-415-83658-6 (hbk)

Typeset in Times New Roman
by Taylor & Francis Books

Publisher's Note
The publisher accepts responsibility for any inconsistencies that may have arisen during the conversion of this book from journal articles to book chapters, namely the possible inclusion of journal terminology.

Contents

Citation Information vii
Notes on Contributors ix

Introduction

1. The 1970s and its legacies in India's cinemas
Priya Joshi and Rajinder Dudrah 1

The cinema of the 1970s

2. Cinema as family romance
Priya Joshi 8

3. 'Relationships which have no name': Family and sexuality in 1970s popular film
Ulka Anjaria 23

4. The affable young man: Civility, desire and the making of a middle-class cinema in the 1970s
Satish Poduval 36

5. The construction of 1970s femininity, or why Zeenat Aman sings the same song twice
Ajay Gehlawat 50

6. Ritual reverb: Two 'blockbuster' Hindi films
Philip Lutgendorf 62

7. The 1970s Tamil cinema and the post-classical turn
Swarnavel Eswaran Pillai 76

8. Aesthetic dislocations: A re-take on Malayalam cinema of the 1970s
Ratheesh Radhakrishnan 89

The legacies of the 1970s

9. The retro noughties: 1970s Hindi films in 2000s Bollywood cinema
Rajinder Dudrah 101

10. The afterlives of 1970s Hindi cinema
Sangita Gopal 120

11. Working Note: From ceiling fans to A/C and juice: Javed Akhtar in conversation with Priya Joshi
Priya Joshi 136

Index 141

Citation Information

The following chapters were originally published in *South Asian Popular Culture*, volume 10, issue 1 (April 2012). When citing material from this journal issue, please use the original page numbering for each article, as follows:

Chapter 2
Cinema as family romance
Priya Joshi
South Asian Popular Culture, volume 10, issue 1 (April 2012)
pp. 7–21

Chapter 3
'Relationships which have no name': Family and sexuality in 1970s popular film
Ulka Anjaria
South Asian Popular Culture, volume 10, issue 1 (April 2012)
pp. 23–35

Chapter 4
The affable young man: Civility, desire and the making of a middle-class cinema in the 1970s
Satish Poduval
South Asian Popular Culture, volume 10, issue 1 (April 2012)
pp. 37–50

Chapter 5
The construction of 1970s femininity, or why Zeenat Aman sings the same song twice
Ajay Gehlawat
South Asian Popular Culture, volume 10, issue 1 (April 2012)
pp. 51–62

Chapter 6
Ritual reverb: Two 'blockbuster' Hindi films
Philip Lutgendorf
South Asian Popular Culture, volume 10, issue 1 (April 2012)
pp. 63–76

Chapter 7
The 1970s Tamil cinema and the post-classical turn
Swarnavel Eswaran Pillai
South Asian Popular Culture, volume 10, issue 1 (April 2012)
pp. 77–89

Chapter 8
Aesthetic dislocations: A re-take on Malayalam cinema of the 1970s
Ratheesh Radhakrishnan
South Asian Popular Culture, volume 10, issue 1 (April 2012)
pp. 91–102

Chapter 11
Working Note: From ceiling fans to A/C and juice: Javed Akhtar in conversation with Priya Joshi
Priya Joshi
South Asian Popular Culture, volume 10, issue 1 (April 2012)
pp. 103–107

Please direct any queries you may have about the citations to clsuk.permissions@cengage.com

Notes on Contributors

Ulka Anjaria is Assistant Professor in the Department of English, Brandeis University, USA, and affiliated with the South Asian Studies Program. Her research interests include realism, the novel, narrative theory and film. She has published in *Novel: A Forum on Fiction*, *Economic and Political Weekly*, and edited collections on post-colonial literature. Professor Anjaria is the author of *Realism in the Twentieth-Century Indian Novel* (Cambridge, 2012).

Rajinder Dudrah is Senior Lecturer in Screen Studies at the University of Manchester, UK. He has researched and published widely in film, media and cultural studies in international journals. His books include, amongst others, *Bollywood Travels: Culture, Diaspora and Border Crossings in Popular Hindi Cinema* (2012), *Bhangra: Birmingham and Beyond* (2007), *Bollywood: Sociology Goes to the Movies* (2006), *The Bollywood Reader* (with Jigna Desai, 2008), and *Theorising World Cinema* (with Lucia Nagib and Chris Perriam, 2011).

Ajay Gehlawat is Assistant Professor of Theatre and Film at Sonoma State University, USA, and the author of *Reframing Bollywood* (2010). His most recent piece, on whiteness in Bollywood, appears in *TOPIA: Canadian Journal of Cultural Studies.*

Sangita Gopal is Associate Professor of Cinema Studies at the University of Oregon, USA. She is author of *Conjugations: Marriage and Form in New Bollywood Cinema* (Chicago, 2011) and co-editor of *Global Bollywood* (Minnesota, 2008). Her current project, "Women Make Movies: Between State and Capital," is on gender and the social network.

Priya Joshi is Associate Professor of English and Founding Director of the New India Forum at Temple University, USA. She is author of *Bollywood's India: A Public Fantasy* (Columbia, 2014), a sequel to her prize-winning book, *In Another Country: Colonialism, Culture and the English Novel in India* (Columbia, 2002), in which she explored public culture and emerging modernities in South Asia.

Philip Lutgendorf is Professor of Hindi and Modern Indian Studies and has taught at the University of Iowa, USA, since 1985. He regularly offers Hindi language classes as well as courses on written and oral narrative traditions of South Asia, including Indian film. His publications include studies of the performance of the Hindi Ramayana (*The Life of a Text*, 1991) and of the popular Hindu "monkey-god" Hanuman (*Hanuman's Tale, The Messages of a Divine Monkey*, 2007). He maintains a website devoted to Hindi popular cinema: www. uiowa.edu/~incinema.

Swarnavel Eswaran Pillai teaches film theory, history, and production at the Michigan State University, USA. His area of research includes documentaries, popular Hindi cinema and the history of Tamil cinema.

Satish Poduval, Associate Professor in Cultural Studies at the EFL University (Hyderabad), India, has contributed to the *Encyclopaedia of Indian Cinema* (1998), edited *Re-Figuring Culture* (2005), and is completing a monograph on the new political documentary film in India.

Ratheesh Radhakrishnan received a PhD from the Center for the Study of Culture and Society, Bangalore. He has been teaching at the Department of Humanities and Social Sciences at IIT Bombay.

Introduction
The 1970s and its legacies in India's cinemas

Priya Joshi and Rajinder Dudrah

The decade

The 1970s were a paradox in India. The global oil crisis, wars with China and Pakistan in the 1960s, and the Bangladesh War of 1971 augured a difficult start to the decade. Labor stoppages stalled an already sluggish economy; widespread corruption stalled redress; and massive shortages in food staples created misery even among the middle classes. By the time Prime Minister Indira Gandhi announced the country ungovernable and declared a state of Emergency on June 26, 1975, it was evident that Indian democracy had reached a nadir. Yet, during this period of political turmoil, economic stagnation, and civic despair, India's cinemas enjoyed a renaissance.

Hindi cinema in the 1970s encountered daring new talent in writing, directing, and acting. New scripts, new topoi, and new kinds of engagement with 'India' emerged in popular film that, in the estimation of some, have not been matched in any decade since. In Tamil cinema, new technologies and hardware released the studio's hold on stars and films, and a cinema characterized by location shooting and new talent was born. Graduates of the decade-old Film and Television Institute of India (FTII) dispersed throughout the country, infusing India's media culture with an expanded repertoire of technical and narrative impulses. Their innovations and a willingness to take risks over style and theme dramatically renewed the cinema in many parts of India and inaugurated debates about the 'popular' and the 'audience' that continue today. The state variously ignored, intervened, and censored the industry, alternately supporting its perceived reach with the development of the Film Finance Corporation and at other times actively undercutting cinema by supporting emerging media such as television.

Some argue that a parallel cinema arose at this moment, but it might equally be claimed that a politically engaged *popular* cinema, with roots in past decades, was consolidated at this moment; that the 1970s was a decade that saw a notably porous boundary between mainstream and parallel, art and popular. Stars, themes, and talent from one cinema easily crossed over to the other as the cases of Naseeruddin Shah, Shabana Azmi, or Smita Patil in Hindi or Kamal Haasan and Mani Ratnam in Tamil illustrate. Debates from the period underscore the cinema's awareness of its potential alongside its attention to the range of products intended to reach a diversity of audiences.

This collection of chapters begins by recognizing the paradox that a golden age of India's cinemas coincides with its most tarnished political moment. The volume's aims are captured in its title ('The 1970s and its Legacies in India's Cinemas'). The linked relationships between its keywords are outlined below and developed more fully in the following pages.

The keywords

Collectively and individually, the chapters in this volume study the 1970s's role in India's cinemas as they probe the relevance of defining a culture through the unit of a decade. Authors ask and try to answer what gets obscured and what extolled in privileging a ten-year unit for critical inquiry, attentive to the pitfalls and opportunities that such division incurs. This is the right time to investigate, from the perspective of the present moment, what occurred in the 1970s that *remains* important today. If the 1970s was a decade in crisis, for whom was it in crisis, and what opportunities might that putative crisis have enabled are questions this volume poses.

Part of the interest in the 1970s question is the long shadow that the decade has cast on India's many cinemas. Thus, the title's second keyword, 'legacies,' invites a reckoning of the extensive half life that the decade has had on the substance and style of much that has followed. Whereas legacies in a primary sense are bequests of will (thus, acts of *subjective* volition), legacies can also proceed *without* will, as when a subject dies intestate and a legacy arrives because of law or lineage. Chapters in this volume consider legacy as both what is willed as well as that which may have been "unwilled" or unintended but is nevertheless passed on. The chapters explore how the legacies of the 1970s are often inadvertent, occurring *despite* will and designs to propel history otherwise. In this regard, the chapters are specially sensitive to the inadvertent consequences and unexpected afterlife of the decade in the cinemas that followed it.

By design and preference, many of these chapters focus on 1970s blockbusters and the different registers that convey this status upon a film. Rather than limiting the volume, the broad selection by contributors makes clear that no single director, actor, or writer guaranteed the box office in the 1970s, nor does a single trope or theme monopolize the status. As these chapters adumbrate, the blockbusters of the decade spoke *of* very much *to* very many. Focusing on blockbusters as these articles do allows scholars to reflect on the decade's wide-ranging aspirations and preoccupations as they are addressed in its popular cinema. Collectively, the articles in this volume convey the range of this decade in both capturing and contesting the zeitgeist, and they invite future contributions to expand the frame.

The interdisciplinary contributions in this volume explore the double role of popular cinema in producing and archiving the many currents in India's history. They are premised on two major themes:

(1) popular cinema's role in fabricating the decade's public culture; and
(2) the powerful and understudied archive of the decade as present in India's popular cinemas.

This collection is an effort to provide a genealogy for film studies and for understanding modern India, as both discipline and nation undergo rapid transformation in the current moment. It is hoped that future volumes will continue to explore these questions as they are elaborated in other cinemas of India, notably Bengali, Telugu, and Kannada; the parallel and art cinemas; the documentary tradition, among others.

The legacies

The legacies of the 1970s on cinema remain palpable today. The parallel cinema, documentary and indie filmmaking, and film industries outside Bombay thrive because of talent and institutional initiatives originating in the 1970s. Likewise, the 'New Bollywood' cinema of the 1990s and beyond continues to reckon with political and social commitments made two decades earlier. The expansion of India's media culture that is so palpable today must likewise reckon with the dramatic expansion that occurred in that culture during the 1970s.

As Indira Gandhi went from Minister of Information and Broadcasting to Prime Minister in 1966, she carried an unerring understanding of the possibilities of the emerging media. Therefore, even as print and film were censored during the Emergency, television enjoyed an expansion. As Satish Poduval outlines in this volume, scriptwriters and directors in Bombay cinema such as Hrishikesh Mukherjee and Basu Chatterjee carried themes and preoccupations incubated in blockbuster 1970s Hindi films to Doordarshan television, and a widely popular 'middle-class' culture of TV serials was born that still thrives today. Mrs. Gandhi's mastery over the media had an ironic coda: her globally televised funeral in 1984 was choreographed in a style closely emulating the cinematic funeral of another Gandhi: the Mahatma, in Richard Attenborough's 1982 film. The flower-covered body, the hushed, Anglicized voices of admiring commentators, millions of white-clad mourners, funeral flames reflected in the faces of a fair-skinned telegenic family: the representation of both Gandhi funerals in film and 'fact' seem eerily to come from the same visual script. Media is the medium, and the origins of this confluence in India can be traced to the 1970s.

Recognizing the dominance of political life as the organizing topos of the decade, this collection takes a cue from Sudipta Kaviraj's suggestion that the 1970s may be more usefully conceived of not as the decade of the Emergency but as the decade of Indira Gandhi. In this context, the decade 'starts' with 1966 and Indira Gandhi's appointment as Prime Minister and concludes with her assassination in 1984. In this volume, thus, the 'decade' is closer to two, and the ebbs and flows of its political culture embody the waning optimism of the Nehruvian era, Mrs. Gandhi's muscular centrist consolidation, and the eventual fracturing of the Nehruvian compact. It would be tempting here to develop some of the political outcomes of this 'Decade of Indira Gandhi' into what followed it: thus, Punjab, Babri Masjid, Assam, the Sri Lankan civil war and its Indian spillover in Rajiv Gandhi's assassination, the Mumbai attacks of 1993, Kashmir, and so on. But that would redirect this volume to writing a political history of India.

The collection seeks, instead, to recover the cinema's history in (and of) a single decade, that has already been made into two. It regards popular cinema as a resource to expand and nuance an understanding of political history. Cinema, in this context, is one of many archives for the nation: literature in the form of novels, short stories, and poetry, formal and informal histories, journalism, painting, economics, legal history, even gossip and graffiti all variously archive the 1970s. Respectful of the findings that are beginning to emerge from these discursive domains, chapters in this collection draw upon them to nuance their readings of film. At the same time, their authors contend that the cinematic archive is a notably precious one. Fabricated by many who were not observers but participants *in* the moment (see Javed Akhtar's remarks in this volume), the cinematic archive from the 1970s contributes a 'response' to events as they were unfolding. Absent the reflection of time or the hindsight of history, the narrative archive thus presented is inchoate at moments, with multiple agents and agencies. Analysis can bring some order to this diversity, but too stringently applied, it can also ignore some of the most prominent (if diffuse) strands for others that are more resonant. Attentive to these pitfalls, the articles in this volume try to avoid them.

The chapters

The chapters in this collection recognize the prominence of the state as well as the nation. Satish Poduval and Priya Joshi outline the pressure placed upon the nation when the state was in crisis as it was during the Emergency. Poduval and Joshi argue, in different ways, that the blockbusters of the day reckon with this sense of crisis in two diametrically opposed ways: Joshi thematizes the prevalence of the Angry Young Man, while Poduval's pioneering chapter urges a long-delayed recognition of what he calls the decade's Affable Young Man, whose seductive tales of desire and consumption recall the cinema of the 1960s (by Raj Kapoor and Dev Anand), even as that cinema is refashioned in a group of massively popular films starring Amol Palekar. Affability, Poduval reveals, is a new kind of patriotism, much as anger also was: both interpellate the citizen into forms of action. If Anger urged collective action (as in *Deewaar*), it also documented the demise of that form of action with *Deewaar*'s depiction of the dispersal of collective labor (literally, in the narrative dispersal of the labor-organizer father). Poduval's chapter, thus, serves as a useful reminder that while Amitabh Bachchan's anger captured a certain structure of feeling in the 1970s, it equally obscured the urgency for individual purpose and middle-class advancement purveyed by the Affable Young Man in the Palekar hits of the period. Affability thus dispenses with confrontation as a form of critique, even as it refashions critique elsewhere and otherwise.

Much as Anger and Affability are rescripted and rewritten across the decade's narrative field, other themes and preoccupations likewise recur and get revised. In some fundamental sense, reviewing the decade in this volume illuminates both its daring narrative interventions as well as the repetitions and revisions to those interventions that are almost as revealing. Ajay Gehlawat persuasively reveals the revisions attending the dramatic *oeuvre* of a single actress such as Zeenat Aman; Ulka Anjaria notes the ways in which 'family' and 'melodrama' expose and obscure intimacies outside both; and Philip Lutgendorf reflects on the very different social purpose of diegetic ritual as depicted in *Jai Santoshi Maa* (1975) and its return in *Hum Aapke Hain Kaun?* (1994).

'Stories are not important,' averred Javed Akhtar of Hindi cinema during the Temple University workshop in which this volume was developed; 'it's how you depict them that matters.' In many ways, it is the cinema's resignification (Anjaria's useful term) of key themes and preoccupations across a body of works that both introduced critique in the form of novelty and then rendered it familiar and even acceptable. Songs and their picturization play a considerable role in this process of repetition: the aural and visual echoes help address and resolve complex issues without the 'logic' of discursive argument. Gehlawat's and Lutgendorf's very different analyses rest on this contention and reveal the work of song, dance, picturization, and poetry on preoccupations over gender, identity, and sexuality.

Swarnavel Pillai and Ratheesh Radhakrishnan help expand the volume's scope beyond the inevitable Bombay-centrism that might otherwise have befallen it. Their chapters invaluably illuminate the very different preoccupations and procedures attendant on two major centers of film production during the 1970s. In Tamil cinema, Pillai shows how the arrival of new hardware such as the Arriflex camera enabled location shooting. The departure from studios that this light-weight camera facilitated also entailed the departure *of* the studios as arbiters of the cinema. Pillai's research documents both the decline in the number of studios operating in Madras as the decade ended as well as a dramatic reduction in films produced by each of Madras's major studios. With the new hardware came experiments not just in lights and location, but also different themes, different forms of editing, and above all, new talent that the colossus M.G. Ramachandran (the actor, director, and producer known by his initials MGR who averaged almost 8 films a year for close to a quarter century), had hitherto kept at bay. One of the legacies of this move away from the classical period of Tamil cinema persists even today: the 1970s 'turn' allowed figures such as Kamal Haasan and Mani Ratnam to come to the fore, and their presence on the national stage today (they work in Tamil, Telugu, and Hindi cinemas), speaks of a far-reaching legacy that invites further elaboration and study.

Radhakrishnan's chapter provides the important reminder that many cinemas in India, as elsewhere, still require a history, however skeletal or contested. Writing such a history for Malayalam cinema could expose some of the major shortcomings that the frame of 'nation' imposes when it tries to understand the region. The preoccupations over aesthetic and style Radhakrishnan traces are consonant with a wider – possibly international – set of cinematic practices. Aesthetics in the Malayalam context are not interventions into the social as a nation-centered narrative might insist, but a set of innovations over form that are in dialogue with both spectator and the medium itself.

In chapters on the legacies of the 1970s, Rajinder Dudrah and Sangita Gopal take two productively divergent approaches on the decade even as both concur that the decade had a porous timeframe that spills beyond it. Dudrah explores the narrative legacies of the 1970s in popular Hindi cinema of the 2000s when the latter cinema repurposed the aesthetic preoccupations of the earlier decade. In A-list blockbusters as well as more indie-inflected hits, self-conscious references to the 1970s and its tropes are rescripted in order to underscore current industrial, economic, and social preoccupations. In Dudrah's provocative reading, the cinema of the 2000s is an ironic reinterpretation of the past, infused partly with nostalgia for it and partly with a suspicion of the new and current. The 'retro noughties' as Dudrah frames it is both an outlook on current cinema as well as a critical account of its genealogy.

In contrast to Dudrah's focus on narrative and aesthetic legacies of the 1970s, Sangita Gopal provides a snapshot of the industry during the 1970s. She reviews the range of practices extant in Hindi cinema during the decade and the many players invested in it, including the state, independent filmmakers, and the film press. She uncovers some of the central debates from the period with regard to questions of audience, genre, and self-reflexivity and shows how they continue to resonate in the present moment. For Gopal, the film product today, its modes of production and exhibition, its expanding media ecology, and its audiences resonate in kind, if not degree, with mutations occurring in form, distribution, and media during the 1970s. Hindi, Bengali, and Tamil cinemas today reflect on these transformations and in key ways locate their genealogy to the 1970s. Gopal's chapter is a reminder that 'New Bollywood' is more Bollywood than 'new,' recalling the decade that gave the Hindi cinema the current name, and possibly also its social purpose.

Conclusion

One of the unspoken themes across the chapters in this volume is pleasure. The focus on blockbusters was not just a matter of canny case selection. Authors chose these particular films because of the immense pleasure they once gave and *continue* to give their viewers. Particular blockbusters tell particular stories, many which are traced in the chapters that follow. But blockbusters also tell a general story in which cinema matters in significant and meaningful ways to very many viewers. It has become the scholar's job to uncover that significance, and the thriving field of Indian cinema studies has done so seriously and extensively. The many references in this collection detail the debt its authors have to these scholars.

As those invested in this field, this collection's authors believe that the practice and recovery of pleasure in its sometimes irrecoverable logics and obstreperous range ought to preserve if not amplify that pleasure. We sometimes find our own pleasures hard to fully articulate and analyze, and we recognize the same must be acknowledged for those of others. These chapters, therefore, take a cue from the decade of our study whose blockbusters so richly incorporated both pleasure and purpose. The analyses that follow are presented in a language and form that try to convey and affirm the pleasures of the cinemas of this decade even as they invite reflection on them from beyond the world of specialist and scholar.

Acknowledgments

This special issue was incubated at an international workshop at Temple University, Philadelphia, in April 2011 funded by Temple's Center for International Business Education and Research at the Fox School of Business, the Center for the Humanities, and the College of Liberal Arts Research Council. Our gratitude to Peter Logan, Arvind Phatak, and Kim Cahill for extensive personal and institutional support. Heartfelt thanks to all who presented papers at the workshop and to Kavita Daiya, Suvir Kaul, Sudipta Kaviraj, Amandeep Sandhu, and Amanda Weidman for their generous intellectual contributions. Javed Akhtar's participation at the event was invaluable. Daniel Ryan Morse, a scholar of media in his own right, provided matchless logistical and practical support for which the organizers and participants are deeply grateful.

Cinema as family romance

Priya Joshi

Temple University, Philadelphia, USA

This essay analyses the narratives and iconographies of India embedded in a trilogy of blockbuster Hindi films from the long 1970s: *Deewar* (1975), *Trishul* (1978), and *Shakti* (1982). These films represent some of the decade's aspirations as well as its repressions that together constitute its public fantasies. Their narratives provide access to the political unconscious of modern India revealing the profound anxieties that pervaded the public culture of the decade. The essay explores the extent to which the traumas of the decade were displaced on the family, and the crisis in political culture was recast in social terms as a Family Romance in popular Hindi film. It analyzes *Deewar*'s tensions at narrating and containing an incendiary critique of the decade, and it exposes the 'revisions' to this film's masterplot as they were rescripted in *Trishul* and *Shakti*. The essay concludes with proposing the social function of cinema as a Family Romance.

> Hindi films can be regarded as contemporary folklore. And a folk hero, in any period, in any decade, is a personification of the moral values of that decade; he reflects the collective fantasies of the time.
>
> – Javed Akhtar (qtd. in Kabir 72)

I. Introduction

This essay analyzes the narratives and iconographies of India embedded in a trilogy of blockbuster Hindi films from the long 1970s: *Deewar* (1975, d. Yash Chopra), *Trishul* (1978, d. Yash Chopra), and *Shakti* (1982, d. Ramesh Sippy). All three were scripted by Salim Khan and Javed Akhtar; all three cast Amitabh Bachchan as a character named Vijay, and all three mobilize the family as a topos around which the nation's imaginary is structured and on which its anxieties are projected. *Deewar* and *Trishul* were blockbusters; *Shakti* is regarded a film to rival Sippy's *Sholay* (1975), though it never quite achieved the latter film's outsize achievement at the box office where *Sholay* remains the #1 all-time top grosser adjusted for inflation (ibos.network.com).[1] These films represent some of the decade's aspirations as well as its repressions that together I call its public fantasies. Through a reading of these blockbusters, this essay explores the extent to which the traumas of the decade were displaced on the family and the crisis in political culture was recast in *social* terms as a Family Romance in popular Hindi film.

For reasons that will become evident shortly, films such as *Deewar* invert the nation's central political conflicts in terms of the family and reframe it around its most cherished social belief – namely, the sanctity of motherhood.[2] In this inversion, the oppositional culture of political life is represented as infecting private life as well, and both are revealed unstable – even combustible. Rather than resolving conflict, the mother is placed as the source and center of it both in political life (where she is symbol of the nation) and in private life (where she is represented, often in highly sentimental terms, as the center of the family).

The biological family and the symbolic nation-as-family become sites of mutual threat in 1970s Hindi cinema, each destabilizing the other in cinema's representation of the period. These narratives of popular cinema, I argue, provide access to the political unconscious of modern India in striking and contestatory ways revealing what the political theorist Michael Rogin in the context of Cold War US cinema identifies as the 'register of anxiety' that pervaded the public culture of the decade (Rogin 238). The nation's political unconscious, like that of human subjects, speaks in symbols in order to evade the strenuous repression of the nation's conscious, and cinema's use of formal symbolism renders it the medium most capable of expressing and evading the apparatus of repression especially characteristic in the decade of the Emergency.[3]

In a series of wildly popular blockbusters such as Salim-Javed's *Deewar-Trishul-Shakti* triptych, popular Hindi cinema imagined the social geography of India, addressed its problems, idealized their solutions, and – to borrow a phrase from Laura Mulvey – generally became the primal scene of many of independent India's modern mythologies.[4] Appearing a few months before the Emergency when the myth of the nation appeared to have devoured its young, *Deewar*'s manifest content initially appears conciliatory if not downright celebratory of the state. It is, after all, a story of a boy who is unjustly rendered homeless, arrives penniless in the metropolis, and nevertheless makes a home and a fortune for himself. When it is discovered that his wealth is the result of smuggling operations, the state comes down hard, and the man is shot by his younger brother, a righteous cop. Both subject and state get their moments of triumph, though in the end, it is the collective, in the form of the state, that prevails over the individual who is punished.

However, rather than restoring the nation's myth of opportunity and justice, *Deewar* exposes its collapse and uncovers a form of violence so grotesque that it is displaced onto the family. Here, the latent narrative is one of a mother who desires her son, commissions his murder when her unspeakable desire is brought to light, and a state that rewards her for it. In short, the film rescripts the Oedipal drama from Jocasta's point of view with her desires and agency at the center. In this script the victim is criminalized and the criminal rendered the victim. However, the ironies of this displacement are cued throughout the film, and *Deewar's* family violence on the child is widely understood to symbolize the state's upon its citizens. Uncovering some of these acts of displacement in *Deewar* and their revisions in *Trishul* and *Shakti* exposes both the social work that the cinema did *in* India and the social work it did *for* the nation.

An important vein of scholarship has posited popular Hindi cinema as a site that produces and reinforces the ideology of the state, a point developed in an influential study by Madhava Prasad who argues for 'cinema as an institution that is part of the continuing struggles within India over the form of the state' (Prasad 9). A host of books with 'nation' in their title or subtitle make similar claims that condense all possible 'Indias' under the term nation.[5] In contrast to these works that regard the 'nation' and 'state' as largely interchangeable, this study insists on distinguishing between the two formations that it regards as fundamentally different and even divergent.

The state refers to those political and administrative components of modern polity that have the power and authority to govern. The nation, in contrast, is the set of imaginative constructions that, ideally, are congruent with the enterprise of the state and underwrite its governance, but more commonly contest and correct the practices of the state. The nation, in this formulation, is both more and less than the state in key ways: it is the repository of ideals and ambitions – not all homogenous – that precede the formation of the state; it can create the state, but it also contests it, diverges from it, or coalesces into it on some issues and diverges from it over others. 'We have to labour and to work, and work hard, to give reality to our dreams,' urged Nehru during Independence, clarifying the difference between the two concepts at stake (Nehru 2). The state marks a 'reality' that is often compromised; the nation, its 'dreams' that are also possibly its nightmares.

In this act of collective dreaming, popular cinema plays a role that is both a revision of reality and a reclamation of its originary impulses. It neither fully represents the state nor the nation as the aforementioned scholars posit: rather, popular cinema in my reading is a contact zone *between* the two, at times corroborating and at others contesting the formation of both in the construction of an ever shifting narrative of 'India.' Popular cinema provides a space for engagement, enchantment, and possibly re-enchantment if not with the nation itself then with the stories that undergird all acts of collective fantasy of which the nation is but one example. At best, it is a third space that fabricates and filters the experience of politics and modernity for its viewers.

The essay proceeds in three main parts. It analyzes the dominance of the trope of the family to represent anxieties of the period; it then explores *Deewar*'s tensions at narrating and containing an incendiary critique of the decade; and it develops the 'revisions' to *Deewar*'s masterplot as they were re-scripted in *Trishul* and *Shakti*. The essay concludes with proposing the social function of cinema as a Family Romance.

II. Film, family, and family romance

The persistent use of the family as source and symbol of national tension is not new to *Deewar*. What is remarkable in *Deewar* is how the deadly national traumas of the 1970s are displaced almost wholesale upon the family which in turn is rendered patently evil in the film. The hitherto mythologized mother is a murderer; the crime she commits an infanticide; and the state a handmaiden in the cover-up. Rather than the family providing solace *from* the state, it provides solace *for* the state which escapes culpability for its crimes through the act of displacement.

Deewar's dystopian account of both family and nation had a rawness hitherto unseen in a commercially successful film. The story was too intense with its exposure of too many wrongs for its ending to be fully satisfying. And so the scriptwriters Javed Akhtar and Salim Khan rewrote the story, and kept rewriting it till they got it right.[6] This essay analyzes *Deewar*, its first revision *Trishul* (1978, which easily outpaced *Deewar* in the box office for the decade and in retrospect)[7] and *Shakti* (1982), the second effort to rewrite *Deewar* from a different directorial perspective. The rewrites are a structuralist's dream. The essential elements remain the same: nation allegorized in the family, conflict between parent and child, youth as a problem, the identity of criminality, and the diegetic use of death to accentuate – or to solve – problems.

What changes across the films, however, is the role each element plays in creating and solving problems. Thus, in *Deewar* the state creates a problem that the family solves; in *Trishul*, a parent creates the problem that the child solves; and in *Shakti*, a cardboard criminal outside the social order creates a problem for both the state and the family that the two together solve.[8] The migration of criminality across the three films from state to a caricatured smuggler external to the social order serves to contain problems and even to render them innocuous by the time they are staged in *Shakti* where the drama of national conflict has devolved into a family melodrama. In each new script, youth goes from indicating a problem (*Deewar*) to being the problem (*Shakti*). The death of the protagonist halts the future in *Deewar*; in *Shakti*, it enables it.

The three films together form a Salim-Javed trilogy that functions as what I had earlier called a Family Romance, and the term deserves some explanation. The Family Romance was fleetingly outlined by Freud in 1909 as a mechanism by which a subject, almost always male, authors fantasies about his origins that are more amenable to him than his real family is. Freud postulated that the child's ability to create an alternate 'reality' through storytelling generally involved 'getting free from the parents of whom he now has a low opinion and of replacing them by others who, as a rule, are of a higher social standing' (Freud 238–239). Read another way, the Family Romance is a liberation narrative that enables the child to master a world in which he is otherwise powerless. The *gesture* of narrating – of telling a story – is a way of liberating the subject from his subjection. In Freud's account, the power of the family is typically inverted in the Family Romance, and its taboos – notably the Oedipal complex – are evaded by the act of fantasy and storytelling.

From this summary, it is clear that the Family Romance serves in understanding two main functions of narrative. It provides a frame for reflecting on the *structure* of stories and also for postulating their *function*, and here is where it has such resonance in domains beyond the couch. In enabling the subject to fabricate an alternative history to the one he lives, it enables him to manage and eventually to accept 'reality,' even as it liberates him from it. The Family Romance can thus be thought of as an epistemological project: its act of narration is also one of interpretation, one that explicates even as it narrates. What matters is not the actual story itself but the *act* of ordering and telling stories that the term Family Romance captures. It is thus both a form of exposure (of the subject's deepest desires and his 'reality') as well as of subterfuge (in which one reality is covered by another more desirable one).

Applied beyond the individual to culture more widely, the concept of Family Romance allows one to probe the work that particularly popular narratives *do* in a specific cultural moment and to ask what traumas they mask, what 'reality' they seek liberation from, and to explore the kinds of fantasies a culture develops in the process. Above all, the application of this concept from individual to society enables one to uncover the structure and function of narratives that were particularly popular and to ask what kinds of unconscious they convey and conceal.[9]

III. *Deewar*, the manifest narrative

Released on 24 January 1975, *Deewar*'s story has a singular preoccupation with provision that captures above all the shortages of the decade. Every character in the film, and every conflict, is driven by the singular desire to provide materially for others, or to withhold provision from others. Workers ask management for a share of the profits from their labor to provide for their families; parents sacrifice to provide for their offspring; children do the same for their progenitors and siblings; the state proves unable to provide basic amenities such as housing and food; and criminals step in at the breach.

Home for the Varma brothers, though, is not where the hearth is: it is where Maa is. In the most famous scene from the film, all its major preoccupations come together: provision, property (moveable and real), criminality, law, justice, kinship, ideals, idealism, and home. Holding them together is the giant figure of Maa. The brothers, Vijay, an underworld employee, and Ravi, a policeman, meet under the bridge where they had lived during their childhood 20 years previously. Vijay warns Ravi of the underworld's price on

Ravi's head and urges him to seek a transfer to a police-station in a different town. Ravi refuses to give up the case against the underworld. 'My ideals won't let me,' he replies.

> Vijay: Your ideals! Bah! What have your ideals given you? A scrappy uniform? A duty jeep? A rundown house? Look at me and look at you. We both came from this same footpath, and now look at what I have today. I have buildings, bank balances, cars. What do you have?
>
> Ravi: Mere pas Maa hain. [I have Maa.]

Countering Vijay's catalog of possessions with the same economy even while putatively critiquing it, Ravi's 'I have Maa' is an awkward locution in any language. But the rhetoric of possession so permeates the film that it is the only way to claim kinship here. It is not that Maa lives with Ravi that matters; it is that he can claim to *have* her that makes him different from Vijay. At a time when very little could be owned, and much less provided, family relations, like ideals, succumb to the rhetoric of property and ownership. Thus, Ravi *has* Maa.[10]

But Maa is not just the mother. She is Hindustan, undivided and free. Not only does the poet Muhammad Iqbal's patriotic anthem, 'sare jehan se achcha,' play each time the brothers are under the bridge, *Deewar*'s *mise en scène* inverts the anthem's jingoistic ethos ('Our Hindustan is the best in the world… ancient Greece, Egypt, and Rome have all vanished without a trace, but we continue to shine in the firmament') in a deeply ironic comment on the bridge and on Hindustan. Rather than Hindustan being better than all lands, it is barely as good as them; rather than bringing the brothers closer, the bridge further estranges them. The bridge, thus, stands witness to the betrayals and failures of state and nation that this film marks, and it is in its presence that some of the most egregious betrayals of the film occur. Thus, it is under the bridge when Maa accepts Vijay's offer to be the man of the house and work so they can together send the baby of the house (Ravi) to school; and it is the consequence of the pact under that bridge that propels Vijay to do the things that men do for their women. But the pact they make is hideously corrupt, far more so than anything the gangster Vijay will do as a grown up.

In accepting Maa's call to replace the father, to give her his childhood in order to be her man even though he is still a boy – her boy – Vijay is fulfilling not the Oedipal wish, but the Jocasta wish: the desire of the mother for her son. For in accepting Vijay's offer to work so that 'their' baby, Ravi, can go to school, Maa has catapulted Vijay from being her son to being her provider. He is the husband she wants, not the husband she married. Her extramarital transgression is monstrous not because it is extramarital, but because it is intrafamilial. In taking her son as her mate, Maa's domination over him is complete. In many ways, she is not just Jocasta; in fact she is worse than Sophocles's doomed mother.

Jocasta's is the submission of desires for her son that comes from ignorance and avoidance; Maa's come from will and design. Having unwittingly 'married' her son, Jocasta punishes herself with death when she discovers what she has done; Maa, in contrast, punishes her *son* with death in order to avoid discovery. Jocasta sought to evade her fate, knowing its horror; Maa sought to embrace her fate, knowing she could evade its punishment.

Maa's is a terrible demand, far worse than Jocasta's in all ways. Whereas Sophocles's mother simply took her child's adulthood away from him, Maa claims her son's childhood. And for this obscene, unspeakable desire, *Vijay* (not Maa) must be punished. The mother cannot and will not accept what she has demanded under the bridge; she cannot and will not take responsibility for the violence for which she is responsible. Maa's disavowal is so complete that it takes two decades and the news that Anandbabu has died riding the rails to permit the stirrings of her repressed to come to the surface. And when it does it is terrible. Her punishment comes brutally, and it is visited upon the son – the object of her desire – rather than on herself, its instigator. Maa conspires with the baby, Ravi, to shoot Vijay. 'I have done my duty. Now I am going to await my son,' she declares, heading off to the temple after handing Ravi his gun. The twinning of her violence with the sanction of the state (the police force) and the piety of religion (the temple) are almost unbearable. But Maa knows that the perfect crime takes no prisoners. Vijay must die and she must do it in such a way as to make it *her* sacrifice, not his. For this the state's participation is crucial. And the state, fully duped, hands Maa a medal for the murder of her son.

The dream that Vijay has offered Maa – a home, respectability, security – cover a nightmarish secret that neither he nor she can speak. It is only when Vijay returns to the primal scene – the bridge – that the rift between them becomes clearest. 'I have buildings, bank balances, cars. What do *you* have?' he asks Ravi. Without missing a beat, Ravi claims Maa as commodity and gloats: 'Mera pas Maa hain.' Their conversation about who 'has' Maa thus devolves into a contest not just about the rightful heirs of the nation, but the rightful vision of the state: one which enables material plenitude ('buildings, bank balances, cars') or purely symbolic substance ('Maa'). In Vijay's depiction, Maa is the nation: a provider. In Ravi's, she is a menacing and vengeful figure akin to the state whose disciplinary power stands behind her.

This dialogue, possibly the most famous in modern Hindi cinema history, forces a latent content on *Deewar* and on its larger narrative of the migrant and home. Ravi's insistent claim that he *has* Maa makes explicit a circuit between mother, home, and nation. To have Maa is to have all three. Yet, the possession of all three is largely symbolic: *Deewar*'s manifest content is a symbolic solution to a problem that cannot be resolved. The dialogue between the brothers underscores the tenuousness of the mother-home-nation circuit. It is unavailable in real, material terms, which is precisely why it must be overstated in such grandiose terms. Maa is neither able to feed nor shelter her children. Roti kapda aur makaan remain elusive in her domain.

Deewar, the latent narrative, or 'India is Indira'

Made in a particularly fraught moment in India's political and economic history, the migrant's journey in *Deewar* plays a key role in dismantling the earlier nationalist myth of nation-as-home. Corrupting the circuit of mother-home-nation, *Deewar*'s Maa not only displaces her children from their natal home, she also insists that they sacrifice their lives for her own depravity. To confront this depravity head on in the film, to give it voice to speak its name, would not just disrupt but topple the vulnerable edifice of the nation c. 1975. It would also be unacceptable in the terms of commercial cinema that *Deewar* enjoyed. So *Deewar* submerges its critique in a powerful latent narrative that connects the specifics of the domestic story with the national one. From the moment Anandbabu leaves Maa, the film portrays him roaming the ends of the nation in third-class rail compartments in which he eventually dies. His journey without destination not only disrupts the settlement narrative Maa promises her children; it also revises it. In fleeing Maa, Anandbabu flees not just the mother-nation-home circuit: he also publicizes its fraudulence. His alternative 'home' is nowhere and everywhere. His is not an alternative to the state's vision so much as an indication of its impossibility and corruption. Anandbabu's aimless 20-year train ride in the temples of industrial modernity testifies to the gulf between the soaring rhetoric and the hopeless reality of his situation. Vijay's tattoo ('mera bap chor hain') is not about the theft by the father, but the theft *of* the father who is exiled from the family along with his efforts to secure roti kapda aur makan.

Assessing *Deewar* two decades after its release, its scriptwriter, Javed Akhtar, offered his perspective on the zeitgeist that the film so starkly captured:

> When we were writing *Deewar*, we were not aware of the sociological causes, implications, or symbolism. But the fact is that writers are also a part of society, and we were perhaps expressing the need prevalent at that time. The Emergency was imposed and the average Indian was losing faith in the various institutions – the police, courts, the government, the bureaucracy, and so on. When that happens, some kind of aggressive individuality develops… In a society that lacked faith, it was natural that the gangster of *Deewar* should take birth. (qtd. in Gahlot 53)

Akhtar's remarks on the period bring a crucial point into focus. Not only did Indira Gandhi's Emergency evaporate the national ideals spawned during Independence, but she insisted on replacing earlier notions of Indian democracy with her own. Thus, 'India is Indira; Indira is India' became her campaign slogan in 1971, and she scripted herself as both mother and nation in speech and image.

Mrs Gandhi's own family psychodrama has unnerving resonances with *Deewar*'s: like Maa, Indira Gandhi too prospered after she absented her husband, Feroze, from public life; like Maa, Indira Gandhi too anointed a younger son, Sanjay, her henchman; and like Maa, Indira Gandhi too commissioned the murder of the nation's young. In this case, the assassinations were accomplished quite literally through Sanjay's massive forced sterilization campaigns and more metaphorically by the Emergency and what Salman Rushdie named her 'sperectomy: the draining-out of hope' (521). Indira Gandhi's reign in the 1970s inaugurated the evaporation of Nehruvian national ideals and their replacement with corruption and cynicism. In this, Mrs Gandhi, like Maa, rewrote the father's legacy and obliterated the father's inheritance from the child. Mrs Gandhi's genius, like Maa's, lay in displacing responsibility for her crimes upon her perceived enemies and fabricating herself as the only figure equipped to save the nation from itself – and her.

The preceding analysis gestures toward two kinds of outlaws and two kinds of gangsters. The manifest law that Akhtar's comments gesture to is that of the state, a law that both the executive and judiciary have broken as the reference to the Emergency highlights. This law must be upheld even if those to do so are the very ones who have corrupted it in the first place. Vijay's transgression against the state must be punished even though his actions regulate society in a way that the state no longer can or will. Meanwhile, the second law is the law of the family. Here the conflict is sharper but also greyer, for the unit of discipline is the family itself, and it is its unspoken laws against desire and incest that Vijay is accused of disrupting. The real outlaw in this context, however, is Maa, the figure who takes a childhood from a son, a family from its father, a future from a brother and returns a bullet in exchange.

Earlier I had compared Maa's infanticide with Mrs Gandhi's and contrasted them with the Oedipal story. Jocasta, in the Greek version, is an unwitting spectator to the initial attempt at infanticide (which was initiated by her husband, Laius) as well as of the later union with Oedipus. Her suicide follows the death of Laius and the revelation of the curse upon him for the long-ago rape of the young boy Chrissipus. *Deewar*'s version of this story uses the same actors but fundamentally changes the point of view. Like Laius, Anandbabu is absent for much of the action, though in marked contrast to the pederastic Laius, Anandbabu's nobility is unquestioned. Whereas the Greek myth focuses on patricide, the Indian version emphasizes infanticide. The difference is key.

According to the folklorist, A.K. Ramanujan, there are scant instances of Oedipal narratives in India, and where they do exist as in Kannada versions, they seldom have tragic consequences. The Jocasta figure marries her son or accepts her fate, and the father figure is *never* overthrown (Ramanujan 379, 388). From this, Ramanujan concludes that

> the modern, Western quest is individualism, achieved through an overthrow of the father, whereas the Indian hero's quest is to fulfill his father... A traditional culture needs to use and absorb the vitality of its young... An innovative culture needs to overthrow its parents. (Ramanujan 394)[11]

Therefore, in the India captured in Ramanujan's folkloric research, stability prevails between the generations, and the father's power is always preserved in the proto-Oedipal oral folktales.

However, *Deewar*'s Oedipal version reveals a very different India than Ramanujan's. It is a society that in Ramanujan's terms is paradoxically both highly modern (in which the father is overthrown) and deeply conservative (where the vital but renegade son must also be killed). At a time of political and social upheaval, youth in the film are a problem; educated and unemployed like Ravi or charismatic and capable like Vijay, they represent challenges to a generational hierarchy and are criminalized or eliminated in the film's conservative plot. At the same time, those elements from the hierarchy (such as the father) that might compromise with youth or share its power with them are exiled, as Anandbabu is. In this, *Deewar* presents a notably *authoritarian* – and eventually unstable – version of the Oedipal drama in which *neither* generation ultimately prevails. *Both* father and child are demolished, and power resides in absolutist fashion with a ruthless central authority that is unwilling to cede or share it. Thus, Maa – and Mrs Gandhi. The oppositional political order has fully penetrated the family, and both are revealed as ruinous.

In its depiction of maternal power, *Deewar*'s mother is closer to Kunti than she is to Jocasta: namely, the figure from the *Mahabharata* who tried to kill Karna her firstborn in order to preserve her social status and then, when he was an adult, asked Karna to sacrifice his life again in order to preserve the mother's future security. It is an impossible sacrifice to ask for, and Karna refuses Kunti. The outcome is the apocalyptic battle in which the House of Pandu is destroyed. Much the same occurs in *Deewar*'s cautionary fable where no happy ending is possible. The mother's infanticide destroys the family just as the state's infanticide deposes the political order and any belief in due process.

Unlike Ramanujan, who sees India's oral folklore providing a flexible and comforting set of narratives that preserve the social order, *Deewar*'s filmlore exposes a political and social order on the brink of collapse, willing to undertake the most egregious violence to kinship loyalties. *Deewar*, furthermore, exposes the violence covered (up) by the mother worship narratives so central to India's political culture and so overplayed in cinema at especially anxious moments of national definition such as the 1970s.

IV. *Deewar* retold, or *Trishul* and *Shakti*

I'll Die for Mama was one of *Deewar*'s English titles that captured both the central plot conflict (for mother, with mother) and the thinly veiled allegory of the nation it signals. Vijay's 'transgressions' in the film were described as inevitable by its scriptwriter: 'In a society that lacked faith,' Javed Akhtar averred, 'it was natural that the gangster of *Deewar* should take birth' (qtd. in Gahlot 53). When asked if a criminal hero like Vijay was 'justifiable,' Akhtar riposted: 'In this kind of society, what do you expect?... A hero at any given time is the personification of contemporary morality and contemporary ambitions (qtd. in Gahlot 53–54).

If Vijay was the outcome of his moment, he was also a marked departure from his cinematic predecessors. The criminal hero was hardly new in Hindi cinema: Raj Kapoor had developed him to popular acclaim in both *Awara* (1951) and *Shree 420* (1955). But whereas Kapoor's heroes eventually repent their crimes (murder and fraud) and are integrated back in society following appropriate penitence, usually in jail, *Deewar*'s hero had no such luck. Vijay, who has done all that his mother asked for (provided for her, prayed for her) is nonetheless killed, and his death meant to signal a sacrifice for Maa. Hence, *I'll Die for Mama*.

The state portrayed in *Deewar* displaces upon the family the problems it creates but cannot solve. It criminalizes those whose efforts at regulation expose the state's ineffectiveness, and then calls upon the social order (in the form of the family) to restrain the monsters it has spawned. In this, *Deewar* exposes the longstanding conflicts at the basis of Indian nationalism: the state espoused democracy but the social order (with its caste and class hierarchies) abjured it. Rather than state and society being partners in a shared enterprise, they became increasingly in conflict. Whereas Nehru's vision tried to develop the state's institutions to nudge society's, his daughter's used the state to divide society. And no film better displays the bitter divisions as they came to a head in the 1970s than *Deewar* in which the menace of public life is reflected in the private.

Javed Akhtar may be correct to insist that Vijay emerged out of his moment, but Vijay's critical and commercial success notwithstanding, his was an uncomfortable emergence that had to be rescripted. If nothing else, the moment had changed with the fall of Mrs Gandhi and the end of the Emergency in 1977, even if its legacies remained palpable. So, Salim-Javed killed Vijay in *Deewar*, but it was not enough to quell the popularity of a hero who captured the day with his fists and his smoldering eyes. He may not have gotten the best line of the film ('mere pas Maa hain'), but he became the best thing about the film. 'A man who dies before his time lives to be a martyr,' cautioned the malevolent mine owner in *Deewar* when his henchmen offer to kill Anandbabu during the labor strike. Anandbabu is allowed to live but become utterly irrelevant; Vijay, on the other hand, achieves his diegetic and extra-diegetic status by his death.

As if wishing to return the monster to his box, Akhtar and Salim Khan returned to *Deewar* and rewrote it twice, revising the basic conflict and looking for more amenable solutions to it. If *Deewar* was a raw exposition of conflict with the state, *Trishul*, which followed it in 1978, placed its conflict solely in society and the family. If *Deewar* was the story of the mother, *Trishul* was largely of the father. If Vijay is deemed a criminal in *Deewar*, he is a successful capitalist in *Trishul*. If Vijay's romantic life follows his doomed family life in *Deewar*, in *Trishul*, he gets conjugal happiness along with restoration into a loving biological family. And where Vijay must be sacrificed in *Deewar*, he thrives in *Trishul*. Above all, if the predominant conflict in *Deewar* is the Kunti conflict in which Maa authorizes the murder of her firstborn, in *Trishul*, it is a more conventional Oedipal conflict in which the son avenges his mother by killing the father.

While the basic structure of the two films remains the same, the point of view and the outcome vary dramatically. And these variations say everything about the decade and about the social work of popular film. Above all, the variations index the different 'India's that popular cinema had to grapple with. In rewriting *Deewar*'s masterplot, its writers were drawing attention to the very different citizen-protagonists in the nation. In this formulation, *Deewar* tells the story of the child who bears witness and cannot forget; *Trishul* the story of an adult who is willing to forgive if not forget. In *Deewar*, Vijay's actions sought to regulate all society; in *Trishul*, they regulate only the family. *Deewar* allegorizes the nation; *Trishul* largely ignores it. If politics and the state *are* the plot of *Deewar*, in *Trishul* both politics and the state are detachable from the plot, and the film is an almost total retreat into family life and its melodrama.

Trishul's revision was a triumphant one; it remains today an all-time grosser at the box office (#23 to *Deewar*'s #50 in figures adjusted for inflation: IBOS). It softens many of *Deewar*'s rawest referential illusions to the faltering state and replays all of *Deewar*'s signal conflicts into happy endings. The preoccupation with roti kapda aur makan is now just a preoccupation with makan (housing); both the protagonists are builders, and in *Trishul*, both Vijay and his father compete for a contract to provide low-cost housing for the middle-classes which they both succeed in providing. The state's ineptitude is irrelevant in *Trishul* because Vijay is allowed to prevail and provide security when the state (in the form of the courts) fails to clear legal title to land occupied by squatters. Vijay's law brings a widely-accepted order. And if *Deewar*'s past is a haunted one that provides Vijay neither rest nor respite, *Trishul*'s past dies out (with the mother) and allows the future to occur and with it a happy ending signaled by the founding of a new corporation called ShantiRaj Enterprises, the name literally meaning the reign of peace. In short, *Trishul* represents a compromise solution to the problem of *Deewar*. The earlier film provided a powerful critique of the state and a stark depiction of its dystopian intrusions into private life. *Trishul*, on the other hand, erases the radical critique and gives the happy ending that was impossible in *Deewar*

In one account, *Trishul* reassured audiences that the problems of *Deewar* could be solved. The private could be separated from the political, and if one could be healed then maybe the other would follow. Above all, *Trishul* diffused the rage of the earlier film and integrated the protagonist not just into the social order, but also as the new head of the order represented by ShantiRaj Enterprises. Vijay is truly a victor in this film, unlike in *Deewar*, where his name was profoundly ironic. (Javed Akhtar has noted a key detail about *Trishul* that bears mentioning in this context: 'The first time we [ever] revised a script was for... *Trishul*' [qtd. in Kabir 56]. It was a script, moreover, that was written with Yash Chopra by their side, though Akhtar would not elaborate on what aspects of *Trishul*'s script or its tone Chopra especially shaped.)

But most happy endings invite one to ask, willfully, what unhappiness awaits around the corner. And in their final take on the 'problem' of *Deewar*, Salim-Javed scripted *Shakti* under Ramesh Sippy's direction. *Deewar*'s legacy is scrutinized in a family setting that is everything that *Deewar* was not: contentedly middle class, professional, and stable. The public sphere doesn't just penetrate *Shakti*'s stable family and ruin it as well: the family *is* the state in the form of a father, a police chief who zealously pursues criminal elements to the letter of the law[12]. The main conflict occurs over whose law best provides justice: the father chooses to observe the state's laws even when his young son is kidnapped ('I refuse your call for a ransom,' he tells the kidnapper). The boy, who overhears this remark, insists that the laws of kinship have been betrayed, and he strays from his father. Explaining his childhood to a lover, Vijay offers: 'My father married twice. My mother and his job. I'm my mother's son; my stepmother's son is the law. The law is my stepbrother [kanoon mera sautela bhai hai].'

Rather than the law as something that protects, *Shakti* reveals it as a weapon that creates a gulf between the weak and strong, men and women, father and son. Rejecting this law, Vijay offers justice to those whom the law does not reach: thus, the woman on the train being harassed by a gang of drunken men is protected by his presence (and his handy fists) when no cop is around. Unable to believe his son over the woman's harassers who then sue for injury, Vijay's father accuses him. Later, when a murder is pinned on Vijay based on circumstantial evidence, his father again believes the charge rather than the evidence. Though the film offers each conflict as a generational struggle, they both also serve as tutorials about law and justice.

At a time when both law and order are shown to have frayed, the policeman's zeal comes with some irony in that rather than burnishing the law, it reveals that even following the law to the letter cannot bring order. The father cannot tell the difference between charge and evidence; for him, an individual (especially his son) is guilty until proven innocent, and in this, his actions unwittingly end up underscoring the widespread view that *Deewar* had captured in the previous decade. Rather than the well-intentioned father redeeming the law by 'believing' it, he ends up revealing that even those best intentioned to uphold the law cannot conceal its utter irrelevance. In this, the law is in fact a stepchild *to* the family *and* to the nation.

Vijay's estrangement from his father in *Shakti* is a parable of the law's estrangement from the nation: Vijay chooses fathers in the film who protect him at the cost of biology; the state chooses laws that protect it at the cost of ideology. In both choices, the mother dies. She is literally shot in *Shakti*, just as the nation and its ideals metaphorically die in the conflict between her son (Vijay) and her stepson (kanoon, the law).

If *Trishul* undid most of *Deewar*'s radical politics, *Shakti* renders those politics obsolete. *Shakti*'s manifest content is profoundly conservative: youth is co-opted into family, family prevails over romance, the authority of both family and state prevail over the individual, and the father is allowed to prosper and to determine the direction of the following generations. Meanwhile, where *Deewar*'s latent content destabilized its manifest order, in *Shakti*, the latent content is harder to discern within the terms of this single film. To do it, one needs *Deewar* and the mythologies embedded in its filmlore.

V. Conclusion

Hindi cinema's Family Romances, as amplified in *Deewar* and its revisions, are neither typical liberation narratives nor exorcisms as psychoanalysis posited such narratives. The traumas they are intended to heal are paradoxically rendered more real on the screen largely because of their projections upon the familiar intimacy of the family unit. Rather than rendering the state abstract and thus distant from the subject, these films render it closer to him in the form of the brother who will gun him and the mother who will authorize the killing as in *Deewar*. Rather than liberating the subject from his nightmares, they bring them to life for him. In this form, the films are a peculiar sort of political tutorial: neither exultant not exculpatory of the national myth, they serve to expose its fraudulence.

Deewar is notable for embedding its extensive critique of India in the 1970s within the terms of popular commercial cinema. If the situation of the decade 'created' the protagonist of *Deewar* and ensured his currency at the time, the film's combustible counter-narrative nevertheless required the formal apparatus of containment that its protagonist's death weakly provided. While Vijay's diegetic death illustrates the incompletely radical nature of popular cinema, it also stands as an indicator of popular cinema's opportunities. Because while Hindi film seldom provides sequels, it narrates the same story numerous times with each retelling exposing or addressing anxieties that the previous one missed or was unable to fully pursue. Thus, *Deewar*'s radical critique kills a semi-criminal Vijay while *Trishul*'s radical revision brings him back an unambiguous hero, and *Shakti*'s radical burial renders him obsolete. Taken together, the three films serve not just as 'contemporary folklore' as Javed Akhtar claimed in this chapter's headnote. They also serve as cautionary fables about the power of stories.

Deewar's volatile family drama with its dramatic critique of family, state, and nation illuminated the corrosion in both biological and symbolic kinship units. Revising this story in *Trishul* generated the happy ending as well as a tutorial on the futility of such endings.

In other words, utopia in *Trishul* proved as unsatisfying as dystopia in *Deewar* was. Stories, in this context, have the power both to satisfy and to unsettle. In the tutorial that emerges from Salim-Javed's cinematic triptych, the pleasures of stories are contingent: they come with attendant cautions to qualify their satisfactions.

But stories also expose and reconfigure the world in which they circulate. *Deewar*'s critique, refashioned in *Trishul* then again in *Shakti*, serves a *restorative* function that first critiques the master narrative (of nation and family) and then provides a series of commentaries on it in the form of revisions. If *Trishul*'s ending of a peaceful ShantiRaj embeds a fantasy, it is a fantasy that powerfully underscores the unrelenting somberness in *Deewar*. In this cautionary account, *Deewar* both exposes the corruption that pervades 1970s India as well as the futility of confronting it, *even while providing the short-lived satisfaction of Vijay's Pyrrhic confrontations*. *Trishul*'s ending is no more fully satisfying than *Deewar*'s, even though both speak to the same desire for social justice.

In short, Salim-Javed's cinematic triptych in *Deewar-Trishul-Shakti* illuminates the many acts of storytelling central to all nation-building projects. The triptych provides a way to reconceive – and perhaps even to restore – the national narrative even while exposing its corruption. It purveys the notion that the art of the story carries the craft of life. And for this, popular cinema is the nation's Family Romance, a space where the nightmares of the collective are addressed and where alternatives can be scripted even if they must eventually be dismissed. Reading the manifest and latent narratives embedded in *Deewar* and unraveled across the triptych exposes a set of pressing anxieties that found expression in the locus of the family and that required the countering impulse of the Family Romance for dissolution, if not resolution. In the Family Romance that emerges, Vijay becomes a symbol condensing all the forces threatening India – both the state and the nation – in the mid-1970s. *Deewar*'s family sanctuary is revealed, like the nation's, as threatened by invasion from without and seduction within (a preoccupation keenly observed by Michael Rogin in his work on US Cold War cinema [Rogin 267]). These threats are narratively 'undone' across the films that comprise the triptych as the originary film's murderous plot is rewritten in more conciliatory terms.

Recovering these acts of making and undoing exposes not just the anxieties of the decade, but also the powerful role popular Hindi cinema played in producing and then containing the combustible energies of the moment. In countering the brutality of a decade on screen if not on the street, cinema served to remind the state of the nation that preceded it. Both were acts of public fantasy, enabled and underwritten by the Family Romance. Cinema in this context stands for a recovered memory: flawed, and faintly gesturing to a truth that cannot be spoken. The cinematic imagination of which the Salim-Javed triptych is a part enables a critique not just of the nation, but of the narrative fabrications that propel it. Suspended below the manifest narrative is a combustible latent critique, one that can only find voice in the displacement and hyperbole characteristic of the Family Romance. Popular cinema's genius lies in providing a space for these narratives that must not be recalled. At best, they have the sharpness and horror of all recovered memories, to which reality is neither as bad, nor as real.

Acknowledgements

Grateful thanks first to the late Michael Rogin who *got* my argument a decade before I did; to audiences at numerous venues for helpful comments: Lewis Gordon's Halloween Lectures on Monsters at Temple University; the Visual Studies Colloquium at Bryn Mawr College; the Madison South Asia Conference; Veena Talwar Oldenburg; the Center for the Humanities at Temple; Javed Akhtar; participants at the 1970s and its Legacies Workshop at Temple in April 2011 (especially Rajinder

Dudrah); Nasreen Munni Kabir; and Russell Berman's seminar at Columbia in the 1980s where Freud's ideas were subjected to the kind of reading that the finest literary critics bring to all texts. Special thanks to Orfeo Fioretos; to Daniel Ryan Morse for research assistance and to the staff of the National Film Archive of India in Pune for many courtesies with research and materials.

Notes

1. "Box Office Results: Biggest Grossers of All Time (adjusted for inflation)."
2. My thinking and phrasing here borrow heavily from Jane Tompkins' work on the popularity of Uncle Tom's Cabin in nineteenth-century America, a work that Tompkins argues 'retells the culture's central myth (crucifixion) in terms of the nation's political conflict (slavery) and its most cherished social belief – the sanctity of motherhood' (Tompkins 134).
3. The tools of psychoanalysis prove particularly useful in interpreting cinema's symbolic language and in uncovering the mechanics of repression and displacement so central to the public fantasies of the decade. For almost a century, psychoanalysis has provided an important interpretive framework for scholarship on India. Research inflected by its tools have come to define numerous disciplines including politics, folklore, religion, and sociology. Film is no exception with foundational scholarship using its tools conducted by Kakar, Nandy, and S. Akhtar.
4. Laura Mulvey's foundational work on early Hollywood melodrama inspired the phrase and insight on cinema's role as primal scene of India's modern mythologies (see Mulvey 121). Inspired by Mulvey's illuminating early work on Hollywood, I too see popular cinema as providing a body of narratives that expose a culture's public fantasies.
5. See Chakravarty and Virdi as important examples. Virdi, for instance, has proposed that Hindi cinema *tout court* 'projects the imagined nation on the terrain of the family... through contestations that throw into relief its social structures and realignments' (7).
6. To a degree hitherto unprecedented in Hindi commercial cinema, Salim-Javed's scripts profoundly shaped the films that emerged from them. The writers were known to present bound scripts to the director who made virtually no changes to them. The director and producer had the choice over stars, music, movement, but little else. ('Prakash Mehra... likes to tell a story, not to disturb the frame... Yashji always zooms, for every shot... Movement means a lot to him,' noted Bachchan of the directors of, respectively, *Zanjeer* and *Deewar* [qtd. in Dwyer, 98].) Recalling *Deewar*, director Yash Chopra observed: 'That was one script and screenplay where you didn't have to delete anything after making, it was such – such a perfect script. We didn't do anything [to it]' (qtd. in Dwyer 100). Both Bachchan (see Somaaya 123) and Shashi Kapoor concur, the latter in a 2003 interview with the author.
7. According to 'International Business Overview Standard,' *Trishul* ranks #23 among world-wide all-time grossers adjusted for inflation, while *Deewar* comes in at #50 (see <ibos.network.com/actualalltimes.asp>, 15 March 2006). If returns just for the decade are reviewed, the gap is considerably narrowed, and the same source has *Trishul* at #9 and *Deewar* at #16 (see <ibos.network.com/topgrosserbyyear.asp?/year + 197>, 15 March 2006). In contrast to the latter, *BoxOfficeIndia.com*, another source, provides returns by decade according to which *Deewar*'s earnings place it at #11 and *Trishul*'s at #15 (see "Top Earners: 1970–79.").
8. Other differences across the films: in *Deewar*, the father's ideals absent him from his family; in *Trishul*, his ambitions absent him from his son but keep him at the center of the family; and in *Shakti*, the father's ideals preserve him in the family and exile the son from it. Mothers are central in all three, but in *Deewar* they are vengeful and prevail till the end; in *Trishul* they are vengeful but die so their sons can achieve a happy end; and in *Shakti*, they seek compromises that eventually kill them, a fate in which their sons join them. Infanticide, or its threat, plays a role in all three: in *Deewar*, it disrupts the family altogether; in *Trishul*, where the threat is headed off, the family reconstitutes itself in a happy unit; and in *Shakti*, infanticide is a sacrifice that is tragic but necessary to assure the stability of a now-truncated family and the nation.
9. Madhava Prasad, among others such as Virdi and Chakravarty, provides a genealogy in which Hindi cinema through the 1960s is characterized by a focus on the family structure that he names 'the feudal family romance' (Prasad 64). Prasad's use of the family romance, however, has no resonance with Freud's definition: for Prasad, the term simply refers to a story in which the ideology of the family is central. In contrast, my usage of the term develops Freud's, and I use the upper case throughout to signal the technical (vs. colloquial) referent (see Prasad 30–31).

10. The historian Vinay Lal regards Ravi's locution of ownership as the 'voice of patriarchy' in which Ravi has become the 'reincarnated husband.' In contrast, my analysis reveals a patriarchy that is overtaken by the castrating figure of Maa who has ambushed its traditional authority. Ravi represents the intrusion of the state on to the family: he is neither the husband Maa married (Anandbabu), nor the husband she chose (Vijay). Unlike both males marked (literally and figuratively) by ideals by which they live, Ravi is a figure marked exclusively by ideology. All his actions require the instruction and sanction of others and the grandiloquence of rhetoric that issues from 'Mere pas Maa hain' (see Lal 241).
11. Javed Akhtar further arguably claims that 'in our country we don't have a strong tradition of bonding between father and son anyway' (qtd. in Kabir 24).
12. In a somewhat ironic biographical detail, Salim Khan was the son of an Indore police officer, which might partly explain the depiction of these police-officer patriarchs in Salim-Javed films such as *Shakti* (and, above all, *Sholay*).

References

Banaji, S.J. "*Deewaar*: They're Hijacking the Matron." *Filmfare* 24.3 (1975): 35. Print.

Banerjea, Koushik. "Fight Club': Aesthetics, Hybridisation and the Construction of Rogue Masculinities in *Sholay* and *Deewar*." *Bollyworld: Popular Indian Cinema through a Transnational Lens*. Ed. Raminder Kaur and Ajay J. Sinha. New Delhi: Sage, 2005. 163–85. Print.

"Box Office Results: Biggest Grossers of All Time (adjusted for inflation)." *International Business Overview Standard*, Web. 15 Mar. 2006. <www.ibos.network.com/topgrosserbyyear.asp?/year+1975>.

Chakravarty, Sumita. *National Identity in Indian Popular Cinema, 1947–1987*. Austin: U of Texas P, 1993. Print.

Devereux, George. "Why Oedipus Killed Laius. A Note on the Complementary Oedipus Complex in Greek Drama." *International Journal of Psycho-analysis* 34.2 (1953): 132–41. Print.

Dwyer, Rachel. *Yash Chopra: Fifty Years in Indian Cinema*. New Delhi: Roli Books, 2002.

Edmunds, Lowell and Alan Dundes, eds. *Oedipus: A Folklore Casebook*. New York: Garland, 1983. Print.

Freud, Sigmund. "Family Romances." Trans. James Strachey. *The Standard Edition of the Complete Psychological Works of Sigmund Freud*. 1909. Ed. James Stratchey. Vol. IX. London: Hogarth Press, 1959. 236–41. Print.

Gahlot, Deepa. "Look Back in Anger." *Cinema in India* III.12 (1992): 52–5. Print.

Goldman, R.P. "Fathers, Sons, and Gurus: Oedipal Conflict in the Sanskrit Epics." *Journal of Indian Philosophy* 6 (1978): 325–92. Print.

Kabir, Nasreen. *Talking Films: Conversations on Hindi Cinema with Javed Akhtar*. New Delhi: Oxford UP, 1999. Print.

Kakar, Sudhir. "The Cinema as Collective Fantasy." *Indian Cinema Superbazaar*. Ed. Aruna Vasudev and Philippe Lenglet. New Delhi: Vikas Publishing, 1983. 89–97. Print.

Kaviraj, Sudipta. "The Imaginary Institution of India." *Subaltern Studies VII: Writing on South Asian History and Society*. Ed. Partha Chatterjee and Gyanendra Pandey. Delhi: Oxford UP, 1992. 1–39. Print.

Khanna, Anil. "Limits of Anger: A Look at the Persona of the Anti-Hero in Popular Hindi Cinema over the Decades." *Cinema in India* 3.6 (1992): 4–9. Print.

Lal, Vinay. "The Impossibility of the Outsider in the Modern Hindi Film." Nandy 228–259. Print.

Lal, Vinay. *Deewaar: The Footpath, the City, and the Angry Young Man*. New Delhi: Harper Collins, 2011. Print.

Mazumdar, Ranjani. "From Subjectification to Schizophrenia: The 'Angry Man' and the 'Psychotic Hero' of Bombay Cinema." *Making Meaning in Indian Cinema*. Ed. Ravi Vasudevan. New Delhi: Oxford UP, 2000. 238–66.

Mishra, Vijay. *Bollywood Cinema: Temples of Desire*. London: Routledge, 2002.

Mulvey, Laura. "'It Will Be a Magnificent Obsession': The Melodrama's Role in the Development of Contemporary Film Theory." *Melodrama: Stage Picture Screen*. Ed. Jacky Bratton, Jim Cook and Christine Gledhill. London: British Film Institute Publishing, 1994. 121–33. Print.

Nandy, Ashis. Introduction. *The Secret Politics of Our Desires: Innocence, Culpability, and Indian Popular Cinema*. New Delhi: Oxford UP, 1998. Print.

Nehru, Jawaharlal. "Tryst with Destiny." *The Vintage Book of India Writing, 1947–1997*. 1947. Ed. Salman Rushdie and Elizabeth West. London: Vintage, 1947. 1–2. Print.

Prasad, M. Madhava. *Ideology of the Hindi Film: A Historical Construction*. Delhi: Oxford UP, 1998. Print.

Ramanujan, A.K. "The Indian Oedipus." *The Collected Essays of A.K. Ramanujan*. 1983. Ed. Vinay Dharwadker. New Delhi: Oxford UP, 1999. 377–97. Print.

Rogin, Michael. "*Kiss Me Deadly*: Communism, Motherhood, and Cold War Movies." *Ronald Reagan, the Movie and Other Episodes in Political Demonology*. Berkeley: U of California P, 1987. 236–71. Print.

Rushdie, Salman. *Midnight's Children*. New York: Avon, 1980. Print.

Somaaya, Bhawana. *Amitabh Bachchan: The Legend*. New Delhi: Macmillan India, 1999. Print.

Tarlo, Emma. *Unsettling Memories: Narratives of the Emergency in Delhi*. Berkeley: U of California P, 2003. Print.

Tompkins, Jane. *Sensational Designs: The Cultural Work of American Fiction, 1790–1860*. New York: Oxford UP, 1985. Print.

"Top Earners: 1970–79." *BoxOfficeIndia.com*, 17 Nov. 2010. Web. <www.boxofficeindia.com/showProd.php?itemCat+124&catName+MTk3MCOxOTc5>.

Virdi, Jyotika. *The Cinematic Imagination: Indian Popular Films as Social History*. New Brunswick: Rutgers UP, 2003. Print.

Virdi, Jyotika. "*Deewar*: Fact, Fiction, and the Making of a Superatar." *Bollyworld: Popular Indian Cinema through a Transnational Lens*. Ed. Raminder Kaur and Ajay J. Sinha. New Delhi: Sage, 2005. 223–39. Print.

Vitale, Valentina. *Hindi Action Cinema: Industries, Narratives, Bodies*. New Delhi: Oxford UP, 2008. Print.

Filmography

Deewaar. Dir. Yash Chopra. 1975. Eros Entertainment. Film.
Roti Kapda aur Makan. Dir. Manoj Kumar. 1974. DEI. Film.
Shakti. Dir. Ramesh Sippy. 1982. Shemaroo. Film.
Sholay. Dir. Ramesh Sippy. 1975. Eros Entertainment. Film.
Trishul. Dir. Yash Chopra. 1978. Eros Entertainment. Film.
Zanjeer. Dir. Prakash Mehra. 1973. Eros Entertainment. Film.

'Relationships which have no name': Family and sexuality in 1970s popular film

Ulka Anjaria

Brandeis University, Waltham, MA

This essay argues that popular film of the 1970s opened up a space for representing new kinds of social relationships specifically by means of its use of melodramatic formulas. Against a dominant periodization of the decade which emphasizes rupture, I argue that over the course of the long 1970s we see a process of repetition and resignification whereby formulas such as the 'lost-and-found' plot and the love triangle were re-presented and their constitutive elements rearranged in order to generate alternatives to conventional kinship and romantic paradigms. Discussing several films from this decade, including *Sangam*, *Yaadon ki Baaraat*, *Deewaar*, *Sholay*, *Amar Akbar Anthony* and *Silsila*, I show how Hindi cinema in the 1970s was engaged in considering how to represent human relationships outside of social sanction or conventionally accepted kinship terms, thus offering a new paradigm from which to read popular film at large.

In the closing moments of Farhan Akhtar's 2001 blockbuster *Dil Chahta Hai*, the dying Tara describes her connection to Siddharth (Sid) by saying, 'There are some relationships which have no name.'[1] This is a redemptive moment in an otherwise tragic scene, as Tara grasps on to the last few minutes of her life and Sid struggles to convey how much she has meant to him. The communication is particularly meaningful for Sid, whose relationship with Tara, throughout the film, exceeded conventional understandings of relationships between men and women, and which, when it was briefly forced into the paradigm of romantic love, all but fell apart.

For a popular cinema so seemingly invested in fixed relationships, a sentiment such as Tara's might seem strikingly novel. Indeed, many critics have heralded *Dil Chahta Hai* (*DCH*) as a new kind of film, which transgressed conventional representations of familial and romantic relationships in Hindi cinema. Sid and Tara epitomize this sense, in part because Tara is older and divorced. But Tara's words suggest that what is significant about their relationship is precisely that it eludes definition, that it cannot be understood by means of any preexisting relational terms. If its undefinability is the source of its transgression, then *DCH* is not entirely new, but furthers a concern with the nature of relationships that popular film has been experimenting with for decades. It is no accident that it is in Farhan Akhtar's film that the idea of a relationship without a name finds form in language, as it mobilizes a sentiment found in the scripts penned by his father, Javed Akhtar, and his contemporaries a generation earlier. Indeed, it is in the films of the 1970s that we see an intensification of Hindi cinema's pressing and somewhat paradoxical interest in representing socially unrepresentable relationships.

A narrative of rupture tends to dominate critical studies of popular film in the 1970s, based in seminal historical moments which are seen to have radically transformed the paradigms of Hindi cinema. Although the particular historical markers vary – from the India-Pakistan war of 1971 (Ahmed 291–292) to the release of *Zanjeer* (d. Prakash Mehra) in 1973, to Indira Gandhi's declaration of Emergency in 1975 – a consensus remains around the idea that somewhere in this decade, Hindi popular film underwent an inalterable change. Central to this narrative is the figure of the 'angry young man' (Mazumdar 1), who represented the deep social angst of the time, and constituted a major shift away from the romantic heroes of the decade before (Ahmed 301).

Yet while this narrative has significant explanatory power, it overlooks the less spectacular undercurrents of change that are more generalizable to popular cultural forms. In what many critics consider the conservative domain of popular culture, change most often does not occur through ruptures or revolutions but by means of small adjustments in conventions, formulas and structures, through which new moral content gradually emerges to reflect or reorient the larger popular moral universe. Indeed, popular cinema in the 1970s, like Hindi popular cinema across the decades, relies on what film theorist Ravi Vasudevan calls 'high contrivance in narrative mechanisms' (Vasudevan 10) such as formulaic plots, tropes and themes.[2] In contrast to contemporary parallel cinema, in which social injustice is described through a harsh realism and original, psychologically probing plots and characters, the social angst of the angry young man is not represented in opposition to formulas but by means of them. The figure is thus often positioned as a son, or a brother, or a lover; familial and romantic structures serve as background against which this more dynamic figure is placed and in relation to which his meaning emerges. In this way, we cannot completely account for the angry young man without looking at the less spectacular changes in conventions for representing family and sexual relationships. This requires considering the significant *continuity* between conventions for representing family and love from the 1960s through the 1970s, preceding and following the Emergency, and even through to the early 1980s.

This essay argues that popular film of the 1970s opened up a space for representing new kinds of social relationships, but within and based on its use of melodramatic formulas. I argue that over the course of the long 1970s we see not radical rupture, but a process of repetition and resignification whereby generic formulas such as the lost-and-found plot and the love triangle were re-presented, and their constitutive elements rearranged, in order to generate alternatives to conventional kinship and romantic paradigms. These alternatives were not paraded, and often not even articulated, but were advanced nonetheless through the insistent suggestion that, anticipating *DCH*'s Tara, the language used by Hindi cinema to describe relationships at times falls short. It is in this indirect way that these films bring to light lived experiences of fraternity, love and desire at the margins of social legibility. These experiences illuminate the complex ways in which popular cultural forms make meaning, and nuance our understanding of the cinema of the 1970s as one marked primarily by radical change.

I. The broken family

Hindi Film scholar Tejaswini Ganti points to the common usage of the 'lost-and-found' formula in 1970s films, which she relates to healing the traumas of Partition. Here, popular film is figured as a utopian space where the land, family and sense of wholeness lost at Partition can be put together again. This certainly accounts for the pathos and popularity of the formula, but it is not quite clear, in Ganti's hypothesis, why the lost-and-found is so prominent more than two decades after Partition. One wonders, by contrast, whether there might be a connection between the lost-and-found formula and the sensibility of angry restlessness that is also seen to define the decade's films. Although seemingly incompatible, their coincidence in the 1970s seems suggestive.

Deewaar (d. Yash Chopra, 1975), although not strictly a 'lost-and-found,' might seem a central text to advance this theory, as the young man's anger against the state is inseparable from his alienation from his family. *Deewaar* tells the story of two brothers, Ravi and Vijay, who take separate paths as they reach adulthood, which lead them to opposite sides of the law. Ravi becomes a policeman and Vijay a smuggler associated with Bombay's biggest gangs. As film and literary scholar Priya Joshi shows (forthcoming), *Deewaar* is in many ways a film about the psychic loss of the mother's love, which is allegorically cast as alienation from the nation-as-mother. Its anger against the state is thus figured via what Joshi calls a 'family romance,' a Freudian parable for filial expulsion and loss.

In this sense, *Deewaar* might be seen to offer a specific, allegorical repetition of the more traditional lost-and-found, such as in the earlier film *Yaadon ki Baaraat* (d. Nasir Hussein, 1973). *Yaadon* begins with the orphaning and separation of three brothers, who watch their father and mother die at the hands of Shakal, a masked thug, and are separated as they try to escape his men. The film flashes forward to their adulthood, where the brothers have taken significantly different paths. They are unknowingly brought together by a series of coincidences that land them all at the same hotel, where Monty, the middle brother and now a pop singer, begins a concert with a song that their mother had sung, the eponymous 'Yaadon ki Baaraat.' The brothers, all attending the concert for reasons of their own, hear the song and are thus reunited.

Unlike *Deewaar*, the separation of *Yaadon*'s three brothers does not carry any obvious allegorical weight, either relating to the mother-as-nation or to Partition. If anything, their separation is attributed to nothing beyond Shakal's villainy. Shakal is a smuggler and runs a gang of thieves and thugs, and there are a couple of indications that he steals high-price jewelry and other valuables so that he can sell them to Robert, a mysterious foreign buyer, and presumably an Englishman. The connection to colonialism is thus invoked, but it is Shakal who continues to be the target of the brothers' rage and it is his downfall that the ultimately united brothers work to effect, even after Robert has made his escape.

Despite this difference, however, both *Deewaar* and *Yaadon* assume the significance of blood bonds, which gives moral weight to the originary losses. In *Yaadon*, the importance of blood as a means of linking individuals within the family is never stated because it does not need to be; the audience only sees the family together in the film's first scene, but otherwise is provided no details about what kind of family they constituted. Likewise, when the brothers meet as adults they have nothing in common except what the audience knows to be their biological connection. Thus we are asked to assume that merely because they constituted a family, their breakup is devastating and, in the moral universe of the film, must be righted.

Deewaar offers a bit more complicated scenario, but here as well the unassailability of the blood bonds is a powerful force within the plot. Vijay, despite his self-assured rebelliousness, is particularly susceptible to it, and thus when one of Dawar's goons suggests killing Ravi, Vijay becomes quickly enraged: 'Yes, he's my brother! And if you talk about him again I'll kill you!' Likewise, Vijay's connection with his mother is portrayed as incontestable, even when his morality in other spheres is compromised. It is in fact his love for his mother that impels his self-sacrifice at the end of the film, rather than any true contrition for his illegal activities. Ultimately then, Vijay's inherent connection with his genetic family is an equally powerful determinant of his fate as his lived alienation from the nation.

Deewaar's Ravi, on the other hand, has a different relationship to his biological identity. When Ravi is first told by the police commissioner of his assignment to capture the smugglers' gang which includes Vijay, he refuses the case, saying,

> Sir, I can't take this case... [hesitates]... Vijay Varma is my brother. He's my brother, sir... You can understand my helplessness. Perhaps I won't be able to carry out my responsibility fully. That's why, sir, please give this case to someone else. I'm sorry...

His hesitation indexes a profound internal ambivalence between his professional and ethical duty and the power of the blood tie. Despite this initial doubt, however, the injustice he continues to see with the eyes of a police officer compels him to reconsider, and he ends up taking the case. Ravi is only the secondary hero of the film, but even so his character begins to put pressure on the *assumption* of the blood tie – the unstated but understood supposition which is generally at the heart of the lost-and-found. In the significance of his decision to choose morality over genetics, the film suggests that blood bonds are not as unassailable as they might appear.

Because of Ravi's decision, the brothers' relationship gets recast outside of the dominant vision of a family united by blood. The brothers exist in relation to their mother, Bharati, whom they both seek to claim, but they are alienated from one another, reborn not as brother and brother, but as upholder of the law and its transgressor. In *Yaadon*, by contrast, the brothers never get to know each other as friends, acquaintances, or in any other non-fraternal capacity. Besides for a few chance encounters, they are strangers to one another. Their *only* relationship to one another is blood and the shared memories of the past. In *Deewaar* it is precisely the conflict between the 'real' logic of the bloodline and the social oppositionality of the brothers' respective positions that determines the film's problematic morality. *Deewaar* is in this sense an ironic lost-and-found, in which the genetic energy that underlies the success of the formula is dissipated by new moral concerns.

Fictive kinship in Amar Akbar Anthony

The unsettling of the assumption of genetic kinship that was gestured towards but not fully developed in *Deewaar* comes to fully inhabit the plot of a film made two years later, *Amar Akbar Anthony* (d. Manmohan Desai, 1977). Desai's film takes the disarticulation between biological kinship and social reality even further to offer a radical reinterpretation of kinship, in which an entirely new morality emerges out of the lived experience of sociality. The film thus encourages its audience not only to rethink the loss of real ties in the wake of Partition but to question the very realness of those ties in the first place.

Amar Akbar Anthony is the story of three brothers separated in childhood when their mother abandons them and their father, fleeing from a group of gangsters who framed him for a murder, leaves them at the foot of a Gandhi statue to await his return. The young boys wander off one by one and are found by three different men, a Hindu policeman, a Muslim imam, and a Catholic priest. The men, unable to trace the boys' parents, adopt the boys and give them new names befitting their new religious identities: Amar, Akbar, and Anthony. The boys grow up under these identities until, in a series of coincidences, all of them are caught up in the lives of the same gangsters. They ultimately come to know of their genetic relations and are reunited at the film's end.

Like *Yaadon*, the film uses a classic lost-and found formula, but layered on this structure is another level of social commentary, as the boys' split represents the separation and alienation of India's religious communities. Conversely, their reunion signifies the utopian harmony of these communities within the larger umbrella of 'Indianness,' conceived as the biological family unit. Like *Deewaar*, then, *Amar Akbar Anthony* imbues the family break-up with social meaning beyond the purely biological violence of separating individuals who share common blood.

Yet early on, *Amar Akbar Anthony* presents the family's separation as a primarily biological one. This is evident in the oversignified credits scene that comes about half and hour into the film. I say 'oversignified' because this scene of blood ties is so protracted and theatrically staged – even by the conventions of Hindi popular cinema of the time – that it exceeds its stated meaning. The credits sequence is an extended tableau of the imagined reconciliation of the broken blood ties, through a deliberate spatialization of the three brothers vis-à-vis Bharati, their birth mother. Bharati has had an accident, the doctors are desperate for blood donations, and by coincidence they call upon Amar, Akbar and Anthony, who do not know their relation to each other or to Bharati, as the donors. The mise en scène – with Bharati lying at one end of the room and the brothers, in parallel beds, at the other – makes it clear that the scene is not supposed to represent an actual transfusion, but instead to serve as a representation of the 'family tree' by which the brothers are literally tied, by the force of blood, to their rightful mother. To add to the staged quality, the camera operates primarily by way of lengthy pans rather than cuts, following along the length of the tubes that connect each son to his mother, while the film's theme song plays in the background, undergirded by the refrain, *Khoon khoon hota hai, pani nahin* ('blood is thicker than water'). On top of this, behind each son's bed is a false window which shows an image of the house of worship of his adopted religion, a temple for Amar, a mosque for Akbar, and a church for Anthony.

While this presentation might seem to lament the loss of the unity of the postcolonial nation using a self-evident biological metaphor, *Amar Akbar Anthony* instead offers an entire plot structured over a parallel set of relationships unrelated to the brothers' blood tie. In this way, the film posits hope not solely in the reunion of lost biological bonds, but in the possibilities for 'fictive kinship.' I use this term as a means of describing the lived experience of kinship, which may or may not relate to real genetic bonds.[3] Thus although the originary point of *Amar Akbar Anthony* is the *broken* family, the substance of the plot is concerned with the 'new' relationships the characters make with people with whom they might or might not be genetically related. These include the three father-son relationships between the boys and each of their adoptive fathers, the closeness of which complicates the idea that blood is thicker than water. The film also traces the coincidental interaction of the lives of the five family members as they negotiate the morally corrupt landscape of 1970s Bombay, in the process of which they meet one other – again, not knowing that they are related – and establish new relationships in the idiom of kinship. Bharati, for example, consistently refers to Amar, Akbar and Anthony as her *bete* (sons) and they to her as *maa* or *mai* (mother).[4] Anthony and Akbar refer to each other as *bhai*. All these relationships constitute the lived experience of fictive kinship that is entirely independent of the fact that the individuals are genetically related.

The concept of 'fictive kinship' has been criticized by scholars because embedded in the term is the assumption that social relationships are false, as compared to their 'true,' biological counterparts (Weston 98–102). However if we retain a sense of 'fictive' not as false but as actively constructed (the word comes from the Latin *fingere*, to contrive or form), we might shift emphasis from the contrast between real and constructed relationships and focus instead on the actual, social process of forming. I suggest that despite its oversignified titular tableau, *Amar Akbar Anthony* invites its viewers to do just that – to focus on kinship as a *process*. Kinship thus becomes significant not because it necessarily *is*, but because it is constantly being made and remade.

This is evident in the scene when Bharati comes to give Amar a flower, and she finds Anthony in prison, where he has been arrested by Amar. Anthony calls out to her from inside his jail cell:

> Anthony: Mai! O Mai!
> Bharati: What's this, this sounds like Anthony's voice!
> Anthony: 'Then what?' Who else could have such a manly voice?
> Bharati: What is he doing here?... *Bete* [to Amar], he's a very nice boy. He also donated blood to me. He's just like my son, just like you are.
> Anthony: He Mai, what are you saying? [laughs] He's your son, I'm your son—according to that logic we should be brothers... Right brother [looking at Amar], what do you think...
> Bharat: Amar *bete*, please release him.
> Amar: Maa ji...
> Anthony: No way, he'd never release me. Even if I were his real brother he'd never release me. He's very strict, very strict.

Then, a few moments later, as Anthony is on his way to the courthouse:

> Anthony: Hey Mai, this is the first time I've come to a police station, and you made the inspector my brother. Today I'm going to the court for the first time... could you give me a flower, for good luck? You know why? If I go there and meet another strict man, I'll give him the flower and make him my father (*apun usko apna baap banaayega*).

In the fictive kin relations described here, their underlying 'realness' is irrelevant; what the dialogue demonstrates is Anthony's deft negotiation of the social landscape through the idiom of kinship. Here, kin terms provide a language in which social relationships are articulated. These sometimes raise contradictions – for instance when two enemies are both called 'bete' by the same 'maa.' But more importantly, the terms are productive, constituting individuals in various relations of proximity through their usage. Thus just as by 'making the inspector [Anthony's] brother' Bharati attempts to mitigate the conflict between the two sides of the law, Anthony believes that by 'making the judge [his] father' he might get a lighter sentence.

This logic of kinship differs from that presented in the credits sequence – or, for that matter, in *Yaadon ki Baaraat* – in which blood bonds, even if they have no social value, constitute the dominant connection between individuals. And it is this fictive kinship that animates the lived experience of sociality in *Amar Akbar Anthony* to such an extent that it comes to overshadow the blood bonds that were so self-consciously staged in the opening. As the film goes on, the dramatic irony of the encounters between the brothers loses its comedy, and the real, social bonds they form with one another begin to acquire greater moral weight. When the five family members finally discover that they are related, therefore, it is more generative of satisfaction than surprise, as the realness of their relations had already been established by their solidarity against Robert and his goons. What the film turns out to advance, therefore, is not the unassailability of blood bonds, but the immensely meaningful possibilities of patching together new families following the loss of an originary one. Insofar as this is allegorical for the disillusionment of post-Emergency India, the film suggests that a connection to the land of one's birth, while psychically very powerful, is not, in itself, enough; the connection needs to be consistently reworked and re-earned as part of the lived reality of the nation. In this way the film puts pressure on the lost-and-found, brother-centric formula seen throughout popular film of the 1970s to suggest a fundamental instability at the heart of the formula. It suggests that equally important, if not more so, to real bonds are those forged in daily life, which cannot be reduced to blood kinship but gain their force from their metaphorical closeness to family. These new relationships – *bhais* who are not necessarily brothers, and *mais* and *baaps* and who are not necessarily birth parents – constitute a world in which the lost-and-found has value, but only partially so: when meaningful ties are lost, new sources of social succor can be found along the way.

II. Homosociality and desire

If lost-and-found is the repeated formula that allows for a reconsideration of the biological family, then the classic love triangle raises similar innovations for rethinking romantic love. As with the broken family, 1970s films offer iterations of the love triangle as a means of unleashing an unstated subtext which, by later in the decade, will offer a glimpse of new kinds of relationships outside conventional representations of desire. These include relationships which allow for the expression of male-male desire in a public cinema with little language to represent overt homosexuality.[5]

An early, and classic, version of the love triangle formula can be found in *Sangam* (d. Raj Kapoor, 1964). *Sangam* is the story of three childhood friends, Radha, Sundar and Gopal, as they negotiate their relationships with one another in early adulthood. The film is a classic love triangle not only because Radha and Gopal love each other while Sundar is in love with Radha, but because of what will become the crucial element as the formula is repeated: the 'dosti' (Mishra 83), or friendship, between Gopal and Sundar. When Sundar leaves for a mission with the Air Force, he makes Gopal promise that he will save Radha for him; Gopal, on his part, is unable to tell Sundar that he is in love with Radha. Underlying this lack of communication is an unstated but ardent relationship between the two men, which is unexpressed in the primary storyline but accounts for the intensity of their clash surrounding Radha. Both men's love for her is charged with desire for the other, which is spatialized most overtly in Gopal's death scene, when the men are finally able to hold each other and only invite Radha into the embrace as an afterthought.

This 'barely disguised homoerotic feeling' (Mishra 6) in *Sangam* is given more space to develop in *Sholay* (d. Ramesh Sippy, 1975). *Sholay* reinterprets the love triangle formula by reducing the role of the woman at the center of the triangulation to a minor character (albeit a memorable one), and thus figuring the relationship between the two men on center stage.[6] This has the effect of highlighting what in *Sangam* was unexpressed – that the triangulated love story is merely an alibi for a representation of homosociality within the censorial parameters of heteronormativity. *Sholay* underscores this by presenting Basanti as forthright and carefree, which immediately makes her unappealing to Jai, and thus precludes the full formation of the love triangle from the start. But Basanti is still the primary site around which Jai and Veeru's relationship is negotiated. For instance, in the dialogue when Veeru, drunk, is asking Jai to discuss his engagement with Basanti's aunt, and Jai jokingly demurs, Veeru pouts:

> You're not my friend ... This is why you're being difficult, right? Because no one else can do this job for me? If my mother were here today, then I would have been long since married. I would have had kids by now. If I had a father, he would have celebrated my wedding in full style. If I had brothers and sisters, they would have touched [Basanti's] Auntie's feet to get us married ... You're not that friend ... What I had thought of you, Jai, but look how you turned out!

As in *Amar Akbar Anthony*, the social value of the men's relationship lives in the discourse around it, which reveals it to be constantly in negotiation. Because of its inassimilability to socially accepted kin or romantic terms, Veeru here has no vocabulary to name it; and thus can only define their relationship by what it is not.

Earlier in *Sholay*, the extradiegetic arena of song had defined the relationship between Jai and Veeru as *dosti*, and it is in this space that most critics have seen the most powerful expression of their homosocial desire (Gopinath 290). In the song, the love triangle is briefly invoked as well, in the form of a village woman whom they both gawk at, and then flip a coin to see who will be allowed to pursue. The entire scene is presented as comedy, with the film speed increased as the woman walks away, turned off by their indecision. The two men shrug and continue their song. This temporary break in the narrative of a song about friendship stages the irrelevance of the female term in the love triangle in a way that *Sangam* alluded to but could not quite pronounce, and in a way that Basanti repeats but cannot quite contain. In the song sequence *Sholay* comes closest of all the films of the decade to making explicit homosocial desire, even as it codes it as the legible and normative *dosti*. But it does so by stretching the love triangle formula to such an extent that it is basically no longer a love triangle. The question of romance is thus sidestepped in favor of the more neutral 'friendship,' and the channels of desire are disarticulated from those of sexuality.

Brotherhood and queer kinship in Silsila

Silsila (d. Yash Chopra, 1981) offers a unique resignification of desire, brotherhood and homosociality by reanimating the female lead which *Sholay* had effaced but retaining the hero's indifference to her. Here, Shobha is too staid for Amit, but perfect for Shekhar, Amit's biological brother. The film's surface text thus narrates two love stories, between Amit and Chandni, who meet at a friend's wedding and fall instantly in love, and between Shobha and Shekhar, who are on the verge of getting married when the film begins. However, early on Shekhar dies in a fighter plane accident and, when it is revealed that Shobha is pregnant, Amit makes the decision to break his engagement with Chandni and marry Shobha instead. He is initially bitter about his decision and is driven to meet Chandni, now married herself, where they begin a love affair that gives them immediate pleasure but whose moral implications eat away at them both. It is not until the end of the film, when Chandni's husband has a near-fatal accident, that Amit realizes the social and personal consequences of their actions and changes his course, returning to Shobha for good.

Silsila reanimates the unexpressed desire that is emptied out at the crucial moment of *Sholay* to reinterpret the relationship between men in the context of the love triangle. For although Amit and Shekhar are biological brothers, their relationship is presented as more complex than what is contained in the kinship term – indexing a potential third 'love story' in the film's subtext. On one hand, their fraternity is assumed, as in *Yaadon ki Baaraat*: the audience expects that the two brothers will be close because of their biological connection. However, the extent of their relationship does not stop there. Unlike in *Yaadon*, the audience witnesses the insistent negotiation of their relationship in a sphere removed from their biological bond. This occurs first in relation to Shobha, the woman whom both men will 'share.' When Shobha picks Amit up from the airport, around 20 minutes into the film, they discuss Amit's relationship with Shekhar:

> Shobha: Why do you call yourself Amit's brother and then start laughing?
> Amit: That was a big problem, which we resolved with some consideration.
> S: I see.
> A: My brother is one-and-a-half years older than me, but we're friends. We started smoking together, and we started drinking alcohol together, at the same time, from the very same glass. But even before that we fell in love at about the same time...
> S: With the same girl...
> A: You know that already? Good. And before that we used to shower together naked.
> S: I heard that.

A: You must not have seen it . . .
[both laugh]
A: We both keep changing our roles.
S: [looking surprised] Changing roles . . . ? I don't understand.
A: I'll explain it to you. When one of us was in trouble, the other would play the role of big brother.
S: [laughs] Amit ji, I'll go crazy listening to your chatter . . .
A: This is just a sample. We still have a whole life together.
S: Meaning?
A: You're related to my brother, I'm related to my brother, so you must be related to me . . . !

We can understand from this conversation that the two men are brothers, but that is in fact the least we understand. The whole conversation ostensibly about brotherhood in fact describes a multi-faceted relationship between two men, of which their genetic bond seems the least important aspect. Instead, the conversation is full of allusions and insinuations that point to a range of relationships that include growing up together, friendship, homosociality and something that borders on sexual intimacy even if not actual sex (showering naked together, falling in love with the same girl). This latter relation, capped off by the allusive suggestion that the two brothers 'kept changing their roles' and the 'joke' that Amit and Shobha are in fact related, verges on an *identificatory* relationship, what Priya Jha calls in the context of *Sholay* '[t]he affirmation of a singular, dyadic identity – two sides of the same coin' (Jha 47), where the two men are so close than they are occasionally replaceable. Pushing the question even further, however, this identity is actually put to the test when Shekhar dies and Amit has to decide whether to marry Shobha. This jocular discussion of the multivalence of the two men's relationship thus gains a moral weight in the plot of the film.

We might not feel that the term 'queer kinship' is appropriate in the context of a film with a heteronormative telos and produced in a context in which sexual themes are restricted by a heavy censorial gaze; however, if we take queer kinship to refer not only to kin relations formed by gay, lesbian, or transgender individuals, but to the 'queering' of kinship more generally, we can open up the focus of kinship analysis to other bonds besides those of the heterosexual family unit. Part of the analytic value of the word 'queer' is that it does not merely point to different kinds of existing relationships but, like the notion of 'fictive kinship' discussed above, indexes the presence of new relationship-possibilities at the margins of the socially intelligible. It is in that spirit that we might label the relationship between Amit and Shekhar as 'queer' in relation to the Hindi popular film repertoire for describing relationships between men.[7] It is also true that their relationship – their 'fraternal friendship' – is laced with desire. For instance, the first communication between the two men in the film takes place in the form of a letter, which Shekhar writes to Amit to invite him to Kashmir; the scene in which Amit reads Shekhar's letter immediately follows another epistolary scene, this time in which Chandni is reading a love letter from Amit. Juxtaposing these scenes draws an implicit relation between the two letters, setting up a second 'triangle' in which Amit, rather than Shobha, occupies the center, and in which desire is repeated in epistolary form.

Evincing a pattern that has come to be central to the triangulation formula, then, Amit's decision to marry Shobha has less to do with his feelings for Chandni or his pity for Shobha, and more with his intense relationship with the dead Shekhar, with whom his relationship is fundamentally ambivalent. At one extreme, they are two individuals who share a biological bond; at the other, they are so close that they are potentially interchangeable ('*we would keep changing our roles*'). In Amit's struggle over his course of action following Shekhar's death, the intense yet ambivalent homosociality of their relationship is put to the test. As a brother, it is unclear whether he has any obligation toward Shobha, and no explicit mention is made – although it might constitute a subtext – of a purely fraternal responsibility. Yet Amit and Shekhar are not 'merely' brothers, but 'two halves of the same coin' – an excess that raises unanswerable questions for Amit, such as How far into domesticity, into *practical sexuality*, ought their fraternal friendship to extend? How much was their sexual intimacy a childhood game, and how much does it produce adult obligations? And, what happens to socially unrepresentable desire when it condenses into social obligation? Despite the putative moral fixity of Hindi popular film, these questions remain largely unanswerable, and *Silsila* is pervaded with a certain moral bleakness that results from such practical obscurity. First, Amit marries Shobha in what he thinks is acting right by his friend – by becoming his sexual equivalent. Yet that proves an unsatisfactory outlet to his desire, which also lies in the socially sanctioned space of heteronormativity represented by Chandni. Then he follows his desire but finds that it leads him back out of social sanction, into the transgressive realm of adultery. These transgressions are not his personal failings, but the impossibility of expressing his multivalent relationship with Shekhar within social conventions. Much like, in *DCH*, Siddharth's short-lived attempt to envision his relationship with Tara through the idiom of '*pyaar*' (socially sanctioned romance), *Silsila* similarly shows how difficult it is for a relationship with no name to survive the rigid paradigms of social life.

Silsila's resolution – its way out of this murky moral territory – is to take literally the metaphor of identification that was used to describe the two men's homosocial intimacy, and thus the film ends with a repetition of the song 'Sar se sarke,' but this time with Amit in Shekhar's place (Dwyer 202). The formal integrity represented by the repetition of this song can only be restored when Amit has returned to his rightful place by Shobha's side. But even within this seemingly conservative ending, the problem of homosocial desire remains unresolved, and the potential multivalence of the two men's relationship continues right until the very final scene.

This is a somewhat counterintuitive reading of transgression in *Silsila*, which has primarily been located in Amit's extra-marital affair with Chandni, a reading buoyed by rumors of a real affair between actors Amitabh Bachchan and Rekha (Dwyer 193). From the perspective of adultery, *Silsila*'s ending could be read as a capitulation to the bourgeois values which uphold the nuclear family. However, in the context of the unarticulated homosociality that underlies the triangulation plots of the 1970s in general, *Silsila* might also be seen as offering another mode of transgression. This transgression irrupts onto the surface of the text only once, in the widely-discussed shower scene, in which Amit and Shekhar, while showering together (now as adults) laughingly express reluctance to bend over and pick up a bar of soap lying on the shower floor.[8] Indeed, this is a moment where the subtext pierces the surface text, but nonetheless it provides a crucial index to the space outside conventional romantic or kin terms where the reality of the men's relationship lies. From this perspective, *Silsila* functions similarly to *Amar Akbar Anthony*, not only repeating the earlier formula but calling into question the assumptions and paradigms it relies on. Coming right at the end of the 1970s, *Silsila* seems a kind of capstone in thinking about homosociality and desire in the decade. It shows with even more intensity the possibilities for incorporating new kinds of social relationships into the registers, even if not the explicit language, of popular film.

III. Conclusion: Reading popular film

I have not intended to suggest that films get 'better,' more sophisticated or more subtle over the years. Indeed, by tracing the sources of Tara's incisive phrasing in *Dil Chahta Hai* to the 'formula-films' of the 1970s, I hope to have shown how what appear to be new innovations often took root long before the current turn towards what appear to be more open representations of family and sexuality in popular film. The films of this long decade constitute a particularly relevant subset of the large body of Hindi popular cinema that was engaged with some amount of persistence in representing human relationships outside of social sanction or conventionally accepted kinship terms. The sheer repetition of the formulas we have seen and the subtle variations that distinguish individual films, along with what are quite radical critiques of normative social relationships, make this set of films not the only, but a particularly interesting case study for the socially radical possibilities of popular film. Moreover, the way individual films build off of generic formulas – and indeed, build off one another – complicates narratives of the 1970s that focus on radical reinvention and rupture. They illuminate the complex ways popular films make meaning and represent new social concerns, even within their conventional formulas.

Thus although the 1970s has often been considered a period of a 'crisis of the state' (Ganti 30), it was also a time in which Hindi films were increasingly receptive to global energies of social ferment, sexuality and rebellious youth. These cannot be accounted for in the language of 'crisis,' yet in many ways their impact on cultural forms is more long-lasting. Certainly the kinds of reconfigurations we see around family and sexuality in popular films of the 1970s are the predecessors of what today is significantly more space in popular culture for representing new kinds of relationships. But if we fixate on radical newness we lose sight of the complex ways in which popular film has always offered alternatives to dominant conventions: by opening up a space of difference where new meanings can emerge outside of the language that conventionally contains them. Without this understanding only anger, crisis and revolution render themselves legible, while the relationships with no name continue to be silenced.

Acknowledgements

The author would like to thank the participants and respondents at the April 2011 conference on 'The 1970s and its Legacies,' and in particular Priya Joshi and Rajinder Dudrah for organizing the conference and for their helpful comments on an earlier draft of this paper. Also thanks to Jayne Ziemba for her research assistance.

Notes

1. *'Kuch rishte hote, jinka koi naam nahin hota.'*
2. Film and cultural theorists Rosie Thomas and Ashis Nandy provide detailed descriptions of the various formulas and tropes of Hindi popular cinema.
3. I want to clarify that although the three brothers do share genetic bonds, the series of relationships they form during the course of the film's plot are not dependent on those biological bonds. Rather, they are 'fictive' bonds because they use the idiom of kinship but are social rather than biological; they are actively made rather than assumed *a priori*.
4. Bharati's constant use of kinship terms is a convention unsurprising to Indian viewers (kinship terms are often used as a marker of respect in intergenerational conversation), but here they are deliberately overemployed, in a classic dramatic irony, to tease the audience towards the resolution presented in the credits tableau.
5. Cultural theorist Gayatri Gopinath defines 'buddy films' (Gopinath 290) as those which focus on homosocial friendship; I emphasize the 'love triangle' because I see shared desire for the woman, which is not common to all 'buddy films,' as a key conduit of homosocial desire in these films.
6. The nature of the friendship between Jai and Veeru has been extensively discussed by critics, including by Jha (46–47), Ghosh (60–61) and Gopinath (290–291); Dudrah (293 and 305n.5)

offers a useful survey of the different queer readings of Bollywood films, most of which include at least some reference to *Sholay*.

7. Film scholar Rajinder Dudrah usefully frames the question of intentionality when he asks, 'Is the Queer Reread in Bollywood or Is Bollywood Inherently Queer?' I follow Dudrah in arguing that although queer subtexts might not be the intention of the films' writers,

> it is possible to argue that in a caricature of selfhood queer Bollywood is not only a matter of the "queer readings" that "queer audiences" bring to the text, but rather Bollywood's investment in caricature makes it a rich cultural resource where meanings of "queer" and "camp" can be readily created and contested. Thus, even the manifest heteronormative content is queered by a representational excess that marginalizes questions of authenticity (of straightness, for example) because both queer and straight are equally caricatured. (Dudrah 301–302)

8. Several critics have noted the homosexual overtones of this scene (Gehlawat 84–114). Ashok Row Kavi writes that '[t]his is the clearest reference to the "penetrating" image of Amitabh Bachchan' (Kavi 311).

References

Ahmed, Akbar S. "Bombay Films: The Cinema as Metaphor for Indian Society and Politics." *Modern Asian Studies* 26.2 (1992): 289–320. Print.

Dudrah, Rajinder. "Queer as Desis: Secret Politics of Gender and Sexuality in Bollywood Films in Diasporic Urban Ethnoscapes." *Global Bollywood: Travels of Hindi Song and Dance*. Ed. Sangita Gopal and Sujata Moorti. Minneapolis: U of Minnesota P, 2008. 288–307. Print.

Dwyer, Rachel. "The Hindi Romantic Cinema: Yash Chopra's *Kabhi Kabhie* and *Silsila*." *South Asia: Journal of South Asian Studies* 21.1 (1998): 181–212. Print.

Ganti, Tejaswini. *Bollywood: A Guidebook to Popular Hindi Cinema*. New York: Routledge, 2004. Print.

Gehlawat, Ajay. *Reframing Bollywood: Theories of Popular Hindi Cinema*. New Delhi: Sage, 2010. Print.

Ghosh, Shohini. "Bollywood Cinema and Queer Sexualities." *Queer Theory: Law, Culture, Empire*. Ed. Robert Leckey and Kim Brooks. Abingdon: Routledge, 2010. 55–68. Print.

Gopinath, Gayatri. "Queering Bollywood: Alternative Sexualities in Popular Indian Cinema." *Queer Asian Cinema: Shadows in the Shade*. Ed. Andrew Grossman. Binghamton: Harrington Park Press, 2000. 283–97. Print.

Jha, Priya. "Lyrical Nationalism: Gender, Friendship, and Excess in 1970s Hindi Cinema." *Velvet Light Trap* 51 (2003): 43–53. Print.

Joshi, Priya. "Cinema as Family Romance." *South Asian Popular Culture* 10.1 (forthcoming). Print.

Kavi, Ashok Row. "The Changing Image of the Hero in Hindi Films." *Queer Asian Cinema: Shadows in the Shade*. Ed. Andrew Grossman. New York: Routledge, 2001. 307–12. Print.

Mazumdar, Ranjani. *Bombay Cinema: An Archive of the City*. Minneapolis: U of Minnesota P, 2007. Print.

Mishra, Vijay. *Bollywood Cinema: Temples of Desire*. New York: Routledge, 2002. Print.

Nandy, Ashis. "The Popular Hindi Film: Ideology and First Principles." *India International Centre Quarterly* 8.1 (1981): 89–96. Print.

Thomas, Rosie. "Indian Cinema: Pleasures and popularity." *Screen* 26.3–4 (1985): 116–31. Print.

Vasudevan, Ravi. *The Melodramatic Public: Film Form and Spectatorship in Indian Cinema*. Ranikhet: Permanent Black, 2010. Print.

Weston, Kath. "Forever is a Long Time: Romancing the Real in Gay Kinship Ideologies." *Naturalizing Power: Essays in Feminist Cultural Analysis*. Ed. Sylvia Yanagisako and Carol Delaney. New York: Routledge, 1995. 87–112. Print.

Filmography

Amar Akbar Anthony, Dir. Manmohan Desai. DEI, 1977. Film.
Deewaar, Dir. Yash Chopra. Trimurti Films, 1975. Film.
Dil Chahta Hai, Dir. Farhan Akhtar, Excel Entertainment, 2001. Film.
Sangam, Dir. Raj Kapoor. Yashraj Films, 1964. Film.
Sholay, Dir. Ramesh Sippy. Eros Entertainment, 1975. Film.
Silsila, Dir. Yash Chopra. Yashraj Films, 1981. Film.
Zanjeer, Dir. Prakash Mehra. Eros Entertainment, 1973. Film.
Yaadon Ki Baaraat, Dir. Nasir Hussain. Nasir Hussain Films, 1973. Film.

The affable young man: Civility, desire and the making of a middle-class cinema in the 1970s

Satish Poduval

The English and Foreign Languages University, Hyderabad, India

A significant counterpoint to the subaltern impatience and revolt that characterized popular Hindi cinema of the 1970s was the staging of middle-class civility and desire, away from the generic conventions of the 'masala-Social.' This paper argues that this new desire for modernity was supplemented with a determination to secure it, and necessarily involved fresh forms of engagement *and* disengagement with the Symbolic pact that had instituted modernity in India during the Nehruvian conjuncture. I trace the emergence of a new cycle of middle-class cinema by focusing on the contrapuntal star personas of the 'angry' and the 'affable' young men (Amitabh Bachchan and Amol Palekar) during this decade. The focus is on selected films by Hrishikesh Mukherjee and Basu Chatterjee which put into play a newer narrative contract, and consolidated the rise of the desiring/consuming screen subjects of the post-liberalization Hindi film narratives.

The 1970s were marked by intense political crisis and change in India, and emergent cinematic trends registered – here directly and powerfully, there through subterfuge and over-coded iconography – the prevailing structures of feeling. Even a cursory trawl through the filmic archives of those transitional years heaps up images of unparalleled despair over the republic's thwarted hopes on the one hand, and on the other flamboyantly wrought vignettes that affirm a sense of desire predicated on the heterotopic possibilities of a new materialism. If certain events (the 'triumph' in Bangladesh, and the early successes in the space and atomic programmes) filled the political leadership and middle-class subjects with a new pride and confidence, others (the widespread protests against inflation and corruption, and widespread labour unrest) prompted the resolve to break from Nehruvian protectionism. Coinciding with the larger shifts in global capitalism and the World Bank's bid to sustain worldwide accumulation through 'third world' markets, the discourse of 'civil society' made its way into elite consciousness during this decade. It is worth considering how this new sense of *civility* began to be refracted through the prism of popular culture in India.

This essay focuses on a cycle of middle-class melodramas within Hindi cinema during the 1970s, especially those by directors Hrishikesh Mukherjee and Basu Chatterjee, in which some aspects of the cultural politics of civility might be discerned. The staging of middle-class domesticity and desire in these films is by no means without precedent in Hindi cinema, but something 'original' does become visible when they are seen as a counterpoint to the theme of subaltern anger and public unrest that had emerged within the masala-Social during the 1970s. While the latter was commonly articulated through the figure of the vigilante superhero or the newly sensitized 'developmental' agent of the state or civil society, middle-class cinema sought a different site of engagement: the insecurities linked to romantic and marital conflict, often under the shadow of aspirations for class mobility. Two crucial elements in these tales of passion and conjugality are (i) the new value accorded to middle-class civility as a strategy of power, and (ii) a re-assembling of middle-class masculine agency through inter-textual face-off between the 'angry' and the 'affable' young man.

Before examining this cycle of films, an attempt will be made in section 2 to describe key features of the historical conjuncture. Following this, in section 3, we shall focus on the ways in which the new aspirations and tensions in Indian society were mediated in the middle-class melodramas of Hrishikesh Mukherjee, featuring Amitabh Bachchan in a set of important films before his formal inauguration as the 'angry young man.' Section 4 will contrast the anger relayed by the masala-Social genre with the affability associated with the persona of Amol Palekar forged in a series of realist romantic comedies by Basu Chatterjee. The conclusion traces the discursive consolidation of affability (or middle-class civility) as a mode of power through influential television serials during the 1980s and the post-liberalization 'Bollywood' cinema since the 1990s.

Periodizing the seventies

Despite the chronic shortage of funds, scarce exhibition avenues, poorly developed distribution infrastructure, high dependence on imported film equipment, prohibitive levels of taxation and censorship regulations, and precious little support from the government, the Indian film industry emerged in 1971 as the world's largest producer of films – a position that has been consolidated in subsequent decades. Notwithstanding the severe handicaps (or perhaps due to them), the industry embarked on untested paths and an autonomous expansion, responding to the public's desire for new cinematic mediations during that crisis-ridden conjuncture. Historians of contemporary Indian political life have argued that the Nehruvian consensus regarding the institutions and instruments for nation-building had begun to unravel gradually during the mid-1960s and with greater urgency during the 1970s, primarily due to the mounting economic crisis, the internal power realignments within the Congress party system, the widespread upsurge of disaffection against a mode of governance perceived as inefficient and uncaring, and decisive shifts in the world economic system.[1] According to the political scientist Sanjay Seth, the privileged classes learned to view distortions in national development not as a function of an 'incomplete' modernity but as necessary structural features of a modernity into which the nation had already 'arrived':

> And so, with an almost audible sigh of relief, these classes... decided to embrace and celebrate this discovery; they have accepted that it is in the very nature of this Indian modernity that the latest consumer goods coexist with extreme poverty. (Seth 353).

Economist Kalyan Sanyal similarly points to a shift in developmental discourse in the early 1970s, with the earlier goal of 'all-encompassing, macro-level transformation' being replaced by an approach that emphasized the emergence of 'a network of interventions aimed at the "management of poverty" in the wasteland produced by the primitive accumulation of post-colonial capital' (Sanyal 88–89). Clearly, however, such a large-scale discursive shift could not be effected merely through the privileged classes' 'sigh of relief' or managerial exhortation from the state. As literary scholars Tharu and Lalita have observed, the mid-1970s was also a period in which 'world capitalism ... made a concerted effort to break the power of national oligopolies' and the '*internationalization of markets, and the transformation of the Indian state essentially into a mediator in that process, required that the nation be imagined anew*' (Tharu and Lalita 49, emphasis in original). There was thus a modification in discourses of nationalism which had until then been ballasted primarily by the imperatives of anti-imperial bonding or the economic and scientific prestige associated with developmentalism. These nationalist discourses, which had ensured dirigistic centrality for the numerically marginal (middle-class, upper-caste) national elite, were increasingly challenged from a variety of locations: potent regionalist demands for redistribution of resources; population groups that convoked electorally around perceptions of long-pending injustices; and a new entrepreneurial class, keen to extricate economic initiative from bureaucratic shackles and confident that competing globally was both possible and profitable. These macro-historical shifts are of not mere contextual 'noise' but crucial determinants in the field of cultural production that came into existence.[2] It might be argued that the new middle-class cinema that emerged during the early 1970s was a key element of a new aesthetic contract[3] that brought the historical shifts into alignment with processes of 'subjectification.'

The origins of this middle-of-the-road cinema have been traced to younger filmmakers who had apprenticed with Bimal Roy during the 1950s. Film journalist Ratnottama Sengupta has listed Hrishikesh Mukherjee, Basu Chatterjee, Gulzar, Rajendra Singh Bedi, and Basu Bhattacharya as representative filmmakers of the new trend, noting that their novelty lay in having 'a sophistication that was in keeping with the recent developments' (Sengupta 89). According to some accounts, this new trend was pioneered by Hrishikesh Mukherjee who 'carved a middle path between the extravagance of mainstream cinema and the stark realism of art cinema' (Gulzar, Nihalani and Chatterjee 592), while others have claimed that it was the 'unexpected commercial success' of Basu Chatterjee's *Rajanigandha* in 1974 that 'helped to open up a new space which would subsequently be referred to as middle cinema' (Ahmed). This cinema drew its thematic, narrative and marketing attributes from a wide variety of sources. Like much of art-house cinema, it was built around 'ordinary' characters, settings, conversations, and events (except that the ambience here was resolutely urban, middle-class and upper-caste). It usually had lesser-known but trained cast and crew (stars, when present, were willing to work at greatly reduced prices and subordinate their roles to the story or directorial vision), and the consequent low production costs allowed a niche market to be cultivated. Commercial viability was also enhanced by *not* eschewing the market-magnetic conventions of popular songs, deft use of comic and melodramatic elements, topical commentary, and cinematic self-reference. The trend was also significantly aided by the fact that between 1971 and 1975, the Indian government allowed what it perceived as a lop-sided agreement with the Motion Pictures Exporters Association of America to expire (for details, see Pendakur), and directed the state-owned Film Finance Corporation to fund independent cinema with a view to turn the medium into 'an effective instrument for the promotion of national culture, education and healthy entertainment' (Committee on Public Undertakings (1975–76) "Report on the FFC," cited in Rajadhyaksha 234). The first step meant that the screen space that had until then been blocked by Hollywood films became available to alternative cinema, while the second ensured that relatively soft loans were in principle available to those willing to make what the government considered 'meaningful films.' It is worth noting that these governmental initiatives ultimately proved unsuccessful and short-lived: many of the successful new wave films were privately funded and promoted, and after 1975 the government chose to pursue its developmental agenda through state-run television rather than through film.

For the inquiry pursued here, more crucial than the formal attributes of this genre are questions concerning what they did, and how they worked. We might usefully take a cue from film scholar Madhava Prasad's suggestion that at the start of the 1970s two broad trends emerged within Hindi realist cinema. The first, set in motion by directors such as Mrinal Sen and Shyam Benegal, was based on a notion of 'progressive realism': it invoked a division within the national space, and positioned the urban spectator to witness a different social world that was nevertheless within the same political unit. The second trend, associated with filmmakers like Hrishikesh Mukherjee and Basu Chatterjee, comprised of films that addressed themselves to a class within (or specifically associated with) the nation, and sought to 'create a world that the spectator would recognize as his/her own' (Prasad 161).[4] Although both sets of films were made almost exclusively for the urban middle-class audience, Prasad points to an inner schism that inflected the narratives in separate directions, leading to different viewing positions generated by the strategies of textual representation:

> [T]he audience of citizen-subjects were called upon to occupy two different positions. One corresponded to the citizen side of the entity and involved a frame of reading that included the perspective of the nation-state while the other was addressed to the subject, the individual in society, faced with the struggle for existence, the locus of desires, fears and hopes. [The latter tendency is] the realist cinema of the subject, or what is commonly known as middle-class cinema. (Prasad 162)

In its turn, the middle-class cinema itself might be seen as oriented *externally* (assuming or asserting the middle-class's reformist role within nationally significant conflicts, thus responding more explicitly to the social tensions and contradictions of the period), or *internally* (focusing on how the class is hemmed in by the larger – presumably 'backward' – society, and seeks to reproduce its identity through a combination of individualist rationality and upper-caste endogamy).[5] The middle class must not be viewed merely in socio-economic terms as the intermediate strata between the upper-class and the working class, but as a constellation defined by its access to significant forms of cultural capital which includes, in addition to ample education and secure employment, the acquisition of crucial 'non-material' attributes such as taste, style, and social networking that facilitates upward mobility. These attributes of 'civility' make the middle class more of an *intermediary* class whose social skills, aspiration, lifestyle and tact play a crucial role in the reproduction of class relations and capitalist culture. The notion of civility tends to be associated most often with the behaviour proper to cultured individuals or decent citizens, and described in terms of the commitment to public reason, courteous social interaction, and tact in the pursuit of economic and political interests. The tendency to regard civility as the 'noble' or 'genteel' protocols of civil society, and its expansion as the solution to many of the problems in a divided world, is increasingly viewed with suspicion by those deemed to be wanting in civilization. As architect and urban affairs activist Jai Sen has noted:

> Beyond good manners, however, a crucial aspect of civility is power... Although the proponents of civility would prefer to be represented as merely a benign and well intentioned rule by those with a superior understanding, in reality civility is interpreted and manifested as power-over – as a force of control, not of emancipation.[6]

Approaching the Indian middle-class along these lines might help us understand how the personas of the 'angry young man' and the 'affable young man' were constructed in the middle-class cinema of the 1970s. Additionally, it indicates why the discourse of affability/civility has had a more sustained inning within mainstream cultural production. We need to examine more closely: *how* did affability work, and *why*? *What* did it convey that the 'angry' stories did not?

To address these questions, we turn now to a closer analysis of selected films from the oeuvre of middle-class cinema, made by Hrishikesh Mukherjee and Basu Chatterjee – arguably the most successful directors of the genre during this period.

The political is personal

Hrishikesh Mukherjee's films of the 1970s with Amitabh Bachchan in key early roles are melodramas of personal tension between intimate individuals, ending in an awkwardly-staged reconciliation that also involves the transformation of the socially-privileged, haughty male protagonist. The 'brooding anger' that would later be associated with the Bachchan persona is already in evidence here, but before it has been yoked through the screenplays of Salim-Javed to the popular impatience with the 'system.' Instead, this smouldering rage takes the form of distressed vulnerability against a loved one's – and indeed society's – ailments, as in *Anand* (d. Hrishikesh Mukherjee, 1971) and *Mili* (d. Hrishikesh Mukherjee, 1975); or an intense ressentiment directed against the rise of the lower-middle-class wife, as in *Abhimaan* (d. Hrishikesh Mukherjee, 1973) or the lower-middle-class friend, as in *Namak Haraam* (d. Hrishikesh Mukherjee, 1973), who suddenly seem to become rivals rather than grateful underlings. These films end in a rapprochement of sorts as the angry (ressentimental) young man learns to recognize the viewpoint of the subordinate subject, but under the condition that order is restored and things move on as they 'ought.' Like most melodramas of reconciliation, these too powerfully evoke a problem that is socially caused and maintained (gender inequality, exploitation of labour, etc.), but resolve them through the narrative contrivance of a personal 'change of heart' in a yet-privileged subject.

Consider *Abhimaan*, made at a time when 'the woman question' was returning to the national agenda under feminist pressure. The film may be viewed not just as a parable about artistic envy but also about the (im-)possibility of companionate marriage.[7]

The questioning of gender norms appears to be the more emphatic point. *Abhimaan* is a solemn enough critique, more acute than in most Hindi films, of patriarchal routines that render marriage and a career so thorny for women. Several insights from feminist debates of the period find an echo in the film. The venerable maestro Brijeswar Rai comments that while Subir's decision to make Uma sing professionally might be a 'mistake' in terms of their marital happiness, it would be a worse mistake if a singer as talented as Uma were to be lost to mundane domesticity. Subir initially affirms to Uma that marriage had merged them into 'one' and so it made no difference at all which of them earned for the family, but when she becomes more successful of the two we see his inability to live up to the consequences of this cogent truism.

There is an effort to break away from prevailing stereotypes about 'proper' femininity: Chitra's lively yet level passion for Subir, both before and after his marriage to Uma, is depicted without grating moralism; and when Subir and Chandru attempt to 'cure' Uma of her depressive apathy after her miscarriage by inducing 'maternal' tears (they show her the little green socks she had knitted for the unborn baby), she walks away saying 'throw them away.' Also noteworthy are several sequences in which the overtly affirmed meanings are possibly undercut by a semiotic doubling, perhaps even subversion, from a woman's perspective. Given that Uma is an artist herself, it is reasonable to assume that her singing stages her complex feelings, perhaps even her 'political' self. Notice the scission at work under the surface of Uma's melodious paeans to marital love: '*Loote koi mann ka nagar ban ke mera saathi*' (A stranger plunders my heart in the guise of a friend), '*Ab tho hai tum se har khushi apni; Tum pe marna hai zindagi apni*' (From now on all my joys are with you; Dying for you will be all my life), or more poignantly, '*Tere saath hum bhi sanam mash-hoor ho gaye; Dekho kahaan le jaaye be-khudi apnee*' (I have attained fame alongside you, my love; Look how far hence my rapture[loss-of-self] takes me). At the film's rather strained climax, we are unsure whether Uma has been able to awaken the right '*an-sunee si dhadkan*' (unknown pulse) in Subir's heart or whether he will merely accept the fact that she will continue to '*nayi ada se sataayegi*' (torment me in new ways), just as it seems ambiguous whether his promise for their future signifies that he would support her or continue to hold her back ('*tujhe thaame kai haathon se*'). Evidently, many scenes in the film pick up aspects of the politics of gender that contemporary feminist critique had broached during the early 1970s. Yet, the personalization of how these problems are (to be) understood limits the scope of that critique in the film. Uma's recuperation is premised on her husband becoming more sensitive and accommodating, not on her connecting up with sites and attitudes that would render her a more assured woman-singer in the world.

At another level, *Abhimaan* offers a perspective on the re-making of the Indian middle-class during the 1970s. The film registers the growing influence of the cultural industries in promoting and naturalizing a materialist ethos within this class: we witness not just the wide dissemination of film culture cutting across public and domestic spaces (through glossy magazines, the radio, cassettes and records, and crowded concerts), but also a commercialized vocabulary (such as 'Binaca smile') passing into everyday conversation. More striking is the candid and largely non-critical depiction of this class's rising affluence through the 'black' economy: Chandru's manipulation of Subir's tax papers and frequent references to the black money they have accumulated – casually suggested in one scene to be almost one-third of their legitimate wealth – is projected as a pragmatic necessity rather than a corrupt or criminal act. It is, in a sense, condoned by the framework of civility.

If *Abhimaan* effectively plays down the *social politics* of gender by prioritizing individualized experience as the framework of interpretation, it forms a pattern with the other key films made by Mukherjee during the1970s. In *Bawarchi* (d. Hrishikesh Mukherjee, 1972), a teacher-turned-chef moves from one squabbling household to the next, working as a servant for a *lower* wage than offered (out of consideration for the inflation that afflicts the masters!) and teaching each family member the virtues of sacrifice and service so that harmony might prevail. *Namak Haraam* (d. Hrishikesh Mukherjee, 1973), perhaps Mukherjee's most directly political film, involves the viewer in a discussion on capitalism versus socialism through a narrative in which a shrewd and ruthless industrialist is confronted by a range of pro-worker positions espoused by diverse key characters. The film is remarkable for its frequent references to class conflicts and socialism; its on-screen debates on social philosophy, industrial policy, and the right principles of effective trade union activism; its semi-documentary montage that references the contemporary working-class sense of ruin caused by hoarding, unemployment, inflation, and destitution. Such themes resonated with Indira Gandhi's contemporary diagnosis of the crisis facing the nation, and were not unusual in the popular cinema of the 1970s,[8] but it might be argued that *Namak Haraam* stages the most explicit discussion on class politics within mainstream Hindi cinema. Yet, as in *Abhimaan*, the narrative here tends to contain the fundamental political questions of its time within the ambit of personal conflicts between the key characters.

Unsurprisingly perhaps, *Namak Haraam* is remembered less for its political impact and more for heralding Amitabh Bachchan's explosive potential for harnessing societal edginess into a charismatic on-screen rage. Hrishikesh Mukherjee claimed that this was Bachchan's 'first angry man role when he didn't pick up an AK-47 and fire at the villains.'[9] Soon after *Namak Haraam* began a cycle of films in which Salim-Javed sculpted that role to perfection, manifesting the impatience and anguish felt by the petit-bourgeois and subaltern classes. However, Bachchan's advent as the quintessential angry young man also had a counterpoint: the appearance of Amol Palekar as an affable young man, laying a timid but deft finger not on the pulse of populist socialism but on newly emerging scenarios of desire and social mobility. We now turn our attention to this new desire for modernity and the re-making of Indian middle-class subjectivity during the mid-seventies.

The advent of the affable young man

Political psychologist Ashis Nandy has rightly noted that by the middle of the 1970s Nehruvian India had become 'a slightly embarrassing inheritance rather than an immediate presence,' although that dispensation with its 'democratic, Brahminic, patronizing socialism' had been instrumental in releasing 'much creative energy at the bottom and peripheries' of the nation (Nandy x). The vigorous effervescence in literary-cultural articulation as well as political mobilization, especially by women, dalit-bahujans and religious minorities, points to the new democratic ferment of this period. We must not, however, lose sight of the fact that crucial transmutations were occurring at the *top* and the *centre* too, where newer hegemonic forms and practices had to be invented in response to the changes that were afoot. A more accommodative socialist populism directed against the 'system' was one aspect of the manoeuvring from above; another was the move to surreptitiously shift the ground from beneath the unruly citizen to the desiring consumer. Discursive shifts of this order evidently required alterations in the prevailing narrative contract, and the rise of contemporary 'heroes' who could clinch a fresh consensus. Gender theorist Michael Kimmel suggests that masculinity be reconceptualized (from the sense of men as custodians and wielders of power) as men negotiating contradictory flows of power *and their sense of entitlement to power*. It might thus be argued that Hindi cinema of the 1970s mediated *both* the discursive shifts mentioned above: Amitabh Bachchan's 'anger' re-directed the masala-Social genre in unprecedented authoritarian-populist directions, while Amol Palekar's 'affability' freed up the urban middle-class/upper-caste male to pursue his self-interest unencumbered by the sense of social(ist) guilt or obligation. Rather than focus on the seeming lack of overlap in the textual forms or market segments within which these two personas were fashioned, it might be useful to attend to how they nevertheless acted in tandem: the angry and the affable young men were both forms of a gendered bildung, enabling a distinctive 1970s *male* subject to negotiate a terrain that he considered to be 'his' due – but was proving increasingly intractable to his occupation as it had to be shared with women and 'lower' class/caste subjects. It is worth noting that the distinction between the 'angry' and the 'affable' masculitines of the 1970s appears to have all but vanished from mainstream Hindi cinema since the 1990s, when affability emerged as the governing tenor.

A bit of film-historical probing might indicate why.

Amol Palekar made a remarkable debut in the mid-1970s with three successive silver-jubilee hits directed by Basu Chatterjee: all films in which Palekar brought to the screen a distinctly ordinary 'hero': clumsy but well-meaning, self-absorbed but likeable, vulnerable but determined, bungling but triumphant. In *Rajnigandha* (d. Basu Chatterjee, 1974),[10] Sanjay is a smooth-talking but befuddled government clerk who feels he is being denied a promotion (which he considers his due) on account of parochialist politics at the office. In *Chhoti Si Baat* (d. Basu Chatterjee, 1975),[11] Palekar plays Arun, a dreamy but feeble-spirited clerk at a private firm in Bombay whose attempts to get close to Prabha are constantly thwarted by her pushy colleague Nagesh Shastri, a competitor for her affection. After a series of failed efforts to impress Prabha, Arun turns to a retired army officer Col. Singh who runs a career-counselling and personality-development centre at Khandala. Col. Singh's expensive grooming helps Arun transform into a canny and self-assured lover; he returns to Bombay, turns the tables on Nagesh, and successfully woos Prabha. At the happy ending of the film, we see Nagesh approach Col. Singh for counselling. Next, Palekar appeared in *Chit Chor* (d. Basu Chatterjee, 1976) as Vinod, an amiable overseer working for an engineering firm: arriving from Bombay to Madhupur village, he is mistaken to be the wealthy engineer by the local school headmaster's family who dream that their daughter Geeta could marry him. Vinod is perceived within the family as being 'agreeable, joyful, sociable, very sweet' and soon even the initially disinclined Geeta falls in love with him. He is flattered with attention till Geeta's parents realize the 'mistake.' When Sunil – the actual engineer and Vinod's boss – arrives, Geeta's parents do their best to court him and he agrees to marry Geeta. Vinod wishes to fade away, but once Sunil realizes the truth he brings the lovers together.

The early Palekar persona thus embodies personal desire and social aspiration tinged with a sense of uncertain entitlement: he is subjected to various trials and taunts, but eventually his goodness and astuteness see him through. It is important to resist viewing this persona as a local variant of the 'good Joe' American social type[12] because, as film- and gender-studies scholar Richard Dyer alerts us, the 'cultural world' articulated by the notion of social types obscures the hegemony of one section of society over another. A striking feature of *Rajnigandha* and *Chhoti Si Baat* is how the narrative constantly flits between the outer world inhabited by the urban middle class (offices, restaurants, bus-stops, streets, apartments, cinemas) and the tense inner desires that structure the experience of 'their' world. The lower classes are absent for most part from the screen; when shown, they are either quietly acquiescent (domestic help, service staff at shops or restaurants) or come across as irritating or mildly menacing (assorted quacks offering psychic cures that never work, swindling mechanics peddling shoddy equipment, lazy and uppity office peons): they are like props on a set, mere local colour or an insignificant blur against which the world of middle-class desire is under construction.[13] The really rich and powerful classes are also not prominently framed, and thus the protagonists propel themselves within these narratives exempt from the polarized economic hierarchies that structure the action in the Social genre.

The conflicts that drive the plots are overwhelmingly emotional, the obstacles the protagonists face are in large measure internal to their class, and the resolutions effected through inter-personal tact and contact rather than the mobilization of dissenting energies. Indeed, any involvement in political activity is subtly derided: Deepa regards Sanjay's union-activities at his workplace as a futile distraction from their leisure-time companionship, and the only good that could possibly result from it would be win him free time to attend to their personal work – when Sanjay says that his office work prevent him from accompanying her to Bombay, Deepa asks '*tum office mein strike kyon nahin kara dete?* (why don't you get a strike organized at your office?).' Again, when the younger Navin requests her to support the student-union's demand for justice from the college management, she declares issues extraneous to her own studies do not concern her. And between the two modes of politics, Sanjay's patient petitioning deemed more acceptable than the younger Navin's more disruptive public activism.

We notice one other subtle narrative stratagem that serves to bracket off the passions of the popular in these films. Above the bus-stop where Arun regularly meets Prabha in *Chhoti Si Baat* is a large poster of the soon-to-be-released Amitabh Bachchan starrer *Zameer* (d. Ravi Chopra, 1975), which simultaneously advertises the mainstream film then being made by B.R. Chopra (the producer of both these films) *and* insinuates a contrast between the realism of the middle-class romance unfolding beneath the poster and the implausible passions that beset a masala-Social film like *Zameer*. When Arun is at the personality development centre at Khandala, we see Amitabh Bachchan (as himself) walk in and briefly consult Col. Singh about his tax returns, a scene that reinforces the 'realism' of *Chhoti Si Baat* and renders more credible the persona of the enthralled Amol Palekar who momentarily star-gazes at Bachchan along with the implied viewer of the film.

This device of contrasting the screen personas and cinematic styles associated with Bachchan and Palekar is later repeated in *Golmaal* (d. Hrishikesh Mukherjee, 1979): in a scene set outside Kamal Studio, the character played by Palekar shakes hands with Bachchan (as himself, shooting for the masala-Social *Jurmana* (d. Hrishikesh Mukherjee, 1979); and in another intrepid sequence, the Palekar character's fantasy of sending Bachchan out of business is filmed through cinematic self-references to *Guddi* (d. Hrishikesh Mukherjee, 1971) and *Amar Akbar Anthony* (d. Manmohan Desai, 1977). We might see this peculiar contrivance as connoting a preference for the ideologies associated with reformist realism (associated with the Palekar persona), and twinkle-eyed disengagement from representational forms that gratify subaltern identification (associated with the Bachchan persona). In the popular films made under the aegis of what film scholar Madhava Prasad terms 'the aesthetic of mobilization,' Amitabh Bachchan's appeal was established through a combination of differentially coded values:

> While the power derived from elite affiliations served to legitimate the persona for the middle class, the personality derived from the subaltern roles was the basis for a new mode of address, which spoke to the proletariat and other marginal sections and mobilized the spectator behind the star. (Prasad 141)

Political scientist Fareed Kazmi has argued that the angry young man embodied a 'fiercely independent Promethean vision' of an extraordinary individual who starts apart from the ordinary and passive masses on behalf of whom he fights – provided he has 'divine benediction and his mother's blessings' (Kazmi 143). Thus, Kazmi concludes that what appears to be social intervention and activism in these films simultaneously naturalizes fatalism and passivity, and 'what is being attacked are the checks and balances of the liberal framework of society' (Kazmi 151).

The affability in middle-class cinema provides not so much a contrast as a *counterpoint* to the anger in the masala-Social film. Middle-class cinema sought to promote the self-identification between its characters and audiences, installing a verisimilitude based on individuated desire and action, and avoiding what it regarded as the un-real phantasms that burdened the masala-Social. This is confirmed in the films by Basu Chatterjee, where the key site of power and economic mobility is located not in organized political action or social mobilization but in the bourgeoisie's discreet charm – that is, in its 'civility.'

In *Rajnigandha*, Deepa's fascination for Navin is built around the sophistication and gainful social connections that help her to get the college job in Bombay; in *Chhoti Bi Baat*, Arun's successful tutelage in 'personality development' under Col. JWN Singh helps Arun not just to defeat Nagesh and get Prabha but also to put in their 'proper' place the likes of lower class mechanics like Gurnaam and the subordinate staff at his office. Cultural capital (fashion, taste, etiquette, contacts within high society, and appropriately gendered behaviour in public) is naturalized as the most prudent and effective resource to be acquired and deployed by the middle-class to promote itself. During the next couple of decades, as the socialist accent petered out of political discourse, the bourgeois hero could emerge from his discreet niche and strut into the high-budget arc-lights of Bollywood.

Conclusion

Madhava Prasad has suggested that since the 1990s, Indian commercial cinema witnesses an ongoing 'process of transformation that, instead of coming in with *alternative* modes ... works on and appropriates the existing mode, bidding to replace the dominant rather than wrest a space beside it' (218). My sense is that this process could be regarded as a longer-term legacy of the 1970s. Clear narrative and institutional linkages may indeed be discerned between (i) the modest genre of middle-class cinema, (ii) the influential tele-serials on Doordarshan during the 1980s which effectively consolidated an Indian middle-class audience of unprecedented size, authority and aspiration, and (iii) the de-politicized and consumerist blockbusters of Hindi cinema of the 1990s.

Hrishikesh Mukherjee and Basu Chatterjee both carried over their success in 1970s middle-class cinema to the emerging field of television entertainment during the following decade. Mukherjee made serials like *Hum Hindustani*, *Talaash*, and *Ujale ki Or*: all of these revolved around contemporary developmental and reformist initiatives launched by the government. Chatterjee was even more prolific and influential – setting a very brisk pace by completing a 30-minute episode in two days each, he made landmark programmes such as: *Darpan*, consisting of dramatizations of short stories with classic liberal-humanist themes from around the world; *Kakkaji Kahin*, a local adaptation of *Yes Minister*, satirizing the ineptness and corruption of the political class in India; and most notably *Rajni*, which made Priya Tendulkar as the eponymous combative consumer-activist a household name and perhaps the first 'television star' in India. Bureaucrat and social commentator Bhaskar Ghose, who was at the helm of Doordarshan during the mid-1980s, praises these serials for being good as well as popular: 'Producers like ... Basu Chatterji (*sic*) had a very clear notion of what they wanted to present and were skilful enough to do it in a manner that attracted large audiences' (Ghose 52).

Media scholars have noted how many of these serials, although commissioned for delivering 'developmental' messages, were forcefully driven by commercial sponsorship and soon created a consumerist ethos that expanded the Indian market almost beyond recognition. By the end of the 1980s, most of the serials on Doordarshan were produced through corporate sponsorship and advertising and 'carried a message of modernity centring on the nuclear family, with two children and aspirations for a better life through education and more consumer goods' (Page and Crawley 154). The transition also saw the emergence of younger entertainers who adapted to, and consolidated, the new market conditions: for example, director Aziz Mirza, who made the serial *Circus* starring Shah Rukh Khan and Ashutosh Gowarikar for Doordarshan in 1989, went on to make two successful films in the 1990s about the struggles and eventual triumph of the dreamy-eyed middle-class hero in the emerging market economy (*Raju Ban Gaya Gentleman* (d. Aziz Mirza, 1992) and *Yes Boss!* (d. Aziz Mirza, 1997); media-magnate Ronnie Screwvala who had already launched India's first cable TV venture in Mumbai in 1981 used his profits to produce significant serials like *Lifeline* (d. Vijaya Mehta, 1991) and *Shanti* (d. Adi Pocha, 1994) for Doordarshan in the early 1990s, moved on to film distribution and production before ending up in the lists of 'the most influential people in the world' published by *Time* and *Esquire*; and superstar Shah Rukh Khan himself, whose initial success came through roles of a confused yet charming and ambitious boy-next-door in Doordarshan serials like *Fauji* (d. R.K. Kapur, 1988) and films like *Raju Ban Gaya Gentleman*, and *Kabhi Haan Kabhi Naa* (d. Kundan Shah, 1993), soon became the iconic 'cool dude' on and off the screen.

During the same phase, the 'anger' associated with the 1970s masala-Social films has largely dissipated. Writing of the transformation in Hindi cinema leading up to *Hum Aapke Hain Koun ...!* (d. Sooraj Barjatya, 1994), film reviewer Nikhat Kazmi noted that there had been a swing away from 'the nasty, brutish hero' and viewers and film-makers were

> turning from revenge, the reason for all that blood and gore... to the family, the nation, and love. There is a ubiquitous demand for good, clean cinema. A demand which is reflected in the stupendous success of *Hum Aapke Hain Koun...!* (qtd. in Uberoi 311)

As is well known, this film financed by Rajshri Productions (which had also funded Basu Chatterjee's *Chitchor*) was a remake of its own 1980s hit *Nadiya Ke Paar* (d. Govind Moonis, 1982) but much more lavishly mounted, and promoted on the newly emerging cable television networks through an emphasis on the family-feeling that went into its making. Rustom Bharucha's incisive critique of the film as 'claustrophobic, homogenized, monocultural, and totalizing' (170), 'its extravagance punctuated with naturalistic details of the contemporary Indian market... [in the process naturalizing] the generic north Indian, upper caste, upper class, extended family, around which the film revolves' (169) prompts a recognition of both its discontinuities *and* the continuities with the aesthetic contract of 1970s middle-class cinema.[14] The major stars of today (including the once-angry young man) function as relays in a libidinal economy of middle-class consumerism and depoliticized aspiration.

The affable young man, that obscure subject of desire who operated through courtesy and tact during the 1970s, might have won the day after all.

Acknowledgements

Priya Joshi and Rajinder Dudrah made invaluable editorial comments, while remarks by Kavita Daiya, Madhumeeta Sinha, and Christine Marran also helped me in rewriting this essay. Specific observations from Sudipta Kaviraj, Javed Akhtar, Anuja Jain, Simona Sawhney, and H. Nikhila (during presentations at Philadelphia, Minnesota and Hyderabad) were useful in reconsidering some points – although I have not been able to take on board everything on offer.

Notes

1. Nivedita Menon and Aditya Nigam (2008) summarize the Nehruvian consensus as combining three basic features: a vision of a self-reliant economy based on an import-substituting industrialization strategy; a broadly secular polity; and a non-aligned foreign policy. Kaviraj (*Trajectories*; *Enchantment*) insightfully discusses the process – and the implications – of the collapse of this consensus.
2. As film scholar Karen Gabriel notes: 'The 1970s constitute a benchmark in Hindi cinema because it was during this period that important changes that began in the late '60s intensified, consolidated and manifested themselves cinematically, in unmistakable ways. These included the political and social upheavals of the time, and organizational and structural changes in the industry – the collapse of the studio and star systems, the flow of unaccounted money, the power of the underworld – which became apparent, cinematically and narratively, in generic changes, and in the emergence of new idioms of gender, sexuality, rebellion, and heroism' (Gabriel xi–xii).
3. Literary scholar Henry Sussman proposes the aesthetic contract as a framework for taking cognisance of the linguistic nature and dynamic of all cultural productions, contrary to the Kantian protocols of individualism. Noting that works of art hold our interest because 'they sustain a certain uneasy balance between public discourse and idiosyncratic personal usage,' Sussman argues that a prevailing aesthetic contract '*incorporates* particular images, sounds, literary styles, and so on, in part because they are as yet publicly *undigested*, not yet reformulated as truism' – and this causes artworks that become the basis for aesthetic contracts to 'hover between an exciting hypothesis regarding possibility and a plausible analysis of existing conditions' (Sussman 166).
4. Film scholar Ravi Vasudevan's magisterial account of historical forms in Indian cinema surprisingly ignores this second trend. He contrasts the 1970s social-realist films of Benegal, Sen and Nihalani which were funded by the government's National Film Development Council and which 'explored various topical issues of social exploitation, and political and moral corruption' with the 1990s realism of Mani Rathnam which 'is privately financed and very much of the

mainstream rather than the parallel cinema' and whose realism celebrates 'middle-class modernity rather than develop a stance of social criticism' (Vasudevan 224–225). I would argue that these features Vasudevan (correctly) discerns in Mani Rathnam's work were also characteristic of the middle-class cinema of the 1970s. It should be stressed, no doubt, that the aspects as well as the prospects of 'middle-class modernity' imagined during the early 1970s by Mukherjee and Chatterjee, and during the 1990s by Mani Rathnam were considerably different.

5. Film historian Valentina Vitali has suggested that middle-class cinema enabled the class which was 'imbricated in religious and casteist structures to re-imagine itself as modern and pan-Indian,' while genre fragmentation enabled the upper-caste audience to further 'construct itself as separate from the lower classes' (Vitali). The new genres of the 1970s – which she names as 'middle-class,' 'action' and 'parallel' cinema – indicate that Hindi cinema had 'found new ways to address a fragmented audience, mediating in a manner that these audiences would deem convincing the contradictions constitutive of the 1970s socio-historical context.'
6. In Sen's view, civility is challenged by two distinct forms of opposition: he categorizes as *incivil* 'the victimised and oppressed who are building insurgent societies and challenging existing power structures dominated by the civil,' and as *uncivil* 'those who, while also resisting civil society and subverting it, do so with motives and acions that are far more limited, material, and in general criminal and exploitative.'
7. Film journalist Raju Bharatan cites Hrishikesh Mukherjee as telling him: '*Abhimaan* was based on the life of Kishore Kumar. As you know, Kishore's wife Ruma (Amit's mother) was no less talented. Since Kishore had a bit of a struggle, early in his career, he was always conscious of Ruma's gifts as a performer.'
8. Such issues are indexed in films as diverse as *Mere Apne* (d. Gulzar, 1971), *Aandhi* (d. Gulzar, 1975), *Roti Kapda aur Makaan* (d. Manoj Kumar, 1975), *Ankur* (d. Shyam Benegal, 1973), *Nishant* (d. Shyam Benegal, 1975), and *Manthan* (d. Shyam Benegal, 1977), *Tarang* (d. Kumar Shahani, 1976), and the political 'trilogy' with Salim-Javed scenarios: *Deewar* (d. Yash Chopra, 1975), *Trishul* (d. Yash Chopra, 1978) and *Kala Pathar* (d. Yash Chopra, 1979).
9. Cited in 'Salute to a Legend,' *Screenindia.com*, 8 Sep. 2006. <http://www.screenindia.com/old/fullstory.php?content_id=13412> (Accessed 19 Mar. 2011).
10. *Rajnigandha* is based on the well-known Hindi short story 'Yehi Sach Hai' by Mannu Bhandari. The narrative is largely focalized through the perspective of Prabha, her ambivalent affection for the lackadaisical Sanjay and her uncertain but intense desire for the suave and successful Navin (named Nishith in Bhandari's version). The film version also relocates the action from Kanpur and Calcutta to the more cosmopolitan settings of Delhi and Bombay.
11. *Chhoti Si Baat* borrows many of its plot elements from the British comedy *School for Scoundrels* (d. Robert Hamer, 1960), and is an interesting instance of a successful – albeit unacknowledged – remake.
12. Sociologist O.E. Klapp had drawn up a list of social types, defined as 'an idealized concept of how people are expected to be or to act' and exemplified through the likes of the Good Joe, the Tough Guy, the Pin-Up, etc. The good Joe is described as 'friendly and easy-going; he fits in and likes people; he never sets himself above others but goes along with the majority...' (qtd. in Dyer 47–48).
13. According to political theorist Partha Chatterjee, the governance of Indian cities underwent a remarkable transformation during the 1970s and 1980s, when unprecedented numbers of low-wage labourers and migrants had to be integrated into urban life through 'paralegal arrangements' (137). This resulted in the passing of the older modes of social-political dominance but also 'more significantly, a disengagement of the middle classes from the hurly burly of urban politics [which was] an important precondition for the transformation of the 1990s' (Chatterjee 142).
14. We might further note that the middle-class cinema of the 1970s set the precedent, in terms of both narrative and business model, for the rise of the 'multiplex film' since the late 1990s. Film scholar S.V. Srinivas's observation regarding attempts by the film-theatre managements in Andhra Pradesh that 'from the 1970s... to alter the composition of the audience by progressively reducing the capacity of the lower class seats in theatres even as they tried to attract middle class audiences' is representative of a wider trend. As film-maker Aparna Sharma notes: 'the multiplex is preceded by and concurrent with a tradition in parallel cinema that reached a peak in the 1970s... [The post-1990s] films occupy the space between the mainstream and art film, reaching audiences without the essential melodrama typical of

Bollywood films in which characters are foregrounded, on occasions distanced, from their milieu... While the attraction of some can be located in the dynamics of stardom and a heady mix of song and dance, all interpellate the audience through commonplace situations, traumas and experiences.'

References

Ahmed, Omar. "Rajanigandha/Tuberose." *Ellipsis – The Accents of Cinema*, Web. 15 Oct. 2011.

Bharatan, Raju. "Hrishikesh Mukherjee: A Cineaste in the Mainstream Cinema." *Rediff.com*. Web. 15 Oct. 2011.

Bharucha, Rustom. *In the Name of the Secular*. New Delhi: Oxford UP, 1999. Print.

Chatterjee, Partha. "Are Indian Cities Becoming Bourgeois At Last?" *The Politics of the Governed: Reflections on Popular Politics in Most of the World*. Ranikhet: Permanent Black, 2004. Print.

Dyer, Richard. *Stars*. London: BFI, 1998. Print.

Gabriel, Karen. *Melodrama and the Nation: Sexual Economies of Bombay Cinema 1970–2000*, New Delhi: Women Unlimited, 2010. Print.

Ghose, Bhaskar. *Doordarshan Days*. New Delhi: Penguin, 2005. Print.

Gulzar, Govind Nihalani and Saibal Chatterjee, Eds. *Encyclopaedia of Hindi Cinema*. New Delhi: Encyclopaedia Britannica Inc., 2003. Print.

Kaviraj, Sudipta. *The Trajectories of the Indian State*. Ranikhet: Permanent Black, 2010. Print.

Kaviraj, Sudipta. *The Enchantment of Democracy and India*. Ranikhet: Permanent Black, 2011. Print.

Kazmi, Fareed. "How Angry is the Angry Young Man? 'Rebellion' in Conventional Hindi Films." *The Secret Politics of Our Desires: Innocence, Culpability and Indian Popular Cinema*. Ed. Ashis Nandy. New Delhi: Oxford UP, 1998. 134–156. Print.

Kimmel, Michael. *Guyland: The Perilous World where Boys Become Men*. New York: HarperCollins, 2008. Print.

Menon, Nivedita and Aditya Nigam. *Power and Contestation: India Since 1989*. Hyderabad: Orient Longman, 2008. Print.

Nandy, Ashis. "Beyond the Politics of Rage." Foreword to *The Flaming Feet and Other Essays*, by D.R. Nagaraj Ed. Prithvi Dutta Chandra Sobhi. Ranikhet: Permanent Black, 2010. ix–xviii. Print.

Page, David and William Crawley. *Satellites over South Asia: Broadcasting Culture and the Public Interest*. New Delhi: Sage, 2001. Print.

Pendakur, Manjunath. "Dynamics of Cultural Policy Making: The U.S. Film Industry in India." *Journal of Communication* 34.5 (Dec. 1985): 52–72. Print.

Prasad, Madhava M. *Ideology of the Hindi Film: A Historical Construction*. New Delhi: Oxford UP, 1998. Print.

Rajadhyaksha, Ashish. *Indian Cinema in the Time of Celluloid: From Bollywood to the Emergency*. New Delhi: Tulika, 2009. Print.

Sanyal, Kalyan. *Rethinking Capitalist Development: Primitive accumulation, Governmentality and Post-Colonial Capitalism*. New Delhi: Routledge, 2007. Print.

Sen, Jai. "Interrogating the Civil. Engaging Critically with the Reality and Concept of Civil Society." n.d. Web. 15 Oct 2011.

Sengupta, Ratnottama. "1962–1975: Wars and Emergency." *Encyclopaedia of Hindi Cinema*. Ed. Govind Nihalani Gulzar and Saibal Chatterjee. New Delhi: Encyclopaedia Britannica Inc., 2003. 75–92. Print.

Seth, Sanjay. "Interpreting Revolutionary Excess: The Naxalite Movement in India, 1967–1971." *New Asian Marxisms*. Ed. Tani E. Barlow. Durham: Duke UP, 2002. 333–357. Print.

Sharma, Aparna. "India's Experience with the Multiplex." *Seminar*, May 2003. Web. 15 Oct 2011.

Srinivas, S.V. "Is There a Public in the Cinema Hall?" *Framework: the Journal of Cinema and Media* 42 (Sep. 2000). Web. 15 Oct 2011.

Sussman, Henry. *The Aesthetic Contract: Statutes of Art and Intellectual Work in Modernity.* Stanford: Stanford UP, 1997. Print.

Tharu, Susie and K. Lalita. *Women Writing in India: 600 B.C. to the Present Volume II: The 20th Century.* New Delhi: Oxford UP, 1995. Print.

Uberoi, Patricia. "Imagining the Family: An Ethnographic Viewing of Hum Aapke Hai Koun . . . !" *Pleasure and the Nation.* Ed. Rachel Dwyer and Christopher Pinney. New Delhi: Oxford UP, 2001. 309–351. Print.

Valentina, Vitali. "The Families of Hindi Cinema: A Socio-Historical Approach to Film Studies." *Framework: the Journal of Cinema and Media* 42 (Sep. 2000). Web. 15 Oct 2011.

Vasudevan, Ravi. *The Melodramatic Public: Film Form and Spectatorship in Indian Cinema.* Ranikhet: Permanent Black, 2010. Print.

Filmograhy

Abhimaan, Dir. Hrishikesh Mukherjee. Amiya. 1973. Moser Baer. Film.

Amar Akbar Anthony, Dir. Manmohan Desai. Hirawat Jain & Co. 1977. Shemaroo. Film.

Anand, Dir. Hrishikesh Mukherjee. Rupam Chitra. 1971. Shemaroo. Film.

Bawarchi, Dir. Hrishikesh Mukherjee. Rupam Chitra. 1972. Shemaroo. Film.

Chhoti Si Baat, Dir. Basu Chatterjee. B.R. Films. 1975. Moser Baer. Film.

Chit Chor, Dir. Basu Chatterjee. Rajshri Productions Pvt. Ltd. 1976. Moser Baer. Film.

Golmaal, Dir. Hrishikesh Mukherjee. Rupam Chitra. 1979. Shemaroo. Film.

Guddi, Dir. Hrishikesh Mukherjee. Rupam Chitra. 1971. Shemaroo. Film.

Hum Apke Hain Koun . . . ! Dir. Sooraj Barjatya. Rajshri Productions Pvt. Ltd. 1994. Ultra. Film.

Jurmana, Dir. Hrishikesh Mukherjee. Shri Lokenath Chitramandir. 1979. Shemaroo. Film.

Kabhi Haan Kabhi Naa, Dir. Kundan Shah. Vikram Mehrotra 1993. Moser Baer. Film.

Nadiya Ke Paar, Dir. Govind Moonis. Rajshri Productions Pvt. Ltd. 1982. Ultra. Film.

Namak Haraam, Dir. Hrishikesh Mukherjee. R.S.J. Production (Combine). 1974. Moser Baer. Film.

Rajnigandha, Dir. Basu Chatterjee. Devki Chitra. 1974. Reliance Big Home Video. Film.

Raju Ban Gaya Gentleman, Dir. Aziz Mirza. Sippy Films. 1992. Pen Video. Film.

Mili, Dir. Hrishikesh Mukherjee. N.C Sippy. 1975. Shemaroo. Film.

Yes Boss! Dir. Aziz Mirza. United Seven Combines. 1997. Moser Baer. Film.

Zameer, Dir. Ravi Chopra. B.R. Films. 1975. Moser Baer. Film.

The construction of 1970s femininity, or why Zeenat Aman sings the same song twice

Ajay Gehlawat

Sonoma State University, Rohnert Park, USA

This paper examines how Zeenat Aman helped inaugurate new forms of sexuality and femininity in 1970s Bollywood. Along with redefining the rules of a screen heroine's identity, Aman also created a range of grey characters such as Sheetal in Manoj Kumar's *Roti Kapada aur Makaan* (1974) and Sheela in Feroz Khan's *Qurbani* (1980). These roles became associated with hugely popular songs of the period, lip-synched by Aman, including 'Aap jaisa koi,' from *Qurbani*, and 'Main naa bhoolunga', from *Roti Kapada aur Makaan*. This paper explores how these repeated song sequences reflect Aman's positioning within these narratives even as they allow her to reshape her role in innovative ways. In this way, this paper examines how Zeenat Aman deviated from earlier binary models imposed upon Bollywood heroines, pitting heroine against vamp and, in the process, created new modes of femininity and female agency within these films.

Alternately touted as heralding 'the 70s look of Westernized, "liberated" young woman in Hindi film' and being 'among the first stars to show that good girls could be unashamedly sexual while fulfilling all the requirements to ultimately become wife to the hero,' Zeenat Aman helped inaugurate a new form of sexual politics and femininity in 1970s Bollywood (Jhunjhunwala 22; Rajadhyaksha and Willemen 41).[1] Along with 'redefin[ing] the rules of a screen heroine's identity,' Aman also created a range of 'grey characters' such as Sheetal in Manoj Kumar's *Roti Kapada aur Makaan* (1974) and Sheela in Feroz Khan's *Qurbani* (1980). These roles became associated with hugely popular songs of the period, lip-synched by Aman, including 'Aap jaisa koi,' from *Qurbani*, and 'Main naa bhoolunga,' from *Roti Kapada aur Makaan* (hereafter *RKM*). Of particular interest is the fact that these two songs – 'Aap jaisa koi' and 'Main naa bhoolunga' – are presented twice in their respective films, with the repeated performance reconfiguring each film's ensuing resolution.[2] In tandem with my inquiry into the construction of a 1970s femininity a la Zeenat, I want to explore how these repeated song sequences reflect Aman's positioning within such a conventional narrative structure even as they allow her to reshape this role in innovative ways. Crucial to this reshaping effect, I shall argue, is the split between a more conventional politics of gazing, in which Aman functions as an object for scopophilic consumption, and the representation of an 'inner view,' in which Aman's own perspective becomes privileged.[3] This paper will examine how Zeenat Aman created new forms of femininity and female agency in these films as well as, in the process, develop a more nuanced understanding of why she sings the same songs twice.

Much has been made of Zeenat Aman's cosmopolitan antecedents, and I would briefly like to examine these, as well as how they have been deployed to shape the subsequent discourse surrounding Aman and her intervention in 1970s Bollywood cinema. While born in Bombay, some biographies have listed her place of birth as Germany, a country she moved to as a young teenager, following the death of her father ('Zeenat Aman', imdb.com). Aman's mother subsequently remarried a German man named Heinz, obtained German citizenship and resettled there with Zeenat. After spending her teenage years in Germany, Zeenat returned to India, graduating from St Xavier's College in Bombay before leaving for California, where she studied on scholarship at USC for a year. Upon returning to India, she began working as a journalist for *Femina* magazine before turning to modeling. She subsequently competed in and won the Miss Asia-Pacific title in 1970, the first time an Indian woman had done so ('Zeenat Aman', imdb.com; Jhunjhunwala 10–11; 'Zeenat Aman', Wikipedia.com). It was precisely this cosmopolitan pedigree that caught the eye of Dev Anand, who went on to cast her as Jasbir/Janice in his film, *Hare Rama Hare Krishna* (1971) (Anand 229–230). Thus Aman's 'chic, westernized manner and cigarette smoking confidence' helped shape her image from the very outset and directly led to her being cast in a role that has subsequently been described as 'mark[ing] a distinct shift' in Bollywood cinema, via which Aman 'naturalized the Western look' (Jhunjhunwala 12; Mazumdar 90).

Janice/Jasbir

Along with being 'a trendsetter of sorts,' *Hare Rama Hare Krishna* (hereafter, *HRHK*) launched Aman's career (Garga 186). Critics have repeatedly claimed that Aman's performance in this film 'ushered in such raw sexuality as never before witnessed on the Indian screen' (Kazmi 235). The film, particularly due to its hit song, 'Dum Maro Dum,' was a success and Aman, who lip-synchs the hit song in the film, became 'an overnight sensation' (Jhunjhunwala 14). Yet, to return to her 'cosmopolitan antecedents,' even while Aman's 'English speech and diction were perfect,' she required a Hindi coach to deliver her dialogue in the film (Jhunjhunwala 14). Precisely for this reason, however, Aman was seen as being 'ideally cast' as the 'hippy chick who can look both Indian and western' (Dwyer 112). Along with her interesting and, in many ways, path-breaking role in this film, what becomes particularly relevant to the current inquiry is how, from the very outset Aman, with all her cosmopolitan aura, was associated with a hit song – as cultural critic Udita Jhunjhunwala notes, 'Even today only the first bars of the tune ['Dum Maro Dum'] need play and Zeenat Aman's face is conjured up in the minds of Hindi movie-watchers all over the world' (Jhunjhunwala 12–13).

While it may be Aman's face that immediately comes to mind when hearing this song, it is her backside that first appears when the song is played in the film. As film theorist Fareed Kazmi notes, 'The camera lingers lovingly while Zeenat, in her introductory shot... seductively wriggles her hips while wearing a suggestively short dress' (Kazmi 195). Thus, if this song has become 'synonymous with Zeenat Aman's image,' it is worth exploring how the song functions in relation to both Zeenat's overall role in the film and, in the process, her (re)construction of Indian femininity in the context of 1970s Bollywood (Jhunjhunwala 13). Aman's character, Jasbir(/Janice) comes of age in what could be called a distinctly modern (read: Western) setting: growing up in Montreal with her brother, Prashant (Dev Anand), her parents divorce while she is still quite young, leaving her to be raised solely by her father (Kishore Sahu), who subsequently takes another wife (Indrani Mukherjee). Making a clean break from her past, Jasbir discards her old identity ('Jasbir') and becomes Janice, Bollywood's first hippie chick. Shedding her old identity and clothes, she dons the garb of her new alter ego ('Janice') and follows the hippie trail to Nepal, where she smokes ganja and practices 'free love' at the local commune.[4]

Yet 'she is haunted by a sense of loneliness and restlessness' (Ray and Mukherjee 139), which is addressed early on in the film via Dev Anand's voiceover to the opening images of Aman, with her back to the camera, dancing by herself to the tune of 'Dum Maro Dum':

> These people whose religion is ganja, opium, hemp, cocaine, LSD, and whose temple is freedom, fun and dance, these people only live from moment to moment for this, lost in the intoxication and stupor to their own folks and their society. These people whom the world knows as hippies, they have no connection with life. Whether they fear or love life, why don't we ask them? There is Jasbir there, my own Jabsir, whom I have loved very much, my own part, my own blood, Jasbir! Tell me what you want, what is in your heart, why are you like this? Jasbir, hey Jasbir! Jassu!

Throughout this opening sequence Aman, in a short red dress, continues dancing with her back turned to the camera. There is a brief shot towards the end of her face in close up, smiling blissfully behind oversized tinted glasses while her lips move as if singing. As Anand, his voice increasingly agitated, calls out her name repeatedly, her tinted glasses fly off and fall to the ground, followed by a match on action shot of another pair of glasses on the ground, accompanied by an off-screen woman's voice continuing the repeated calling of Jasbir's name. The camera pulls backs to reveal the young Jasbir, kicking her glasses and refusing to drink her milk while her nanny reprimands her. Anand subsequently freezes the image of the young Jasbir while continuing his voiceover, noting that no one ever asked her what she wanted from life. The next time we see her, following the ensuing dissolution of her parents' marriage and the break-up of her family, the transformation is complete: she is now Janice, again wearing tinted glasses and selling hippie garb from a bus with her boyfriend in Nepal.

Thus, in what became a staple in the representation of this 'new woman' of Bollywood, Aman is introduced via a song sequence, which is reprised at a later point in the narrative, further associating her with its sentiment (of simultaneous pleasure and isolation).[5] As in the opening sequences, though she is surrounded by others, Janice remains essentially alone, dancing by herself or, to extend the metaphor, to her own tune. In playing the female protagonist of *HRHK*, Aman established herself both as 'an iconic figure of the seventies' – what film theorists Manas Ray and Madhuja Mukherjee call 'a child-woman caught in a whirlpool of "wrong" notions and right "traditions"' – and, thus, as a woman incapable of reconciling the twin elements to her identity or, put another way, as a woman unable to come to terms with her severed past (Ray and Mukherjee 139). In an echo of the typical scenario facing the figure of the 'vamp' in popular Hindi cinema, 'the guitar-playing, beer-guzzling, cigarette-puffing' Janice kills herself at the end of the film even as her family, reunited in their attempt to regain their 'Jassu,' arrives in Kathmandu and desperately entreats her to return to them (Ray and Mukherjee 139).

One might say, then, that even as Aman ushered in a radically new type of heroine to Bollywood via her breakthrough performance in *HRHK*, she was also made to suffer for it, at least within the story. The important role of the recurring song also becomes apparent in this first feature, as Aman takes her own life (via an overdose of pills) when her brother sings the same song he sang to her when they were children ('Phoolon ka Taaron ka'). Apparently overwhelmed by the repressed recollections this song brings about, Janice, who in many ways is defined by her association with (another) song, comes to her tragic end via the reenactment of a long forgotten melody. In this way, the film seems to suggest the incompatibility of these two roles (via their corresponding songs) as her long-lost brother (and director of the film), in his attempt to remind her of who she once was, pushes her to the point of no return.

Aman went on to play another successful role soon after, in *Yaadon Ki Baraat* (d. Nasir Hussain, 1973), which directly references the popularity of *HRHK* in one of its first songs. When Aman's character, Sunita, attends a concert early on in the film (again wearing a short red dress), the singer (Tariq) invites her to join him on stage and, after singing the song, 'Aap ke Kamare Mein' together, the guitar-playing singer segues into 'Dum Maro Dum,' as Zeenat/ Sunita reprises this now-famous song's opening lyrics and the young people in attendance sway along to the tune. Even as *Yaadon Ki Baraat* similarly employs the repeated use of a song as a key element of the plot – in this case, the title song, which unites the three brothers separated as children – it is for a different song, again 'sung' (i.e., lip-synched) by Aman's character, that the film gained its greatest fame. This song, 'Chura liya hai tumne jo dil ko,' sung by Asha Bhosle, has been called 'the main merit' of the film and simultaneously acknowledges Aman's association with the 'disco era' (Rajadhyaksha and Willemen 420). In this song sequence Aman, sporting a white bellbottomed outfit, guitar and sparkling, oversized hoop earrings, 'sings' to the young man, Vijay (Vijay Arora), who has come to her house for a party, as the rest of the guests look on. In this way, Aman again demonstrates how she 'could play the modern sort of woman, very different to the old style actresses of Bollywood' (Bose 304). Furthermore, Aman's performance as a new type of Bollywood heroine is again directly linked to a popular song, and it is via the performance of this song – openly declaring her love for a man she has just met before her assembled guests – that she arguably 'violat[ed] several moral codes advocated by earlier melodramas to control female sexuality' (Rajadhyaksha and Willemen 41).

Sheetal

It was in the following year's *Roti Kapada aur Makaan* (*RKM*), however, that these aspects of Aman's persona became most evident. In this film, directed by Manoj Kumar, Zeenat plays Sheetal, a young woman with grand aspirations and the girlfriend of Bharat (Manoj Kumar), a young man who is having difficulty attaining a job. These issues are addressed early on in the film via a conversation in a gazebo, in which Bharat and Sheetal take shelter from the rain. After asking Bharat when he will be able to acquire employment, Sheetal goes on to describe her dreams:

Sheetal: Bharat, I'm telling the truth. When, four years ago, you received this engineering degree, ever since then I've been having this dream that you will land a nice job. Then we won't have to stand in bus lines, we'll have a car, too. We'll have a huge, beautiful house. We'll have wardrobes full of different clothes, I'll wear the finest jewelry and then, sitting on a plane, we will fly the skies.
Bharat [snapping his fingers in her face]: Hey, high flying queen.
Sheetal: Why, don't you like my dreams?
Bharat: When I like you, I like everything that you like.

Hearing these words, Sheetal jumps out of the gazebo into the pouring rain, crying out, 'Oh! I could die for that,' and inviting Bharat to join her. When he demurs, pointing out that he will get drenched and that he has a job interview in half an hour, Sheetal interrupts him via the first song sequence, 'Hai Hai Yeh Majboori.' In this classic 'wet sari' song sequence, Aman (as Sheetal) cavorts and sings in the rain, while Bharat remains standing under cover of the gazebo, gazing on ruefully as he clutches his rolled up diploma.

This sequence is coded as taking place in the private sphere (the intimate couple caught alone in the rain) yet the framing splits the subject and mode of identification to bifurcate the viewing experience, coming closer to what film theorist Lalitha Gopalan refers to as 'cinema of attractions... and scopophilia' (Gopalan 109). This doubling of modes of address is mirrored in Aman's conflation of vamp and heroine characteristics that had previously been diametrically opposed and only began to be combined in the 1970s (Kasbekar 300–301).[6] Sheetal's materialistic aspirations, which become a recurring theme in the film, typify this conflation – though in love with Bharat (metonym for India), she also wants more out of life, e.g., a car, a big house, wardrobes full of clothing, etc. – and in this way, i.e., via her materialistic aspirations, she simultaneously embodies the 'new woman' of Bollywood and functions as a hyperbolized echo of the sentiment underlying the film's title, championing basic needs (i.e., bread, clothing, housing) in a time of economic uncertainty. That she herself becomes an object (read: attraction) for the camera's gaze in the song sequence's visualization of her (materialistic) fantasies could thus be seen as an apt reflection of both her (self-)commoditization and the film's larger critique of such predilections, embodied, aptly enough, in the figure of the 'new woman'.

It is via the ensuing song sequence – 'Main naa bhoolunga' (I Won't Forget) – and its subsequent role in the film's narrative, that these apparently conflicting (though ultimately resolved) tendencies are most vividly on display. Before singing the song for the first time with Bharat (as part of a televised broadcast and as a way of making some money), Sheetal is given a ring by Bharat for her birthday, featuring an image of a Hindu god. Wearing this ring, Sheetal tells Bharat, 'Today, let's sing such a song that everybody will remember'. The sequence begins in the recording studio, where Bharat and Sheetal are filmed by the television crew, before moving into a fantasy sequence (via a transition shot through the shiny hub of a BMW car wheel) which is again coded as a private fantasy yet features moments of direct (i.e., public) address, primarily by Aman. In this fantasy sequence, Sheetal and Bharat enjoy all of Sheetal's previously professed desires – new car, new house, and multiple colorful costumes – and even partake in an imagined wedding ceremony before the sequence returns to the recording studio. This fantasy's disjuncture from the world of the narrative is further reinforced in the following scene when Sheetal's new boss, Mr Mohan (Shashi Kapoor), points out that she has only worn two outfits in the past ten days and offers to purchase some new clothes for her. When Sheetal initially objects, Mohan interjects by noting that, as an employee, she is under the company's (and thus his) purview and that, furthermore, she should not argue over such 'little things.'

Thus begins Sheetal's gradual transformation or, put another way, her relationship with Mohan initiates the actualization of her materialistic desires.[7] When she meets Bharat one day after work, sporting a new outfit and matching flower in her hair (both provided by Mr Mohan), she asks him what he thinks of her new appearance. 'Flowers look better on plants,' Bharat coolly replies. Sheetal responds by telling him that she sometimes wishes he were more like Mr Mohan and, in response to Bharat's ensuing question ('Then what would happen?'), adds, 'Then all my dreams would have been fulfilled. Life wouldn't have passed waiting in line for buses. If you were Mr Mohan, then life would have sped by in big fast cars.' In a continuation of this trajectory of desire, Sheetal misses her date with Bharat the following day (to celebrate the fourth anniversary of their first encounter), in order to accompany Mohan on a business meeting. Later than evening when Bharat stands waiting with another man at the bus stop, he sees Sheetal leaving with Mohan in the latter's 'fast car.' When the other man says, 'Looks like the bus has come,' Bharat replies, 'And it looks like I've missed it.' Sheetal, after apologizing for missing their date the next day, excitedly informs Bharat that she will soon be going to America with Mr Mohan. This sequence is followed by a cut to a plane flying overhead while Bharat intones, in voiceover, 'Sheetal went to America with Mr Mohan and I began to feel she was slowly drifting away from me.'

Upon returning to India, Sheetal and Mohan announce their engagement and have a party. However, Sheetal is unable to remove Bharat's ring from her finger, try as she may, and finally extends her hand to Mohan before all the assembled guests, telling him, 'Cut it off.' Mohan demurs, noting the image of the Hindu god on the ring even as he states, 'It's only a ring,' slipping his ring on her other hand's finger. Thus wearing both men's rings, Sheetal, the 'new woman,' proceeds to clink champagne glasses, only to drop hers when Bharat, singing a somber song, appears on the television. Breaking her glass, Sheetal takes a new one yet, even as she drinks, seems conflicted. Compounding Sheetal's indecision is a flashback sequence, featuring images of Sheetal together with Bharat, following which Mohan finally switches the television off, thus abruptly ending Bharat's dolorous song. Yet in an ironic follow-up to this, Mohan proceeds to whistle Bharat's tune while smiling and twirling Sheetal around in his arms in slow motion, even as the grim undertone of the song's melody continues to play, thus bracketing this moment and calling attention to the artificiality of its frivolity.

In keeping with the dynamics of this film, Sheetal's subsequent return to Bharat comes via a song sequence – a reprise of the earlier 'Main naa bhoolunga.' This sequence also further illuminates the simultaneous deployment of both privately and publicly coded modes of representing Sheetal, in which there is a shift from depicting her as the object of men's gazes to the enactment of her own 'inner view.' This reprised sequence also illuminates the triangular nature of Sheetal's desire, even as this triangle's embodiment in this song sequence allows for Sheetal to deviate in some ways from the typical position afforded to the woman in such a structuring, i.e., one in which she functions primarily as an object of exchange between the two men, to instead manifest attributes associated with the previously noted 'new woman' (Kasbekar; Sedgwick).

The (re)enactment of 'Main naa bhoolunga' (which, in turn, leads to Sheetal's return to Bharat) comes at a party at which Bharat is also present. Mohan introduces Sheetal as his fiancée who, in turn, is addressed by one of her old friends from the recording studio days where the song was originally 'sung.' When this man chastises Sheetal for failing to recognize either him or Bharat, Mohan realizes that Sheetal and Bharat knew each other previously. Mohan encourages Sheetal to sing a song with her old 'friend' but she replies that she has 'forgotten everything.' Bharat then agrees to sing by himself and, after glimpsing his old ring still on Sheetal's finger, begins 'Main naa bhoolunga' for the second time. While Bharat sings, Sheetal steps away from Mohan and slips into the bathroom. From here there is a cut to Sheetal inside this private sphere, which features a mural of a woman struggling in a body of water. Sheetal leans again the shut door and cries, covering her face with both hands (bedecked by both men's rings), the camera cutting from her to the image of the suffering woman in the painting as she pounds her fist against the wall. She gazes at her reflection in the bathroom mirror (below the mural of the anguished woman), then dries her eyes. There is a cut back to the outer (public) realm, where Mohan and Bharat are both shown looking off-camera in separate shots, followed by a cut to Sheetal, who reemerges, calm and dry-eyed, from the bathroom.

Bharat resumes singing while Mohan and Sheetal hold hands and listen. Then, as Bharat comes to the end of his lyric, the camera zooms in on Sheetal's and Mohan's enjoined hands as Sheetal lets go of Mohan's grip. The camera pans from Mohan's confused expression back to Sheetal's face as she finally begins to 'sing' her lyrics to the song. As Bharat subsequently joins Sheetal in singing the song, the camera pulls back to present the three – Bharat, Sheetal and Mohan – standing in a loose triangular formation with Mohan, now by himself, in the background and Sheetal and Bharat occupying the foreground. The camera further emphasizes this triangulated structure by engaging in a series of whip pans from Sheetal to Mohan to Bharat (with Mohan always appearing between the other two) and, as Bharat and Sheetal conclude the song with their backs now turned to Mohan, this latter figure leaves the gathering with a confused expression on his face. Thus, even as Sheetal moves from one man to another, she does not merely function as an object in this exchange but rather, via her 'departure' from the song's (public) setting and the ensuing depiction of her inner turmoil, emphasizes her own subjective agency in this process, choosing to act on her own inclinations rather than in direct accordance with the desires of either man who, in many ways, become sidelined in the process.

Sheetal subsequently breaks off her engagement to Mohan and, when Mohan asks her why she failed to marry the one she loved and still loves, Sheetal replies, 'That was my mistake.' Mohan's subsequent rejoinder – 'Not a mistake, call it a sin!' – as well as Sheetal's acceptance of his point illuminates the religiously inflected paradigm at play here, and also foreshadows her subsequent fate. Though she now remorsefully concludes, 'I considered wealth to be more precious than love, and blackened the Taj Mahal of my dreams,' this realization comes too late, a point Sheetal also acknowledges when Mohan offers to take her back to Bharat, replying, 'I know that this is not possible now.' Indeed, though Sheetal is temporarily reunited with Bharat, she is subsequently gunned down while helping him evade the police and, in accordance with the role whose fate she now resigns herself to, conceals her gunshot wound from Bharat until it is too late, at which point, even as 'Main naa bhoolunga' is again repeated on the soundtrack, she smiles and tells Bharat to go on, only crying (and dying) after he leaves.

Thus, even as Aman's character straddles the divide between vamp and heroine, she, like the vamps of previous films, is ultimately punished for her decadent ways, signaling both the lingering presence of this older binary logic and its religiously inflected morality. As she dies, Sheetal is referred to as 'the Sita of [Bharat's] life.' Sheetal however disavows this parallel, stating that 'Sita stands by her man even when he is exiled in the forest. I deserted him when he went through difficult times.' In the process, Sheetal paradoxically resigns herself to the morality associated with this (repudiated) figure and, thus, to the necessity of her own demise. While one can point to Aman's role in *RKM* as a decided break from previous female roles, in which the heroine was entirely pure (and purely devoted to the film's protagonist), this film also signals a return to the narrative of the earlier *HRHK*, in which Aman's character, Janice, also has to die because of her excessive deviation from the (proper) role of the (upright) heroine. These films, then, simultaneously reveal Bollywood's willingness to entertain as plausible the figure of the 'new woman,' replete with her independence from a male counterpart and interest in pleasure, self-fulfillment and material gain (or, indeed, self-fulfillment through material gain), even as they ultimately censure her for embodying these very characteristics. It is in the following film, Feroz Khan's *Qurbani*, then, that we see a further reformulation of the role of the Bollywood heroine and a deviation from the older narrative order in which such radical reformulations, while paradoxically indulged within individual segments of the film (most notably in song sequences), were ultimately discredited.

Sheela

Qurbani (1980), a 'hugely successful action movie,' was made even more famous by its song, 'Aap jaisa koi,' sung by the Pakistani-British singer Nazia Hassan and featured twice in the film, lip-synched in both instances by Aman's character, Sheela, a nightclub dancer

(Rajadhyaksha and Willemen 448). In this film, again featuring a triangular romantic structure in which Aman's character is desired by two different men, several of the previously addressed components of the Bollywood film are significantly reworked. As with *HRHK*, Aman's character is introduced via a song – the first rendition of 'Aap Jaisa koi' – which she 'sings' at a nightclub. In the first version of this hit song, Aman appears in a sexy red outfit with her back again turned to the camera (and the internal nightclub audience), before turning around to 'sing' the song. Rather than direct address, the sequence features several shot/reverse shots between Sheela and Feroz Khan's character, Rajesh, who appears in the nightclub for this first enactment. Indeed, the first instance of a direct address by Aman comes halfway through the four-minute song sequence, via a heart-shaped frame within a frame, in which Aman looks directly at the camera and winks as she sings.[8]

Following this sequence formally introducing Sheela, she leaves the nightclub with Rajesh and, on their way out, she is briefly detained by several of her fans who pay her compliments while Rajesh grows increasingly impatient. When one such fan, a man with a particularly large moustache, stops Sheela, placing his hand on her and commenting on how sexy she is, Rajesh grabs the man by his moustache and tells him to leave. When Rajesh says goodnight to Sheela in the following shot at her door, he tells her, 'No more dancing in the nightclub from now on,' while Sheela looks at him demurely, with only the hint of a smile on her lips. Unfortunately Rajesh, a jewel thief, is subsequently arrested and sent to jail, and so Sheela resumes her career as a nightclub dancer, performing the second rendition of 'Aap jaisa koi' for the second man to come into her life, Amar (Vinod Khanna).

In the second version of this song, which is half as long, Sheela wears a figure-hugging yellow outfit and engages in much more direct address than in the first rendition. Furthermore, while this second version also features several shot/reverse shots between Khanna and Aman, in this instance these looks – or, more precisely, Aman's looks off-screen at Khanna – are interpellated into the direct address. Thus, at the level of gazes, one could say that while Sheela is much more the direct (private) object of Rajesh's gaze in the first version, the second time around she is not only on display for Amar but also, via the overlapping of shot/reverse shot and direct address, for us, the film's external audience.[9] Zeenat's dancing in both versions is 'poor,' as film theorist Rachel Dwyer notes, 'but the camera, clothes and movements all emphasise her curvaceous body' (Dwyer 196). All of these elements seem to frame Sheela as a vamp figure, 'dressed in a shimmering tight-fitting gown,' while 'perform[ing] a cabaret number . . . at a night club, to seduce' both the internal male protagonist(s) and, by extension, the audience (Kasbekar 300) – as Jhunjhunwala notes, 'No vamp has gyrated as seductively as Zeenat Aman to the 'Aap jaisa koi' number in *Qurbani*' (Jhunjhunwala 22–23).

Yet there are also significant deviations from the previous articulations of this figure. To begin with, Sheela is not just relegated to this (vamp) setting but, indeed, operates beyond it as well.[10] Whereas the vamp was 'an outsider' and 'a home breaker,' Sheela, while embodying several vamp attributes (e.g., an unrestrained sexuality and 'Westernness'), is not coded as a vamp figure but rather as a heroine (Mazumdar 86, 90). Similarly, whereas the nightclub was formerly coded as 'an illicit landscape,' in which the dancer performed for her 'customers,' the nightclub setting of *Qurbani* is more benign, featuring 'a backing group . . . who seem to have no idea how to mime playing their instruments' and, rather than an underworldly 'clientele' (with this term's implicit associations with prostitution), the occupants of *Qurbani*'s nightclub could more accurately be described as Sheela's fans who dance along (rather than remaining seated, an element again associated with the earlier paradigm of [illicit] dancer and [paying] client) while smiling and waving their arms (Mazumdar 86, 88; Dwyer 196). Furthermore, whereas some theorists have argued that such 'mandatory cabaret sequences' violated the recipe of classical cinema, where voyeurism is mediated through the gaze of another (internal character), Sheela's twin performances of 'Aap jaisa koi' illuminate the differing ways in which she engages the look(s) of both internal and external audiences (Prasad qtd. in Mazumdar 87–88). Rather than being a case of either one or another (i.e., the look of classical cinema or that of direct address), in Sheela's case both forms are utilized, at times, within the same number. All of this is to illuminate how such sweeping formulations (of such sequences' placement in Bollywood films and their internal structure, as well as their coding of this [vamp] figure) are disrupted or, indeed, made redundant via Aman's performance in films such as *Qurbani.*

Thus even as Aman reworks the previous Bollywood premise, in which the vamp is opposed to the heroine, she simultaneously avoids the fate meted out to her previous enactments of such a hybrid role (e.g., Janice in *HRHK* or Sheetal in *RKM*). One could argue that such a fate is avoided because Aman's character does not overstep the redefined parameters allotted to the 'new woman,' in the sense that, even though she performs 'Aap jaisa koi' for Amar (and, in the process, signals her attraction to him), she also reaffirms her (monogamous) commitment to Rajesh once he is released from jail, simultaneously disavowing her previous attraction to Amar. In this way Aman, as Sheela, embodies 'a working woman' who 'pursu[es] a career... as singer in bars and discotheques [...] without jeopardizing her virtue' (Kasbekar 301).[11] In defying this binary and the fate normally allotted to those who attempt to do so, Aman (as Sheela) embodies a new type of femininity in Bollywood which, in turn, reflects a shift in the make-up of other elements of the Bollywood film formerly associated with the vamp figure (e.g., the decadence of the nightclub). Via Aman's performance as Sheela, the heroine could now be said to occupy the space of the vamp which, in turn, undermined several older boundaries regarding the display of female sexuality (Mazumdar 90). Indeed, to employ the current lexicon, one could point to Aman as the first 'item girl' who also played the heroine (or, conversely, one of the first heroines who also doubled as an 'item girl').[12] Via her performances in these films – *HRHK, Yaadon ki Baraat, RKM*, and *Qurbani* – one can also chart the evolving role of the 'new woman' in Bollywood during the 1970s, when the construction of femininity was gradually liberated from the stifling binary model that previously regulated on-screen desire and forced actresses to either (entirely) embody the heroine or a woman comfortable in her own sexuality. Whereas the repetition of the songs in *HRHK* and *RKM* illuminated Aman's characters' inability to fully sever ties with this binary model (and the fate it afforded those who transgressed), her repetition of 'Aap jaisa koi' signals her decision to continue her career as a nightclub dancer (despite Rajesh's injunction) and, in the process, to fulfill her own desires. Rather than functioning as mere renditions, Aman's repeated songs reflect her agency in the unfolding stories and become a way for her, via playback, to express this agency.

In this manner, Zeenat Aman has helped pave the way for more recent Indian actresses such as Kareena Kapoor, Aishwarya Rai, and Katrina Kaif who have 'blurred the identities of a heroine and a seductress... in recent years' (Amin 112). This legacy itself becomes a way of charting Aman's inextricable link with the films of the 1970s and their ensuing reformulations of the Indian heroine. If one could argue that it was in the 1970s that one first saw heroines who pursued professional careers while maintaining a high level of sensuality, then one can see a continuation of this confluence in the roles of actresses in today's Bollywood films. Kareena Kapoor, for instance, plays an attorney in *Aitraaz* (d. Abbas-Mustan, 2004), defending her husband against charges of sexual misconduct even as she retains her own seductiveness in song sequences such as 'Gela Gela Gela' and 'Woh Tassawur'; in *Kambakkht Ishq* (d. Sabir Khan, 2009), meanwhile, she plays both a doctor and a model. These are strong female roles with a high degree of female agency – in both, it is Kapoor who takes the initiative, particularly in her relationships with men – and the heroine's sexuality subserves, rather than detracts from, this agency. If Zeenat Aman, as Amitabh Bachchan has claimed, 'epitomized' the 'greater sociological changes that were beginning to emerge in [India]' during the 1970s, then her 'instant acceptance by audiences,' as well as the continuing success of contemporary actresses who, following in her footsteps, have effectively merged previously dichotomized identities, are testaments to both Aman's constitution of a new feminine subjectivity and the enduring legacy of the 1970s, particularly in its revamping of female sexuality (qtd. in Jhunjhunwala 20).

Notes

1. One can gauge Aman's new form of femininity and sexuality in Bollywood by comparing her screen presence with those of some of her more well-known predecessors. For instance, one of the earliest female stars in Indian cinema, Nargis, whose performances were considered 'authentic to a degree unprecedented in Indian cinema' during her time (1940s–50s), was 'often presented as the femme fatale doomed to destruction by her beauty' (Rajadhyaksha and Willemen 161); at the same time, in a classic film such as *Shri 420* (1955), the role of the westernized proto-vamp is played not by Nargis, who is portrayed as 'simple, sari-clad, and incorruptible,' but by another actress (Kasbekar 300). On the other hand Bollywood's classic vamp, Helen, 'provided the antithesis to the ideal [Indian] woman's embodiment of chastity,' but was regulated to only playing the role of sexually promiscuous Other in Hindi films, never appearing as the heroine and usually being punished for her sexual promiscuity with death (Kasbekar 298). Meanwhile Mumtaz, 'another firebrand actress who walked the seductive route' and was 'already bridging the traditional-western divide' in the 1960s, turned down the role ultimately given to Aman in *Hare Rama Hare Krishna* (1971), that of the 'hippie-chick,' Janice, choosing instead to play the more traditional heroine/love interest, despite this role's lesser importance (Amin 105, 110; Jhunjhunwala 13).
2. While the repeated song sequence is not unique to Aman's films but, indeed, somewhat of a staple of popular Hindi cinema, such a repetition typically functions as either a recognition device, i.e., as a way of revealing the true identity of a character and/or the hidden relationship between two or more characters, or as a form of reprise, i.e., the iteration of an earlier theme conveyed in the first enactment of the song. Aman's repeated songs, on the other hand, deviate from this standard model in some interesting ways, as we shall see below.
3. As a film scholar, I am particularly interested in coming to terms with the cinematic techniques employed in these films and how they, in turn, adhere to and deviate from a conventional politics of gazing in which, as film theorist Laura Mulvey has famously noted, the woman traditionally functions on two levels: 'as erotic object for the characters within the screen story, and as erotic object for the spectator' (Mulvey 719). It is particularly with regard to what Mulvey calls the woman's 'to-be-looked-at-ness' in the conventionally coded context of (voyeuristic) cinema that I would like to (re)consider the representation of Zeenat Aman in some of these song sequences (Mulvey 719). Indeed, one of my aims in this paper is to deconstruct what at times has been the assumption of either absolute adherence to or deviation from these codes, particularly in the context of Indian cinema and particularly in the timeframe of the 1970s, a period which saw not only the advent of psychoanalytic film theory but also, in the Indian context, a new, at times unconventional form of popular cinema and, with it, the unconventional 'new woman' of this cinema, e.g., Zeenat Aman.
4. The homonym of Janus is worth noting in relation to Aman's dual identity/ transformation in this film as, in many ways, a part of her remains looking back at her older self (Jasbir), even as her other persona (Janice) insistently moves in the opposite direction. This 'split' is a key factor shaping her identity, as we shall see below.
5. One can see such an introduction of the female via song becoming a staple in Bollywood not only through Aman's various films during this period, e.g., *Hare Rama Hare Krishna* (1971); *Roti Kapada aur Makaan* (1974); and *Qurbani* (1980), but also through subsequent films featuring actresses such as Rekha (*Muqaddar ka Sikandar* [1978]; *Silsila* [1981]); Madhuri Dixit (*Tezaab* [1988]; *Ram Lakhan* [1989]); Kajol (*Dilwale Dulhania le Jayenge* [1995]); Karisma Kapoor (*Dil To Pagal Hai* [1997]); Aishwarya Rai (*Hum Dil De Chuke Sanam* [1999]; *Devdas*

[2002]); Kareena Kapoor (*Kabhi Khushi Kabhie Gham* [2001]); and, most recently, Katrina Kaif (*Tees Maar Khan* [2010]).

6. As film theorist Asha Kasbekar notes, 'The vamp provided the antithesis to the ideal woman's embodiment of chastity, by her demonstrations of uncontrolled female lust and wantonness' (Kasbekar 298). Aman's roles in the 1970s, e.g., in *RKM*, can be seen as typifying what Kasbekar goes on to call 'the new woman,' a modern, independent woman who was 'willing to execute the erotic dance performances that used to be the raison d'etre of the seductress' (Kasbekar 301).
7. This transformation subsequently comes to an end via the second iteration of 'Main naa bhoolunga,' which commences her rehabilitation.
8. The only other time that she engages in direct address in this first version is briefly near the very end of the song.
9. That is to say, the audience is interpellated much more into Amar's point of view than we are in Rajesh's the first time around.
10. Another way of putting this would be that Sheela's displays of sexuality are not limited to certain spaces, e.g., those of the nightclub, but, rather, featured throughout the film.
11. Indeed, one could argue that because of Sheela's discretion in her involvement with Amar and her subsequent concealment of this relationship from Rajesh (unlike in *RKM*, where Aman's character Sheetal publicly 'betrays' Bharat via her engagement to Mohan), it is Amar who must 'sacrifice' himself in order to make way for the monogamous relationship of Sheela and Rajesh. *Qurbani* thus signals the advent of the 'new woman' (who no longer need perish for embodying such a role) even as it reaffirms the importance of the homosocial bond between the two male leads, in whose name Amar sacrifices his life.
12. It is worth noting that in the recent film, *Dum Maaro Dum* (2011), the actress who appears in the remixed and recreated version of this song, Deepika Padukone, only appears in this song, i.e., she merely functions as an 'item girl,' unlike Aman who both performed such a 'risqué' song (in the original *HRHK*) and played a key role in the film story.

References

Amin, Tushar A. *Bollywood Themes*. Noida: Brijbasi Art Press, 2010. Print.

Anand, Dev. *Romancing with Life: An Autobiography*. New Delhi: Viking, 2007. Print.

Bose, Mihir. *Bollywood: A History*. New Delhi: Roli Books, 2006. Print.

Dwyer, Rachel. *100 Bollywood Films*. London: BFI, 2005. Print.

Garga, B.D. *The Art of Cinema: An Insider's Journey Through Fifty Years of Film History*. New Delhi: Viking, 2005. Print.

Gopalan, Lalitha. *Cinema of Interruptions: Action Genres in Contemporary Indian Cinema*. London: BFI, 2002. Print.

Jhunjhunwala, Udita. "The Elegant Zeenat Aman." *Women in Indian Film*. Ed. Kabir Nasreen Munni. New Delhi: Zubaan, 2009. 9–32. Print.

Kasbekar, Asha. "Hidden Pleasures: Negotiating the Myth of the Female Ideal in Popular Hindi Cinema." *Pleasure and the Nation: The History, Politics and Consumption of Public Culture in India*. Ed. Rachel Dwyer and Christopher Pinney. Oxford: Oxford UP, 2001. 286–308 Print.

Kazmi, Fareed. *Sex in Cinema: A History of Female Sexuality in Indian Films*. New Delhi: Rupa, 2010. Print.

Mazumdar, Ranjani. *Bombay Cinema: An Archive of the City*. Minneapolis: U of Minnesota P, 2007. Print.

Mulvey, Laura. "Visual Pleasure and Narrative Cinema." *Critical Visions in Film Theory: Classic and Contemporary Readings*. Ed. Timothy Corrigan, Patricia White, and Meta Mazaj. Boston: Bedford/St Martin's, 2011. 715–25. Print.

Rajadhyaksha, Ashish and Paul Willemen. *Encyclopaedia of Indian Cinema*., Rev. ed. London: Fitzroy Dearborn, 1999. Print.

Ray, Manas and Madhuja Mukherjee. "Bollywood in Diaspora: In the Tracks of a Twice-Displaced Community." *City Flicks: Cinema, Urban Worlds and Modernities in India and Beyond.* Ed. Preben Kaarsholm. Copenhagen: Roskilde UP, 2002. 113–46. Print.
Sedgwick, Eve Kosofsky. *Between Men: English Literature and Male Homosocial Desire.* New York: Columbia UP, 1985. Print.
'Zeenat Aman.'. *Imdb.com*, n.d. Web. 24 Feb. 2011.
'Zeenat Aman.'. *Wikipedia.com*, n.d. Web. 26 Feb. 2011.

Filmography

Aitraaz. Dir. Abbas-Mustan. Mukta Arts, 2004. Film.
Devdas. Dir. Sanjay Leela Bhansali. Eros International, 2002. Film.
Dil To Pagal Hai. Dir. Yash Chopra. Yash Raj Films, 1997. Film.
Dilwale Dulhania le Jayenge. Dir. Aditya Chopra. Yash Raj Films, 1995. Film.
Dum Maaro Dum. Dir. Rohan Sippy. Ramesh Sippy Entertainment, 2011. Film.
Hare Rama Hare Krishna. Dir. Dev Anand. Navketan Films, 1971. Film.
Hum Dil De Chuke Sanam. Dir. Sanjay Leela Bhansali. Bhansali Films, 1999. Film.
Kabhi Khushi Kabhie Gham. Dir. Karan Johar. Dharma Productions, 2001. Film.
Kambakkht Ishq. Dir. Sabir Khan. Eros International, 2009. Film.
Muqaddar ka Sikandar. Dir. Prakash Mehra. Prakash Mehra Productions, 1978. Film.
Qurbani. Dir. Feroz Khan. Eros Entertainment, 1980. Film.
Ram Lakhan. Dir. Subhash Ghai. Mukta Arts, 1989. Film.
Roti, Kapada aur Makaan. Dir. Manoj Kumar. DEI, 1974. Film.
Shri 420. Dir. Raj Kapoor. R.K. Films Ltd., 1955. Film.
Silsila. Dir. Yash Chopra. Yash Raj Films, 1981. Film.
Tees Maar Khan. Dir. Farah Khan. Hari Om Entertainment, 2010. Film.
Tezaab. Dir. N. Chandra. Video Sound, 1988. Film.
Yaadon ki Baraat. Dir. Nasir Hussain. Nasir Hussain Films, 1973. Film.

Ritual reverb: Two 'blockbuster' Hindi films

Philip Lutgendorf

University of Iowa, Iowa City, USA

This essay re-examines a highly successful and much discussed film of the mid-1970s, *Jai Santoshi Maa*, along with a comparably celebrated hit released two decades later, *Hum Aapke Hain Koun..!* Theorizing that the unexpected success of both these films may lie in their structuring around popular forms of ritual, it situates each in the context of its production and reception and considers the nature and implications of some of the forms of participatory practice that each film, at very different historical moments, encouraged.

> In ritual, the world as lived and the world as imagined, fused under the agency of a single set of symbolic forms, turns out to be the same world.
>
> Clifford Geertz[1]

Popular Hindi films contain a great deal of visual, aural, and thematic content that may be termed 'religious,' and most often Hindu, in character. Such content has dominated the narratives of this cinema in its historic inception, since films of genres variously identified as 'mythologicals' (based on epic and puranic scriptures) and 'devotionals' (based on the hagiographies of religious exemplars) formed the bulk of productions during the first decade of India's silent era (1913–1922).

Despite changing labels, and the comparative rarity of 'mythologicals' in post-1920s Bombay cinema, religious content – often expressed through ritual – has remained a ubiquitous feature of popular films, a fact recently underscored by an ambitious survey (Dwyer). Diurnal rites such as 'taking *darshan*' and receiving *prasad* and performing *arti* in temples and before home altars, women greeting male relatives with a lamp and auspicious forehead-mark, as well as seasonal and life-cycle rituals, such as the annual festivals of Holi and Divali and (especially) the rites of passage attendant on marriage and death – all are recurring motifs in popular films, which have developed certain conventions for their representation. Their common uses include the alteration of mood (through an injection of solemnity, mourning, or festal gaiety), the development of character (e.g., through the representation of piety), or the suggestion of the passage of time, as in the repeated ringing of temple bells in the 1975 hit *Deewaar*, which signals the lapse of 20 years in the lives of the main characters. Moreover, in *Deewaar*, the early representation of a pious and long-suffering mother's *darshan* at a Shiva temple, participated in by her younger son but boycotted by his angry elder brother, prefigures the latter's climactic confrontation with the deity and offering of himself as a sacrifice (*balidan*) to save his mother's life.

Although the introduction of such portentous vignettes is commonplace, the most celebrated Hindi films of the past half century include two that are more centrally structured around ritual performances: *Jai Santoshi Maa* (1975; hereafter, *JSM*) and *Hum Aapke Hain Koun..!* (1994; hereafter, *HAHK*). Although classed in different cinematic genres ('mythological' and 'social,' respectively), these films show a number of intriguing similarities as well as some striking differences. Since each has enjoyed a success that may, without exaggeration, be termed phenomenal – exerting, in the opinion of both admirers and detractors, an impact on popular culture that has proven to be lasting – each has also become the subject of a modest body of critical literature.[2] In the remainder of this essay, I will revisit these well-known films with a focus on their ritual dimension, which has been largely neglected in previous analyses, and which functions in each in both a narrative and prescriptive manner. That is, within the film, the enactment of rituals is central to the unfolding of the plot and to its satisfactory resolution, and in the context of the film's reception, these practices have come to be widely emulated, in part through 'ritualized' re-viewings of the films themselves.

Yet in focusing on one comparatively neglected dimension of these films, I do not intend a reductive argument, suggesting that their popularity depends primarily on this element of their structure. In closely examining a few scenes from each film, I seek to supplement existing scholarly analyses by giving greater emphasis to specifically cinematic dimensions of film 'texts' (e.g., cinematography and framing, *mise-en-scène*, sound and music) that may convey equally compelling (and sometimes internally-contradictory, resistant, or even subversive) 'messages' to audiences. The lyrics and staging of song sequences have been especially neglected in scholarship on Hindi cinema, although songs constitute one of its characteristic features, typically account for 20 to 30% of a film's running time, and enjoy wide post- and extra-filmic circulation.[3] Even scholars who concede the importance of song sequences tend to treat them as 'interruptions' in the flow of the narrative, allowing for the eruption of 'excess' in the form of emotion and spectacle (e.g., Gopalan; Thomas, 'Indian Cinema'). Yet in the case of both *JSM* and *HAHK* it is precisely during song sequences that the most significant and imitated ritual activities occur. This is perhaps not surprising, since the repetitious and harmonious structure of music mirrors that of ritual, and may also serve (as in the musical setting of the Catholic mass or the lyrics of a Hindu *arti*) to script and prescribe ritual practice. If filmmaking in general has been compared to ritual as a 'world-making' activity that creates an alternative, self-contained universe structured according to orderly rules (Plate 1–13), then the Hindi filmsong, with its typical format of rhyming verses and echoing refrain, accompanied by complex and artfully choreographed 'picturization,' may be said to present a world-within-a-world that both encapsulates and mirrors the larger structure of the film, and that accordingly warrants close analysis within the larger filmic 'text.'

In the concluding section of this essay, I propose that the unusual success of both films rests, in part, on their supplying scripts for individual and collective mimesis both through ritual practice and ritualized re-viewing. I also discuss an apparent shift that this focus on cinematic ritual suggests, from the turbulent 1970s to the decade of growing but uneven plenitude that characterized the 1990s: that *JSM*'s subversive critique of dominant familial and religious structures appears largely undone in *HAHK*, which reaffirms those structures around a smiling but triumphalist brand of Hinduism.

The fast that satisfies

The screenplay of *Jai Santoshi Maa*, attributed to Pandit Priyadarshi of Hardwar, is unusual in that it is based on the genre of popular literature known as *vrat-katha* ('ritual fast-narrative'), usually encountered as inexpensive and crudely printed chapbooks sold in religious bookstalls and used primarily by women in the performance of domestic rituals. These texts detail the procedures for observing a *vrat* and then offer a story, the recitation of which will constitute one of its essential rites. The story may tell of the origin of the rite, or alternatively (and sometimes additionally) of its paradigmatic performance by an individual who struggles against obstacles to complete the *vrat* and obtain its 'fruit.'

Historically, Santoshi Maa ('Satisfaction Mother') seems to have originated in the 1960s in Rajasthan or western Madhya Pradesh, when a local goddess acquired this name. Whereas many such 'mothers' are simply regarded as autochthonous protectors of a given locality, Santoshi Maa acquired an origin story identifying her as the daughter of elephant-headed Ganesha and his wives, Riddhi and Siddhi ('prosperity' and 'success'). This story links her with a pot-bellied deity known for his beneficence and also places her within an extended family that ultimately includes, as her paternal grandparents, the powerful Shiva and Parvati. This familial placement of Santoshi Maa, which is in contrast to the relative autonomy of many other goddesses, seems important both for her general appeal to women and for the film narrative, and indeed may have contributed to the latter's most innovative plotline: a divine 'family quarrel' that pits senior goddesses against the young 'newcomer' Santoshi Maa.

Like her father and grandfather, Santoshi Maa is regarded as 'easy to satisfy.' Her preferred offering is raw sugar and parched gram, among the most inexpensive foodstuffs, and her *vrat* simply requires, on Friday (the day sacred to her), an offering of a small amount of these accompanied by abstention from sour foods and the reading of her *katha*. This is to be observed for a cycle of successive weeks (16 in the film, but 14 or 12 in some printed sources), followed by the celebratory feasting (with a menu from which sour foods are likewise banned) of a group of boys. The completion of this extended ritual is said to grant any wish of the devotee. Limited evidence suggests that the popularity of this *vrat* was slowly spreading – by word of mouth, printed booklet, and through a religious poster illustrating its key elements – among lower-class women for at least a decade prior to the film's production. Indeed, Bombay-resident filmmaker Vijay Sharma is said to have made, at his wife's suggestion, a pilgrimage to a Santoshi Maa temple, where he received the inspiration to direct the film (Hawley and Wulff 4). It is equally clear, however, that large numbers of women had not heard of the goddess or her *vrat* prior to the release of the film, which repeatedly alludes to the 'newness' of the cult.[4]

Incorporating both the birth story of Santoshi Maa (with which it opens) and the tale of a heroic performance of her *vrat* by a sorely-tried human devotee named Satyavati (Kanan Kaushal), the film thus literally presents itself as the cinematic equivalent of a *vrat*-pamphlet, complete with its obligatory story and with the prescribed sixteen-Fridays ritual graphically and dramatically illustrated. To these narrative elements is added another: an audacious story in which the goddesses Lakshmi, Parvati, and Sarasvati (the latter here called 'Brahmani' or 'Mrs Brahma'), egged on by the mischievous and meddlesome sage Narada (played by the comic actor Jeevan), attempt to stop the worship of their new 'rival,' Santoshi Maa, by destroying the happiness of her exemplary devotee, Satyavati. This narrative, enacted through witty and colloquial dialogue, exemplifies the kind of 'domestication' of Hindu deities that is as common in the Sanskrit Puranas as it is in the regional folktales on which they may often have drawn, and was reportedly greatly relished by theatre audiences (Kurtz 14). But quite apart from its entertainment value, the story of the jealous goddesses, brief episodes of which alternate with longer ones devoted to the central tale of the long-suffering Satyavati, allows the film to develop a remarkable parallelism that is absent from its written precursors (Das 49). By continually juxtaposing the assault on Santoshi Maa by senior divine women with the persecution of Satyavati by her jealous sisters-in-law, and then ultimately thwarting both through Satyavati's successful completion of the sixteen-Fridays *vrat*, the film makes a 'theo-visual' assertion of the oneness of deity and devotee. That such empowerment is potentially available not only to the film's heroine but also to any woman who undertakes the *vrat* is underscored by the changing manifestations of Santoshi Maa in the course of the film: as a girl-child in the opening scene (wished for and welcomed by her adoring mothers, but 'created' only reluctantly by her frowning father); as a beautiful young woman (Anita Guha) who thrice rescues Satyavati and her husband, Birju (Ashish Kumar) from the consequences of the goddesses' and sisters-in-law's wrath; and as a white-haired, gap-toothed crone who hobbles up on the sixteenth Friday of Satyavati's fast and miraculously provides her with the handful of offerings that her in-laws and a greedy merchant had withheld, enabling her to complete her vow.

The film's four catchy devotional songs (*bhajans*) are all performed during acts of worship of Santoshi Maa, thus establishing liturgical texts that may be used by worshipers – and indeed, these songs have remained popular and may still be heard on Fridays in temples and homes throughout India. The first, *Main to arti utarun* ('I perform [Santoshi Maa's] *arti*'), immediately follows the scene of Santoshi Maa's birth, and similarly introduces Satyavati, who sings it with an ensemble of female dancers in a large and apparently flourishing temple to this 'new' goddess. The camerawork during this lively number provides a visual intimation of the unity of worshiper and deity that I have noted above, as well as a striking cinematic demonstration of the bodily and affective practice of *darshan*. Many of the long shots offer near-symmetrical views of the temple in which either the goddess or Satyavati are framed by the moving dancers. Close-ups of Satyavati's face alternate with comparable shots of an icon that resembles the young actress; in a third variant shot, the camera peers over the deity's right shoulder to approximate the view of Satyavati and the dancers that (in the understood reciprocity of *darshan*) Santoshi Maa sees. Indeed, one full verse of the song revels in this theme of 'visual communion.'

> Satyavati (seen in long shot over the goddess' shoulder): There is great affection, great love in Mother's eyes.
>
> Chorus (long shot of dancers): ... In Mother's eyes!
>
> Satyavati (in close-up, followed by reverse-shot of goddess' face): There is great mercy, power, and affection in Mother's eyes.
>
> Chorus: ... In Mother's eyes!
>
> Satyavati: (in medium shot, followed by close-up) Why shouldn't I gaze, again and again, into Mother's eyes?
>
> (in long shot over goddess's shoulder) At every instant, a new miracle is seen in Mother's eyes!
>
> Chorus: (close-up of goddess)... In Mother's eyes!

Satyavati's performance of this song, and her prayer to the goddess for a worthy husband, leads to a chance encounter with Birju, the youngest of seven sons in a family of farmers. It is love at first *darshan* for the two young people, and (unexpectedly, given the usual protracted trials preceding cinematic 'love marriage') their match is quickly sanctioned. This development is accompanied by several allusions to the auspicious union of Rama and Sita in the *Ramayana* story.[5] But albeit made in heaven, this marriage, like that of Sita, is soon to be sorely tried, when Satyavati runs afoul of the internal politics of her husband's extended family – her brothers- and sisters-in-law's jealousy of the pampered, artistic Birju and resentment over the ease with which he has acquired a beautiful and self-chosen bride. When, through the machinations of the equally jealous celestial women (whom Narada has informed of the growing popularity of Santoshi Maa), Birju learns that he is being fed the leavings of his brothers' meals, he storms off to seek his fortune, leaving his bride at her in-laws' mercy.

What ensues generally follows the *vrat* story, though with repeated digressions to the innovative heavenly subplot. Although Birju is believed to have drowned while crossing a river, he in fact prospers as the trusted assistant to a fabulously wealthy merchant. Meanwhile, Satyavati, branded an inauspicious widow, suffers as the slave of her in-laws, while the gloating goddesses regularly applaud from their perch above the clouds. When the family's abuse drives Satyavati to attempt suicide, she is stopped by Narada, who tells her about the sixteen-Fridays fast for Santoshi Maa. The performance of this ritual – against the opposition of sisters-in-law and heavenly powers – is one of the climactic events of the film, and is accompanied by a moving *bhajan*, '*Karti hun tumhara vrat main*' ('I perform your *vrat*'). Satyavati's pleading verses, accompanied by visuals that show the passage of time by the increasing number of oil lamps on her *puja* tray and the darkening circles around her eyes, alternate with musical passages dominated by a solo flute, and accompanied by scenes of the Krishna-like Birju (whose name is an epithet for the amorous flute-player), sporting in flower gardens with his employer's voluptuous daughter – a risqué episode facilitated by goddess-induced amnesia. His apparent total abandonment of his wife gives special poignancy to her cry (accompanied by visuals that again largely alternate between Satyavati's now-anguished face and that of a more somber Santoshi Maa icon) for the Mother's help:

I perform your *vrat*; accept it, O Mother!

I am caught in mid-current; carry me across, O Mother!

O Mother Santoshi, O Mother Santoshi!

I sit with high hopes in your court,

Why do I weep while you look on, in this cruel world?

Amend my fate, O amend my fate; make a miracle, O Mother!

I am caught in mid-current; carry me across, O Mother!

O Mother Santoshi, O Mother Santoshi!

When, after many trials, the *vrat* is successfully completed, Santoshi Maa restores Birju's memory, and he rushes home with the wealth earned in the merchant's service. Discovering his wife's plight, he builds a palatial new house for the two of them, complete with its own temple to their patron goddess. It is here that the film's earthly plot reaches its climax, during Satyavati's final feasting ceremony, which her sisters-in-law, inspired by the goddesses, attempt to ritually thwart by introducing sour food. This provokes Santoshi Maa's wrath, which shakes both the earthly and celestial worlds. It leads, following another song in which Satyavati entreats Santoshi Maa (once again, a series of close-up shot-reverse-shots alternate between the weeping wife and an icon that now appears sorrowful), to the goddess' miraculous epiphany in the courtyard, the in-laws' repentance, and, in a brief coda, the three celestial women's acceptance of Santoshi Maa as an honored member of their divine family – Parvati's own granddaughter. The successful completion of the *vrat* thus signals both Satyavati's triumph on earth and that of her chosen goddess in heaven.

Two weddings, a funeral, and a dog

Whereas *Jai Santoshi Maa*, a 'mythological' film about the tribulations and rewards of faith, drew on the folk literary genre of the *vrat katha*, *Hum Aapke Hain Koun..!* ('Who am I to you?'; hereafter, *HAHK*), a largely comedic 'social' film about the marital alliances of two uncommonly wealthy and harmonious families, intertextually cited a number of previous hits of Bombay cinema. Most notably, it referenced director Sooraj Barjatya's own first film,

Maine Pyar Kiya ('I fell in love,' 1989), which was similarly set in a palatial home awash in consumer goods, cast six of the same actors in major roles, featured the same male star, Salman Khan, playing a romantic hero likewise named Prem ('love'), and included the plot motif of a miraculous messenger-pet (a white pigeon in the 1989 film, a white dog in *HAHK*) who intervenes at a crucial moment in the narrative.[6] Whereas *JSM* opens with a prologue set in Ganesha's heavenly mansion, *HAHK*'s opening shot establishes an opulent earthly estate with verdant lawns big enough to allow family members to stage their own cricket matches. One is in progress as the film begins, played by gendered teams with caps that declare 'boy' and 'girl' respectively, announced by the comical servant Lallu Prasad (Laxmikant Berde), and umpired by the family pet, a straw-hatted Pomeranian named Tuffy. Astute viewers who guess, from the first moments of this 195-minute film, that its lighthearted plot will unfold in game-like permutations, focus principally on romance, and involve Lallu and Tuffy as channels of Higher Authority, will not be disappointed.[7]

As in *JSM*, the *Ramayana* is cited early on, in the context of a prospective marriage. Kailash Nath (Alok Nath), a self-made industrialist who has foregone conjugal life in order to raise the two orphaned sons of his deceased brother and sister-in-law, now seeks a match for the elder boy, Rajesh (Mohnish Bahl), who is already a partner in the family business. A close relative arranges a meeting, at a pilgrimage place known as Ramtekri ('Rama's hill'), with the family of Prof. Siddharth Chaudhuri (Anupam Kher), who has an eligible elder daughter named Puja (Renuka Shahane). Given that Prof. Chaudhuri and his wife (Reema Lagoo) turn out to have been old school chums of Kailash Nath's, the meeting of the two families is especially warm; soon Rajesh and the lovely, domestically-inclined Puja meet and shyly assent to an engagement.

The 'Ramtekri' shrine is an idealized soundstage set not unlike the temple depicted in *JSM*, and it echoes with recitation of the *Ramcaritmanas*, and indeed with an excerpt from the episode of Rama and Sita's marriage cited in the earlier film (1.271.1). These mythic allusions are emphasized by the first diegetic song, '*Vah vah Ramji*' ('Bravo, Mr Ram!'), in which members of both families celebrate the engagement of Rajesh and Puja while simultaneously participating in the temple *arti* ceremony of Rama and Sita. This occasions – at the conclusion of a 'secular' song that playfully 'congratulates' the deity for having made such a good match – a *darshanic* shot-reverse-shot not unlike those seen in the opening song sequence in *JSM*. Meanwhile, Rajesh's younger brother, Prem, has met and been charmed by Puja's spirited younger sister, Nisha (Madhuri Dixit), though their romantically-tinged mutual teasing goes unnoticed by other family members in the excitement of the elder siblings' match. These initial rituals are soon followed by others that occupy much of the film's running time: a second, formal betrothal and gifting ceremony (*tilak*, *milni*), held at Kailash Nath's mansion; the wedding itself, incorporating a number of subsidiary rites; the elaborate ceremony held to celebrate Puja's pregnancy; and then, unexpectedly, a heartrending funeral and wake, followed by a climactic second wedding.

By Hindi cinematic standards, *HAHK*'s plotline is sparse and linear, especially given the film's unusual length – a fact much remarked on in both popular and critical writings. During the course of Rajesh and Puja's engagement, marriage, and production of a son, Prem and Nisha gradually fall in love. Puja, learning of this (two hours and 36 minutes into the film), is about to 'arrange' their engagement when she dies tragically in a fall, leaving both families devastated and her infant without a mother. When Prof. Chaudhuri proposes that his younger daughter take her sister's place as Rajesh's wife, Prem and Nisha realize the need to sacrifice their love for the greater good of the family.[8] Only the faithful servant Lallu knows their secret, and, just as Rajesh' second wedding is about to be solemnized, he prays to the idol of Krishna in the Chaudhuri family's shrine room, asking for a 'miracle.' Krishna provides this by causing the dog, Tuffy, to deliver Nisha's farewell love-note, intended for Prem, to Rajesh instead. The latter, after a dramatic confrontation, magnanimously sanctions the lovers' union, declaring that Nisha can give no less love to his son as a '*chachi*' (paternal uncle's wife) than she could as a mother.

The relative simplicity of *HAHK*'s storyline is, however, compensated for by the baroque density of the film's *mise-en-scène*: the hyperbolic plenitude of the lifestyles of the two families, in homes overflowing with consumer goods, well-stocked with foodstuffs that are constantly being prepared, served, and consumed, and usually thronged with relatives, friends, and well-wishers observing joyous or solemn occasions – which unfold in a long series of comic and celebratory vignettes dense with jokes, songs and dances, and allusions to popular culture. For foreign viewers, it may be challenging merely to keep the familial relationships straight, though Indians are guided by the nearly complete lexicon of Hindi kinship terms that pepper the dialogue; these terms are nearly always accompanied, in this world of ultra-rich *noblesse*, by the respectful suffix '*-ji*' This plethora of labels gives an ironic twist to the film's titular question – twice posed by Nisha to Prem: 'Who/what am I to you?' Yet, paradoxically, it also highlights a key feature of *HAHK..!* that was remarked on by many viewers: its displacement of a central couple by a diffused focus on (what sociologist Patricia Uberoi terms) 'the emblematic family' – an idealization of the patrilineal joint family from which all systemic stressors have been carefully removed (Uberoi 311, 328, 338–340).

Indeed, the darker side of affinal relations in north India, which is so prominent in *JSM* – the often agonistic relationship between bride-givers and bride-takers both during and after marriage – is, as Uberoi notes, smoothly elided in the familial world of *HAHK*. Greed for dowry is displayed only by a single character: a crassly materialistic and apparently sexually frustrated maternal aunt ('Mami-ji,' played by Bindu), who is as close to a 'villain' as the film provides, but whose attempted interventions pose no real danger and are usually played for laughs.[9] Other common manifestations of the traditionally perceived inequality between bride's and groom's families are either downplayed through hyper-polite dialog and body language, or transformed into vestigial but spectacular ritual practice, displayed in two lavish ensemble numbers (discussed below). Interestingly, these satirical allusions to real domestic tensions were – like the expressions of jealousy by the three senior goddesses in *JSM* – reportedly especially relished by audiences, and these two numbers remain among the most popular of the film's twelve songs (Uberoi 317, 328; cf. Kurtz 14).

That *HAHK*'s opening rituals at Ramtekri are staged as celebratory fun rather than pious worship sets the tone for the depiction of most of the life-cycle rites that follow, and the songs accompanying these center around elaborately choreographed send-ups of folk customs (here termed *shakun* or 'good omens') rather than Sanskritic rituals. Thus the actual 'marriage' of Rajesh and Puja, solemnized by a Brahman's Vedic chants and the couple's circumambulation of the sacred fire, forms a mere background prelude to the spectacular ensemble number '*Jute do paise lo*' ('Give the shoes and take the money'), which depicts the attempts of the bride's junior female kin to steal the bridegroom's slippers and then 'sell' them back to him for a substantial bounty – a teasing reversal, observed by some north Indian communities, of the dowry prestation. Prem and his co-conspirators Lallu and Tuffy try to thwart the theft by hiding the slippers in a fancy sweetmeat box, but are outsmarted by the ladies. The song's lyrics are presented as a verbal duel between male and female soloists and choruses, and the *mise-en-scène* takes full advantage of the Chaudhuri home's vast two-storied atrium and grand staircase. The frenetic choreography features chases, as well as the dispensing (also celebrated in the lyrics) of abundant food – here intended to distract the 'boys' from their attempt to regain the shoes.

(female singer) Have a cool drink. (male singer) Not in the mood!

(female) Take some *dahi bada.* (male) Not in the mood!

(female) Eat some *kulfi* (male) I've had plenty!

(female) Take some *pan.* (male) I've had plenty!

(male chorus) We've had plenty, we've had plenty!

Although critics of the film condemned the materialist excess of such sequences (Bharucha), the conspicuous display of both wealth and food has long been a central component in the non-Vedic rituals associated with Hindu marriage – e.g., Tulsidas twice 'interrupts' the first book of his epic with multi-page descriptions of weddings that feature feasts served on golden platters as well as such non-Sanskritic rituals as women's song sessions in which the groom and his relatives are mocked, and his description is said to have influenced popular practice, even becoming, in some regions, a liturgical text to accompany weddings.[10] In *HAHK*, the '*Jute do paise lo*' song similarly offers a model for wedding planners and an auspicious tableau of lavish consumption, even as its male-female duel serves the larger narrative by highlighting the developing romance between Prem and Nisha – who end up, after a final chase, in an 'accidental' embrace on a double bed, beneath a huge color portrait of Nisha licking an ice cream cone.

An equally elaborate number occurs after the film's intermission, when Puja's female relations and friends come to bless and celebrate her pregnancy, placing a coconut in her lap and honoring her with oil lamps. In some families, such rites include a women's singing program (*sangit*) in which risqué songs are performed that satirize male kin. Here, this custom – somewhat sanitized, yet hyperbolically visualized – takes the form of the showstopping '*Didi tera devar divana*' ('Big sister, your brother-in-law is crazy!'), in which Nisha (as herself) dances with and mocks 'Prem,' impersonated by a cross-dressed female cousin. The accusative refrain charging that he 'flirts with girls' (*kudiyon ko dale dana*) is graphically pantomimed, culminating in brisk activity under a sheet and Nisha's own feigned pregnancy. The song draws on the long and robust tradition of sexually-tinged humor and slang regarding the 'joking' relationship of sister- and brother-in-laws (*bhabhi-devar*) within the extended family, a 'natural friendship' understood to include the frisson of possible sexual attraction and even intimacy. This is indeed a common subject of women's folksongs, as well as of both men's and women's pranks and skits during occasions of social license such as the Holi festival.[11] There is also a cultural tradition (dramatized in the film by Prem and his friends Lallu and Bhola) of men attempting to 'crash' women's singing programs in order to enjoy the salacious lyrics as well as to find out what is being said about them. Here, the friends' several attempts earn them abuse and mockery from the ladies, but ultimately result in Prem's successful replacement of his drag-double to complete the song in a saucy duet with Nisha. In a further ludic reversal, the song ends with Prem himself outfitted in a flimsy negligée and apparently pregnant.

Ritual cinema, ritual practice

Before I consider some of the practices that have developed around these two ritual-laden films, I would like to briefly place the initial success of each in its historical context. *JSM* appeared in the same year in which Prime Minister Indira Gandhi, faced with growing labor unrest, mass political agitation, and charges of electoral corruption, declared a state of National Emergency and assumed draconian powers. In retrospect, this move and the circumstances that provoked it revealed widespread disillusionment with the performance of the Indian government and economy since Independence and presaged the end of the Congress Party's long mandate. The decade that followed saw the rise of regional and caste-oriented parties as well as the increasingly strident assertion of rights by traditionally disadvantaged groups. Scholars of Hindi cinema have similarly identified this period, in terms of its predominant narrative themes, as marking the end of the optimism of the post-Independence 'Nehruvian' era. Tejaswini Ganti thematically labels the next wave of films, beginning in c. 1973, the 'crisis of the state,' and M. Madhava Prasad speaks of a new 'populist cinema of mobilization' centered on 'angry' proletarian heroes, often played by Amitabh Bachchan (Ganti 30–33; Prasad 118, 138–159). Although such a typology clearly fits the 1975 action hits *Sholay* and *Deewaar*, I apply it as well to that year's other, more unexpected cinematic success story.

Despite the demure piety and apparent non-assertiveness of *JSM*'s rural heroine Satyavati, she gradually achieves many of the pragmatic goals to which large numbers of Indian women aspired during this period: a companionate marriage to a man of her liking, an extended 'honeymoon' with him (in the form of a pilgrimage to far-flung temples to Santoshi Maa), and ultimately, a prosperous household of her own, independent of her in-laws. The husband she chooses is a restless young man with similar aspirations, who tells his mother early in the film, 'I don't want to spend my life like my brothers: same old plow, same old fields! Mom, my life will be something amazing, extraordinary!' With the blessings of the 'upstart' goddess Santoshi Maa, and through his wife's steadfastness and his own hard work, he achieves his goals, becoming, in effect, a 'white collar' businessman who has broken free of the rural subsistence economy. The catalyst for this couple's transformation is an extended ritual that is tenaciously performed by the young wife in the face of tremendous opposition: Satyavatis *vrat* is pious worship, but also an 'act of resistance' defying both heavenly and earthly powers. The 'fruit' of her ritual is not merely confirmation of her near-identity to the goddess she adores as well as the attainment of undreamed-of prosperity, but independence from an 'idealized' joint family that has gradually been revealed as dysfunctional and abusive. The reprise of the film's opening *bhajan* just before its climax – when Satyavati and Birju host Santoshi Maa's feast in their opulent new home – suggests, in the costuming of the female dancers, both chronological and economic maturation: village belles in mirrorwork skirts and blouses are replaced by prosperous-looking matrons in 'Georgette' printed saris. Through a female-oriented plot, and without recourse to themes of violence and revenge, *JSM*'s tale of a new goddess of 'satisfaction' displays in its own way the unsatisfied aspirations that fueled the 'crisis of the state,' and offers its own model of 'mobilization' to obtain desired fruits.

The period that saw the release of *HAHK* is likewise associated by film scholars with another major thematic shift, and Sooraj Barjatya's first film, *Maine Pyar Kiya* (1989), with its 'adoption of advertising imagery: rich, saturated color effects constantly emphasizing surface' (Rajadhyaksha and Willemen 451), has been identified as a key cinematic text presaging the 'consumer revolution' of the 1990s, which reflected policies of 'economic liberalization,' and the growing political influence of the urban middle classes, with their links to a global diaspora of successful 'NRI' ('Non-Resident Indian') families (Ganti 33–43). Although these developments brought new prosperity to many Indians, they also sharpened the divide between haves and have-nots, and contributed to the rise of reactionary religio-political movements seeking to impose a majoritarian ideology of *Hindutva* ('Hindu-ness') on India's diverse population (Rajagopal 35–50). *HAHK*'s 'feel-good' saga of a wealthy joint family epitomized many trends of this period: appearing to smoothly balance an opulent, consumer-oriented lifestyle with reverence for 'tradition,' expressed through kinship terms and the cheery observance of gendered and age-ranked hierarchy – though this is tempered (as in the *Ramayana*) by the voluntary mutual 'sacrifice' of loving brothers. Rama-related imagery indeed looms large (despite the intervention of the playful Krishna through his canine agent), and the film has been declared symptomatic of 'a deep internalization of the Hindu Right in popular and mass culture' (Bharucha 804). It is the spectacular performance of rituals – from the initial *arti* at Ramtekri through the choreographed rites of passage that occupy much of the film's running time – that seamlessly blends its diverse and even paradoxical themes. Rites generally associated with upper-caste, north Indian Hindus are presented as normative expressions of a valorized 'Indian' identity, based on patrilineal extended-family 'love' and reverence for (Hindu) tradition. These are trends that can be detected in many Hindi films of previous decades, and indeed are connected with the rise of a more generic and mass-mediated 'public culture' in India throughout the twentieth century, but they arguably acquired a particular force in the economic and political climate of its final decade.

It may appear that I am advancing – and, to an extent, I am – a reading of *JSM* as an unexpectedly 'subversive' and progressive film and of *HAHK* as a far more conventional, even regressive one. Some of their contrasts may be summarized through a chart (Figure 1):

Yet, having identified these contrasts, I must remind readers of the complexity of cinematic texts and the diversity of 'messages' that individual viewers may draw from them. It appears, from Uberoi's interviews, that at least some who enjoyed the exuberant energy and inventive dialogue of *HAHK*'s 'comedy of manners' also maintained a critical distance, recognizing that the film's depiction of 'good relations' within a joint family was a fantasy 'not generally found in families,' or identifying the film as a nostalgic evocation of a bygone era (Uberoi 312, 323, 328). To paraphrase a view that I once advanced in relation to the ideology and performance of the *Ramcaritmanas* of Tulsidas: a thorough consideration of what a popular text 'says' also ought to consider what it 'does' – or rather, what people do with it (Lutgendorf, 'The Life,' 439). And this brings me back to the ritual content of these two films and to practices that have developed around their re-presentation.

	***Jai Santoshi Maa* (1975)**	***Hum Aapke Hain Koun..!* (1994)**
Setting:	Rural economy of scarcity	Urban economy of abundance
Highlighted ritual practice:	Innovative, individual	Traditional, collective
Gender orientation:	Female	Male
Presiding diety:	Unmarried Shaiva goddess	Vishnu (Sita-Rama, Krishna)
Socio-political context:	'Crisis of the state', lower-class assertion	'Cconomic liberalization', middle-class consumerism, *Hindutva*
Family depiction:	Oppressive joint family, ultimately abandoned	Harmonious joint family, continually reaffirmed
Plotline(s):	Strong and multiple, with several villains	Weak and singular, lacking villains
Principal textual reference:	Folk narrative genre (*vrat-katha*)	*Ramayana*; previous Hindi films

Figure 1. Comparison of *JSM* and *HAHK*

The conventional assumption that film-viewing belongs to a 'secular' sphere of human activity that is categorically separated from the 'sacred' or 'religious' sphere, has been challenged by a number of recent studies that call attention not simply to the mythic and theological content of films, but to the formalized practices that surround their reception by audiences (Lyden 108–136; Plate 1–17, 78–91). The experience of periodic, congregationally-shared viewing of massively-projected, dream-like images and stories, suggests participation in mythic and ritual performances, and the assumed 'passivity' of cinema audiences may merely reflect the relative lack of research devoted to film reception. In India, 'moving pictures' of deities, like other forms of representational embodiment, have readily elicited a devotional response from some viewers – e.g., the reported prostrations that greeted the first on-screen appearance of Krishna in one of Phalke's early films – that has been the butt of scorn from critics who assume (as did early writers on cinema in the West) that 'credulous' audiences mistook projected images for 'real' phenomena. Indeed, that such behavior was repeated during screenings of *JSM* has been cited as evidence of a lack of 'progress' in educating 'the people' (Dharap 82–83). But such dismissive attitudes avoid the larger issue of how cinema viewers worldwide react to screen images of 'stars' and 'idols' and the powerful narratives in which they appear, generating responses that often take the form of mimesis.

JSM, with its explicitly 'religious' subject matter and its roots in the *vrat* tradition, offers, not surprisingly, the more obvious example of cultic behavior on the part of audiences, which began soon after the film's release. An article that appeared in the trade journal *Screen* in August 1975, noted the repeated garlanding by filmgoers of signboards advertising *JSM* in the lobbies of theatres, and observed that 'every Friday thousands of men, women, and children, particularly women, rush to the theatres showing the film like they were going to a temple to pay their oblations [sic.] to the all-merciful Goddess' (John). The reporter also noted the phenomenon of repeat participatory behavior engaged in by audience members ('. . . as soon as a bhajan in the film begins a section of the crowd slowly starts chanting the same bhajan and sometimes the whole hall gradually gets into a mood and there is rhythmic clapping and singing in the hall'). Subsequent writings on the film described periodic revivals in Friday matinee screenings that drew largely female audiences; later, the advent of videocassettes enabled women to view the film at home as part of their *vrat* ritual. The choice by viewers to engage so repeatedly with *JSM* did not, however, mean that they would favor the film industry's own attempts at repetition: several 'mythological' spin-offs inspired by the success of *JSM* (including a 2006 remake that updated the storyline and boasted digital special effects) were commercial flops.

HAHK also famously prompted repeat viewing along with several kinds of participatory and mimetic behavior. As with *JSM*, lore circulated regarding the number of repeat viewings indulged in by some fans; the most famous example was that of painter M.F. Hussain, who claimed to have seen the film 67 times. But, like *JSM*, *HAHK* also inspired varieties of domestic performance, particularly in the execution of family life-cycle rituals. The popularity of grandiose weddings, of course, owes little to the film, yet the latter is credited with having helped popularize certain styles of nuptial celebration, including details of costuming and décor, as well as subsidiary rites (such as the theft of the groom's shoes), which would now often be accompanied by songs from the film. Notably, *HAHK* is said to have provided a model for wedding planning among some diasporic South Asians, especially those born or brought up outside the Subcontinent.

Indeed, the critics' dismissal of *HAHK* as an interminable 'wedding video' misses a key element of the film's 'ritual' appeal. The opportunity to record and memorialize family celebrations on film, long enjoyed by the Western middle classes, became increasingly available to Indians following economic liberalization, and began to 'trickle down' from the elite – who could afford personal camcorders – to lower-middle-class families, who would engage local photographers to produce 'custom VCDs' that combined footage from family rituals with still photos, animation, special effects, and songs from Hindi films – including, of course, *HAHK*. This reflexive loop between popular practice and its mass-mediated simulacra is in fact twice celebrated within *HAHK* itself: when Prem watches a video of Nisha's performance, at Rajesh and Puja's wedding, of '*Jute do paise lo*,' at one point pausing the tape to gaze adoringly at her face (and thus revealing his love for her to the observing Lallu); and when Prem and his friends attempt to 'crash' the ladies' *sangit* session by barging in with a video camera and lights and insisting that they must record the event (they are, however, driven away with the threat of a ritual 'shoe-beating').

To observe that *JSM* and *HAHK*, albeit inspiring similar forms of mimetic behavior among viewers, were fundamentally different in their class ethos and address may be accurate in the immediate historical context of each film, yet this assessment overlooks the aspirational dimension of film-inspired mimesis, as well as the impact of India's material 'progress' – however unequally delivered – over several decades. Viewers of *JSM* in 1975 lived in a country in which the majority of people lacked access to electricity, motorized transportation, television, and high-speed communication, and in which the modest aspirations of many – for material prosperity, homes of their own, and greater independence in choosing careers and spouses – were appropriately shown as the kinds of 'satisfaction' that could result from propitiating Santoshi Maa. Two decades later, massive if uneven infrastructural and market changes had considerably upped the ante on the kinds of possibilities to which lower and middle-class people could aspire. The ostentatious life-cycle rites in *HAHK* celebrate the satisfaction of sometimes conflicting wants, and indeed, suggest the possibility that one might 'have it all': partake in a consumer cornucopia and yet espouse 'simple, traditional' values; be a rich capitalist and yet a democratic humanist (Prem eventually heads his own automobile company, yet continues to treat the family servant as a fictive 'brother'); be materially successful yet artistically sensitive (Rajesh paints and Prem plays the balalaika); be obedient to elders yet free to make key choices for oneself. Such goals may have remained impossible dreams for many of the film's enthusiastic fans – but then, cinema, like ritual, is about (among other things) the satisfaction of temporarily real-izing the impossible.

Acknowledgements

A longer version of this essay will appear in a forthcoming anthology, *Hindu Ritual at the Margins: Transformations, Innovations, Reconsiderations*. The author wishes to thank the editors of that volume, Linda Penkower and Tracy Pintchman, and the University of South Carolina Press, for permission to include this abridged version in the present collection.

Notes

1. Geertz 112–13, qtd. in Bell 27.
2. On Jai Santoshi Maa, see Das; Erndl 141–52; Kurtz esp. 111–31; Lutgendorf, 'A Superhit Goddess.' On *Hum Aapke Hain Koun..!*, see Bharucha and Uberoi.
3. E.g., one of the most influential monographs on popular Hindi cinema, M. Madhava Prasad's *The Ideology of the Hindi Film* (1998), ignores their musical component entirely. More recently, several studies have offered insightful readings of song sequences: e.g., Mazumdar esp. 79–109; Gopal and Moorti.
4. For a detailed synopsis and fuller discussion of the film, see Lutgendorf, 'A Superhit Goddess,' 26–34.
5. Thus Satyavati's pious, widowed father (played by former male star Bharat Bhushan in a cameo role), is reciting from the popular Hindi retelling of the epic, the *Ramcaritmanas* of Tulsidas,

when his daughter returns from her first encounter with Birju, and he chants a verse in which the goddess Parvati, to whom Sita has prayed for a husband, assures her of the fulfillment of her request (1.236.7).

6. An explicit reference to the earlier film occurs during the first wedding sequence in *HAHK*, when Prem receives a prank phone call from one of the bride's cousins, who identifies herself as 'Suman' (the name of the heroine of Maine pyaar kiya), and says she was his girlfriend 'in a previous life.' In addition to allusions to Barjatya's previous film, *HAHK* includes a 'pass the pillow' game played during a family gathering, which features several well-known filmsongs as well as the performance, as the 'penalty' exacted from 'losers,' of famous speeches from *Mughal-e-Azam* (1961) and *Sholay* (1975).
7. It is worth noting that the family's cricket match, like their staging of other 'rituals,' is elaborate, carefully coded, and parodic (thus, Lallu pretends to be a sportscaster, 'announcing' the game into a fake microphone), and helps to establish the film's surreal and comic tone. The initial match, which serves to introduce several principal characters, is reprised later to introduce a song in which the daughter-in-law's pregnancy is revealed.
8. Prem initiates this act of renunciation. Nisha at first misunderstands, thinking she is to be married to Prem, but when she learns the truth, she too accepts the propriety of the elders' choice. For some women viewers' critique of this sequence, see Uberoi 322.
9. Uberoi astutely examines the manner in which this character is permitted to voice conventional and cynical attitudes that are otherwise repressed in the film's sanitized and sunny narrative (330–33).
10. See *Ramcaritmanas* 1.92–1.102; 1.286–1.342.
11. The recent tendency for such songs to be co-opted by male singers, and for the spectacle of female performance of them to be presented to a male gaze – both evident in this *HAHK* sequence – has been illuminatingly explored by Jassal.

References

Bell, Catherine. *Ritual Theory, Ritual Practice*. New York: Oxford University Press, 1992. Print.

Bharucha, Rustom. "Utopia in Bollywood: '*Hum Aapke Hain Koun.!.*'" *Economic and Political Weekly,* 15 Apr (1995): 801–4. Print.

Das, Veena. "The Mythological Film and Its Framework of Meaning: An Analysis of *Jai Santoshi Ma*." *India International Centre Quarterly* 8.1 (1980): 43–56. Print.

Dharap, B.V. "The Mythological or Taking Fatalism for Granted." *Indian Cinema Superbazaar*. Ed. Aruna Vasudev and Philippe Lenglet. New Delhi: Vikas Publishing House, 1983. 79–83. Print.

Dwyer, Rachel. *Filming the Gods*. Abingdon and New York: Routledge, 2006. Print.

Erndl, Kathleen M. *Victory to the Mother*. New York: Oxford UP, 1993. Print.

Ganti, Tejaswini. *Bollywood*. London and New York: Routledge, 2004. Print.

Gopal, Sangita, and Sujata Moorti, eds. *Global Bollywood: Travels of Hindi Song and Dance*. Minneapolis: U of Minnesota P, 2008. Print.

Gopalan, Lalitha. *Cinema of Interruptions*. London: British Film Institute, 2002. Print.

Hawley, John Stratton and Donna Marie Wulff, eds. *Devi: Goddesses of India*. Berkeley and Los Angeles: U of California P, 1996. Print.

Jassal, Smita Tewari. "Taking Liberties in Festive Song: Gender, New Technologies, and a 'Joking Relationship.'" *Contributions to Indian Sociology* 41.1 (2007): 5–40. Print.

John, Ali Peter. "The Miraculous Success of a Mythological." *Screen* (29 Aug. 1975): 10. Print.

Kurtz, Stanley N. *All the Mothers Are One*. New York: Columbia UP, 1992. Print.

Lutgendorf, Philip. *The Life of a Text.* Berkeley and Los Angeles: U of California P, 1991. Print.

Lutgendorf, Philip. "A Superhit Goddess/A Made-to-Satisfaction Goddess: Jai Santoshi Ma Revisited." *Manushi, a Journal About Women and Society* 131 (2002): 10–16, 24–37. Print.

Lutgendorf, Philip. "Is There an Indian Way of Filmmaking?" *International Journal of Hindu Studies* 10.3 (2006): 227–56. Print.

Lyden, John C. *Film as Religion.* New York and London: New York UP, 2003. Print.

Mazumdar, Ranjani. *Bombay Cinema.* Minneapolis: U of Minnesota P, 2007. Print.

Plate, S. Brent. *Religion and Film.* London and New York: Wallflower Press, 2008. Print.

Prasad, M. Madhava. *Ideology of the Hindi Film: A Historical Construction.* Delhi: Oxford UP, 1998. Print.

Rajadhyaksha, Ashish and Paul Willemen. *The Encyclopaedia of Indian Cinema.* New Delhi: Oxford UP, 1995. Print.

Rajagopal, Arvind. *Politics After Television.* Cambridge: Cambridge UP, 2001. Print.

Thomas, Rosie. "Indian Cinema: Pleasures and Popularity." *Screen* 26.3–4 (1985): 116–31. Print.

Thomas, Rosie. "Melodrama and the Negotiation of Morality in Mainstream Hindi Film." *Consuming Modernity: Public Culture in a South Asian World.* Ed. Carol A. Breckenridge. Minneapolis: U of Minnesota P, 1995. 157–82. Print.

Uberoi, Patricia. "Imagining the Family: An Ethnography of Viewing *Hum Aapke Hain Koun . . . !*" *Pleasure and the Nation.* Ed. Rachel Dwyer and Christopher Pinney. Delhi: Oxford UP, 2001. 309–51. Print.

Filmography

Deewaar. Dir. Yash Chopra. Trimurti Films Pvt. Ltd., 1975. Film.

Hum Aapke Hain Koun.! Dir. Sooraj R. Barjatya. Rajshri Productions (P) Ltd., 1994. Film.

Jai Santoshi Maa. Dir. Vijay Sharma. Bhagylaxmi Chitramandir, 1975. Film.

Maine Pyar Kiya. Dir. Sooraj R. Barjatya. Rajshri Productions (P) Ltd., 1989. Film.

Sholay. Dir. Ramesh Sippy. G.P. Sippy, 1975. Film.

The 1970s Tamil cinema and the post-classical turn

Swarnavel Eswaran Pillai

Michigan State University, East Lansing, USA

This paper explores the way significant Tamil films of the 1970s were distinct from most of the films made by and largely in the major Madras studios – Modern Theaters, AVM, Gemini, and Vijaya-Vauhini – during the earlier decades. It interrogates the seminal moment in the history of Tamil cinema when films such as *Aval Appadiththan* (1978), *Agraharathil Kazhuthai* (1978), *16 Vayathiniley* (1977) and *Uthirippookkal* (1979), marked by ambiguous and dark protagonists, avoidance of clichéd and cathartic closures, experiments in cinematography and editing, and shooting on locations and new subjectivity, signaled the transition of Tamil cinema from the classical period of the studio system to the post-classical. All these films epitomize a unique period punctuated by the changing power of studios and stars and dramatic changes in technology.

The 1970s in Tamil cinema marks a unique time when a distinct transition from the old to the new occurs. The studio system, which was on the decline from the mid-1960s, loses its influence over the film industry and in its place emerges a powerful network of independent producers and technicians who redefine Tamil cinema by dictating the form and content of its films. Simultaneous to the fading away of the centrality of the studio system, its biggest stars MGR (Maruthur Gopalan Ramachandran) and Sivaji Ganesan too, have lost their preeminence as key players who substantially dictated the economics of the industry through their dominance of the box-office for over two decades. These changes mark a dramatic shift of power away from a studio system that was arguably the biggest in the private sector outside classical Hollywood. This decentering of the power and control of the Madras studios, which dominated not only Tamil but also Telugu, Kannada, and Malayalam cinemas for over three decades, marks the 1970s as the most significant decade in the history of South Asian Cinema.

Although the 1950s and the 1960s are often nostalgically referred to as the 'golden period' of the Madras studios, their dominance was already undermined in the 1960s by the rising power of individual stars. However, the studios could still coexist with the stars and exercise control over production and distribution by financing and offering their facilities to outside producers. It was only in the 1970s that Tamil cinema established its identity as a cinema driven by independent producers and technicians, who moved away from the studio infrastructure and its formulaic narratives in search of a new style. In this paper, consequently, I engage with the significant Tamil films of the 1970s to interrogate a unique decade when all the films made cannot be classified as Madras studio pictures given that the form and content of many of these landmark films are distinct from most films made by, and largely within, the Madras studios during earlier decades – particularly such major ones as Modern Theaters, AVM, Gemini, and Vijaya-Vauhini. I argue that this period, therefore, signifies a seminal moment in the history of Tamil cinema – the transition from the classical period of the studio system to what may be viewed as the post-classical era. And while 'postclassical' has emerged as a loaded and contested term within film studies, my reference to it in its hyphenated form is intentional; I believe that within the context of Tamil cinema in the 1970s, it informs us of the ringing-out of the old and the ringing-in of the new, with the hyphen serving to symbolize the conflation of the echoes of the old within the emerging and new.

My reference to the classical period (of Tamil cinema) serves to emphasize a certain 'classicism' of style, storytelling, modes of production, and technology deployed by the (Madras) studio system (Bordwell, Staiger, and Thompson). Until the late 1960s, Tamil cinema was marked by uniformity of narrative, with a marked preference for the predominant genre of the melodrama. Equally evident is the consistency of the modes of production driven by the studio system and the stars and the use of technologies for production and postproduction accessed primarily through the studios. With the fading away of the studio system in the 1970s, however, we begin to see a heterogeneity replace the visible homogeneity of all of these practices. While the standardization of an earlier industrial practice was, similarly, defined and dialectically driven by variance as exemplified by the films of auteurs like Shridhar, it is the 1970s that mark Tamil cinema's uniqueness as predominantly driven by differentiation, in contrast, not only with the earlier, more classical style but also among the various kinds of films that begin to emerge from that point onwards.

My point of departure, consequently, is Bordwell's (later) observations on continuity and change in Hollywood from the 1960s onward and his claim that classical narrative has the stability to explain contemporary change in storytelling and style as it has the potential to subsume difference by co-opting variations (Bordwell 14). My contention is that while traces of the classical can be observed within 1970s Tamil films, it is the 'post' which defines the decade – the period *after* the complete domination of the studio system and its stars, when Tamil cinema is redefined by films which exemplify a spirit of experimentation.

Before exploring the 1970s Tamil films, let us look at the discourse surrounding the post-classical which is inextricably tied to (classical) Hollywood: following their compelling analysis of the film *Die Hard* (d. John Mctiernan, 1988), and their argument that it may be defined as falling under the rubric of both the classical as well as the postclassical, Thomas Elsaesser and Warren Buckland conclude by comparing their act of classification to the interpretive malleability of rotating a crystal (Elsaesser and Buckland 289). Within their reading, *Die Hard*, 'can neither be situated conceptually in a linear, progressive, chronological line nor pictured as a dialectical or directly antagonist relationship (to the classical)' (79). Elsaesser's analysis correctly foregrounds the tenuousness in labeling randomly chosen films. For my claim regarding the post-classical in Tamil cinema that is not predicated on any one film, therefore, I examine the 1970s in linear, progressive, and chronological order for films that epitomize the provenance and entrenchment of the post-classical period. I interrogate the decline in the productivity of the major Madras studios as well as of its primary stars to demonstrate how the studios become a nonentity, particularly during the second-half of the 1970s when challenging the studio-inflected classical narrative and style becomes a specific factor that attracts audiences to theaters.

Such a critical evaluation of the 1970s, I believe, can enhance our understanding of the significance and uniqueness of the post-classical turn that begins to fundamentally define the specificity of Tamil cinema by undergirding narratives with regional and native ethos – unlike Hollywood where postclassical 1970s cinema becomes a conduit to the expansive New Hollywood of the 1980s. In Madras, the experimentation with form and theme of the 1970s serves as a means to uncover the singularity of Tamil cinema/culture by differentiating it from stereotypical Madras(i) studio picture/melodramas. To trace the unique ways in which Tamil cinema was redefined in this period (and after detailing the decline of the studio system and its major stars), I focus on the seminal films involving such iconic directors as Bharathiraja and Mahendran and the graduates of the Pune and Madras film schools, who seek Tamil identity beyond the clichéd rhetoric of the uniqueness of Tamil/Tamilians through films shot primarily in the city of Madras and mostly within its studios.

Major Madras studios and Tamil films: the rapid decline in the 1970s

Tamil cinema scholars differ widely in their assessment of the number of studios that were in Madras: while Theodore S. Baskaran accounts for 98 by the end of 1998 (89), Venkatesh Chakravarthy argues that the total could never have exceeded 30 (Interview). This significant discrepancy can be traced to the lack of a standard definition where even a standalone dubbing facility could often be counted as a studio. Nonetheless, as studios that were active for at least three decades and offered all the facilities for production and postproduction (including a laboratory) under one roof, only five qualify as major ones: The Modern Theaters, AVM, Gemini, Vijaya-Vauhini, and Prasad Studios. And given that Prasad Studios focused on post-production facilities in the 1970s – *Piriya Vidai* (d. Srikanth, 1975) being their only Tamil production – it becomes less significant in this discussion.

The Modern Theaters Ltd., oldest of the majors, produced 116 films between 1937 and 1982 (Venkataswamy 169–174). During the 1950s it produced 36 films but only 24 in the 1960s, a number that dwindles further to five in the 1970s (none of which were box-office successes). After three further productions in the early eighties, The Modern Theaters Ltd. closed down in 1982 (150–161). The Modern Theatres was once at the forefront of innovation (exemplified by its special effects particularly during the inaugural 'title sequence,'), and the unparalleled pioneer among the Madras studios. It was the producer of the first Malayalam film *Balan* (d. Notani, 1938); producer of the first color film in Tamil – *Alibabavum Narpathu Thirudargalum* (d. T.R. Sundaram, 1956); and well known for its international collaborations, including seven films in Sinhalese in partnership with Ceylonese producers, and one in English – *The Jungle* (d. William Berke, 1952). From being on top of the market in controlling stars, genres and the scales of production in the 1950s, its influence begins to decline in the 1960s, and decline steeply in the 1970s.

In contrast to the now defunct Modern Theatres, the AVM Studios recently announced its 175th feature film. Nonetheless, the 1970s marked its lowest output ever since it began production in 1945 – from 1976 to 1980 AVM did not produce a single film.[1] Chakravarthy reasons this low output of AVM in the 1970s to three major factors: the 1968 strike when workers demanded salary on par with the workers of Vijaya-Vauhini studios, which led to a shutting-down of operations for 18 months; the second major strike again in 1975; as well as the general economic crisis for the studios during the later half of the seventies: it was a time of recession, and many studios in Madras had to rent their floors to organizations like the Food Corporation of India that were looking for warehouse space; AVM, however, sought to survive this crisis by reorganizing their studio space into a massive theater, a postproduction sound unit, and retaining four of its studio floors (Chakravarthy, 'Naam Iruvar' 50–53). From 1947 onward, AVM had produced an average of four films a year with 22 major hits by the end of the 1960s. The 1970s, therefore (with an average of less than two films per year) indicate, as in the case of Modern Theaters, a sudden fall in the level of operations at AVM (Anandan, Sadhanaigal 7–43).[2]

When AVM released carefully mounted and well publicized films every quarter till the 1960s, the box-office success of most of its films and their innovative scripts which anticipated the changes in the tastes of the audience, became the signifier of the 'pulse of the masses' for most producers (Suryanarayanan). In addition, AVM Studios regularly signed 'package' contracts with outside producers by offering them their entire facilities including raw stock and the processed final prints on credit for a share in the profits. Thus, AVM became the nucleus of the Tamil film industry in this period; Sivaji Ganesan's highly successful and landmark films in the early 1960s, for example, were produced in partnership with AVM but released by producers under their own banners (Anandan, Interview).

The decline in the 1970s is mirrored by the history of Vijaya-Vauhini Studios as well. With 13 floors (Vahini-13 and Vijaya-2), this, arguably, was the biggest studio in Asia in the 1950s and 1960s, producing 45 films from 1950–1980; 15 films in the 1950s; 18 films in the 1960s; and 12 films in the 1970s. Vijaya-Vauhini's significance lay in the trends it could generate through its bilingual films in the Tamil and Telugu market through sophisticated production values achieved with a team of such technicians as the legendary cinematographer Marcus Bartley. Nevertheless, like AVM, Vijaya-Vauhini did not produce any Tamil film during the second half of the 1970s, which signifies the end of Madras studios as the predominant production houses of Tamil cinema.

Gemini Studios too, reeling under the death of its visionary founder S.S. Vasan – the DeMille of India known for his spectacles like *Chandralekha* (d. S.S. Vasan, 1948) on 26 August 1969, saw its output shrink in the 1970s: in the 1950s it had produced seven Tamil films; four in the 1960s; and two in the 1970s; the corresponding numbers in Hindi being eight, seven, and seven. Thus, it was interested in maximizing income by catering to a national market in the 1970s rather than producing Tamil films. The highly successful Hindi version of Chandralekha (1948) established Vasan's reputation as an unparalleled producer/director and enabled his collaborations with stars like Dilip Kumar and Dev Anand in *Insaaniyat* (d. S.S. Vasan, 1955), and Dilip Kumar and Raaj Kumar in *Paigham [Message]* (d. S.S. Vasan, 1959). Later, though, Gemini studios continued to work with iconic figures like Rajesh Khanna (Aurat, d. S.S. Vasan, 1967) and Amitabh Bachchan (Sanjog, d. S.S. Balan, 1971), stars who were yet to attain their subsequent superstardom. The dwindling of Gemini's productions from epic scales to medium budgets illustrates the dramatic shift in power equations between the studios and stars from the 1950s to the 1970s.

MGR and Sivaji Ganesan: the vicissitude of star power

MGR and Sivaji established themselves as bankable stars by the end of the 1950s – MGR through the huge success of *Madurai Veeran* (d. D. Yoganand, 1956) and Sivaji through his double role in *Uthamaputhiran* (d. T. Prakash Rao, 1958) (Baskaran 57). As a consequence, the 1960s saw them becoming power centers with the industry reorganizing itself around these two stars toward the goal of releasing almost a film every week. Of the 485 Tamil films produced in the 1960s, Sivaji acted in 75 and MGR in 60; thus, acting as heroes, between them, in 27.8% of the total films produced. But the 1970s saw a decline: Sivaji only acting in 72 films, and MGR only in 30, of a total of 641, together accounting for only 15.9% of the films (Anandan, Sadhanaigal 13–28).

The decline of MGR is marked; he did not act in movies towards the end of the decade as he became the first popular star in India to become the chief minister of Tamilnadu in 1977. MGR, a member of the Dravida Munnetra Kazhagam/Dravidian Progressive Front and of the Legislative Council elected from the St. Thomas Mount constituency in Chennai (in 1967 and 1971), was not happy when he was given the party treasurer's post instead of a ministry after his mammoth win in the 1971 elections. The chief minister at the time, M. Karunanidhi, who wanted to undermine MGR's enormous popularity and the unparalleled network of his fan clubs, launched his son Mu Ka. Muthu in a film scripted by himself, with a protagonist based on MGR's persona. The subsequent growth of Muthu fan clubs facilitated by DMK party functionaries and their generous financial incentives angered MGR's fans. In fact, 'the secretaries of eight hundred of his fan clubs threatened to disaffiliate their clubs from the DMK, forcing Karunanidhi to disband the Muthu clubs' (N. Subramanian 243–244). When an increasingly alienated MGR, responding to charges of corruption against the party by the media, asked for the disclosure of the assets of party members and their relatives, he was suspended from the party on 10 October 1972. Within a week, on 17 October 1972, MGR had formed his own party, the ADMK (Anna Dravidian Progressive Front). Later, the ADMK would go on to win the state legislative elections in 1977, leading to MGR becoming the chief minister and serving in that role through his triumphs in the elections of 1980 and 1984 until his death in 1987 (N. Subramanian 243–330; T.S. Subramanian). The 1970s, therefore, was the most crucial decade in the career of MGR, arguably India's most popular star of the last century. While the number of his films declined, MGR's successful transition from celluloid to politics as a mass hero both blurred the line between cinema and life and prefigured the increasing visibility of stars in active politics.

The year 1977 saw the aura surrounding MGR reach its teleological fruition and validate the Dravidian movement's investment in film as a preeminent tool for ideological dissemination. From the 1950s onward, MGR's persona was carefully constructed by a team of writers, directors and producers who borrowed the swashbuckler action-hero stereotype from Hollywood (especially from the films of MGR's own idols, Erroll Flynn and Douglas Fairbanks Jr.,) and effectively juxtaposed it with the melodramatic staple of indigenous folklore or the mythos of an Oedipal son who could balance the excessive attachment for his mother with the taming of the shrew(s) while freeing the downtrodden. In addition, MGR's charisma as an innocent yet rebellious villager against injustice appealed to his fans in every nook and corner of Tamilnadu, contributing to the entrenchment of the industry, particularly in terms of box-office returns from villages.

By the 1970s, MGR's persona subsumed the protagonist and the narrative of his films, as exemplified by *Nam Naadu* (d. Jambulingam) released in November 1969. This film produced by Vijaya-Vauhini, recycled for its narrative, the growing resentment of the masses over corruption within the DMK government, especially following the demise of Annadurai and Karunanidhi's assuming leadership in 1969. In *Nam Naadu*, MGR plays an honest clerk in the mayor's office who is forced to contest the elections due to rampant corruption. MGR utilized the film to critique his own party, the DMK, through a staple of most MGR films, the idiom of the propaganda song. For example, the lines 'Vizi Pola Enni Nam Mozi Kaakka Vendum/Like the eyes we must protect our language; Thavarana Perku Ner Vazikaata Vendum/Show the right path to the misguided ones; Jana Naayagathil Naam Ellorum Mannar/In democracy we are all kings; Thennattu Gandhi Annaalil Sonnar/As told by the Southern Gandhi (Annadurai),' allude to the Dravidian ideology by invoking Tamil language, but is used by MGR to critique Karunanidhi and recall the greatness of Annadurai.

Later, once MGR founded the ADMK and his party's candidate, Maayathevar, had won the by-election at Dindugal in 1973, *Nam Naadu* was re-released to capitalize on the euphoria and stock shots of MGR and Maayathevar celebrating the electoral victory inserted into the film at the point of the narrative when MGR's character celebrates his success in the mayoral elections (Suryanarayanan). In addition, the black and red colors of the DMK flag depicted within the film at the mayor's office was changed to the tricolored – black, white and red – of the ADMK flag. MGR's persona, thus, not only subsumed the characters he played on screen and prescribed the way his films were to be showcased and exhibited, but also undermined the reputation of Vijaya-Vauhini as producers of classical films with seamless narratives designed to sustain illusions of reality. This rupturing, within the narrative, of the national through the regional and the allusions to a 'Naadu' (country) while evoking a 'southern or regional Gandhi' led to the emergence of a space that allowed for the juxtaposition of both mayoral/metropolitan electoral success with that of regional success within the Dindugal district.

Though MGR's persona as the stereotype of the oppressed, alluded to by the titles of such films as *Mattukara Velan [Cowherd Velan]* (d. M.A. Thirumugam, 1970), *Rickshawkaran [Rickshawpuller]* (d. M. Krishnan, 1971), and *Meenava Nanban [Fisherman's friend]* (d. Sridhar, 1977) continued through the 1970s, the ageing star's draw at the box office was waning; only nine of his 30 films in the 1990s enjoyed significant success (30%). The paucity of fresh ideas from his regular writers to feed an aging star's young romantic persona led MGR to look elsewhere for narratives. The 1970s marked significant remakes in MGR's career, including three consecutive remakes from Hindi – *Ninaithathai Mudippavan* (d. P. Neelakantan, 1974)/*Sacha Jhutha* (d. Manmohan Desai, 1970), *Naalai Namathe* (d. K.S. Sethumadhavan, 1975)/*Yaadon Ki Baarat* (d. Nasir Hussain, 1973), and *Pallandu Vazhga* (d. K. Shankar, 1975)/*Do Aankhen Barah Haath* (d. V. Shantaram, 1957). None of them, however, were to enjoy as much success as the Hindi originals (Suryanarayanan).

This mirrors Sivaji's career which included 12 remakes in the 1970s (accounting for one out of every six films), clearly underscoring a changed landscape when producers were eager to play safe. 1972, however, was a year of phenomenal success for Sivaji – he had six hits leading up to his first 1973 release – *Bharatha Vilas* (d. A.C. Tirulokachandar). But the very next film was to presage Sivaji's fading charisma as a hero at the box-office and his transformation into a character actor by the 80s. *Rajaraja Cholan* (d. A. P. Nagarajan, 1973), the first cinemascope film in Tamil on the life of the Chola emperor Rajaraja, bombed at the box-office, marking a dwindling success rate for Sivaji's films (Hariharan). Post 1974, many of his films remained in production for extended periods of time, plagued by persisting financial hurdles and faring miserably at the box-office when they were finally released (Anandan).

Nevertheless, Sivaji, more than any other figure, epitomized the efficiency of the Madras Studios. In 23 years, from *Parasakthi* (d. Krishnan-Panju, 1952) till *Avan Than Manithan* (d. A.C. Tirulokachandar, 1975), he had acted in 175 films, i.e., an average of 7.6 films a year. In a career spanning more than four decades, he acted in 306 films, of which 288 were lead roles. With Sivaji's career in decline and MGR's gradual exit from films, the mid-1970s marked the end of an era not only defined by the dominance of the studio system through its own productions and that of its collaborators (the independent producers who functioned like satellites around the stars,) but also by the preeminence of studio-trained technicians and their aesthetics of indoor lighting (inspired by the three-point Hollywood style), the use of the sturdy Mitchell camera, of in-camera special effects, continuity editing, as well as of seamless narratives centered on melodrama and action framed in city/village locales mostly designed within the studio.

Time of the technicians: the 1970s and the transition to the post-classical

The mid-1970s was also the time when graduates of the Film and Television Institute of India, Poona, and the Institute of Film Technology, Madras, began to make their presence felt. Scholars regard the 1970s as the only decade when Tamil cinema had the semblance of an art movement. Films like *Thagam* (d. Babu Nandancode, 1974), *Thikkatra Parvathi*

(d. Singeetham Srinivasa Rao, 1974), *Sila Nerangalil Sila Manithargal* (d. A. Bhimsingh, 1977), *Agraharathil Kazuthai* (d. John Abraham, 1978), *Aval Appadiththan* (d. C. Rudraiah, 1978), *Oru Nadigai Natakam Parkiraal* (d. A. Bhimsingh, 1978), and *Kudisai* (d. Jayabharathi, 1979) mark the only period in the history of Tamil cinema that witnessed a sustained attempt toward an alternative form of cinema.

Of these films, *Aval Appadiththan* is perhaps the most reflective of the aspirations for change harbored by Tamil filmmakers and audiences in a changed environment. In 1978, the International Film Festival was held in Madras which, along with the film appreciation course conducted by the National Film Archives, served to energize the film society movement in Madras. Against this backdrop, a young director from the Madras film school, Rudraiah, teamed up with his classmates and cinematographers, Nallusamy and Gnansekaran, to make a film on the triangular relationship of a documentary filmmaker, an independent woman and her sexist boss, and signed-up the emerging stars of the 1970s. Within this narrative, Arun (Kamalahasan), invested in documenting the plight of women, arrives in Madras from Coimbatore and falls in love with the enigmatic Manju (Sripriya), who is haunted by her past and the life of her 'wayward' mother. She works for the male chauvinist Thyagu (Rajinikanth). Arun falls in love with Manju, proposes and waits for her response, but by the time the reluctant Manju could make up her mind regarding marriage, he leaves for his hometown and returns with his new wife. The final sequence has Thyagu, along with Manju, driving from the station with the newlyweds. Along the way, Manju asks Arun's wife for her opinion on women's liberation. When Arun's wife expresses her ignorance on the subject, Manju responds by telling her: 'that's why you're happy,' before abruptly asking Thyagu to stop the car. The car pulls away from her in the last shot:

> All this could have been avoided if she only had a "proper" mother! The last shot of the film leaves her on the road where liberated women end up. This final visual detail reveals the entire content of the film,

observed Tamil's preeminent feminist writer, Ambai (Lakshmi 25), in her critique of the representation of women in Tamil cinema. On reevaluation, however, *Aval Appadithan* emerges for many to be a landmark Tamil film that refrains from the cliché of the pseudo-feminist, a staple of the 1980s and 1990s' Tamil cinema (Kumar). The climax of the film, while showcasing Manju's criticism of the complacent Arun's wife/Tamil women, complicates any easy access to her subjectivity by immediately positing her in a no-woman's land from the audience's point of view – the any-space-whatever denies both the cathartic as well as a Brechtian understanding of her subjectivity (Deleuze 109).[3] Manju's characterization resonates with the atypical representation of women within such films by the legendary K. Balachander as *Arangetram* (1973) and *Aval Oru Thodarkathai* (1974).

More importantly, to focus only on the narrative would be to miss the real significance of the film. *Aval Appadiththan* is reminiscent of the 'film school brats' of Hollywood and Bombay in its French New Wave-inspired technique, replete with the use of jump cuts, repeated zooms, extreme close-ups and handheld camera. The easy availability of the lightweight Arriflex 35-2c cameras in the 1970s enabled location shooting, while the film school training helped cinematographers to use minimal lights privileging realism with high intensity key lights and the soft filler-lights for the shadows, and vastly different from the studio style. The film within the film – the documentary shot by Arun – reflexively reveals the enthusiasm of these young filmmakers through a handheld camera which, even as it documents the documentary, records the spontaneous and insightful reactions of women to Arun's question about equality, freedom and choice. The music was composed by another star on the horizon, Elaiyaraja, whose songs are used to punctuate the interiority of the characters rather than as a spectacle or as a device to move the plot forward.

The search for a new idiom is also underscored by John Abraham's *Agraharathil Kazhudhai*. John, and his cinematographer Ramachandra Babu, both graduates from the FTII, drew their inspiration from their mentor, Ritwick Ghatak as well as from Robert Bresson (particularly *Au hasard Balthazar*, 1966), the political cinema of Latin America (mainly that of Glauber Rocha) and the surrealism of Bunuel. They narrate the story of Prof. Narayana Swamy who provides refuge to a donkey (whose mother has been killed by a mob) and a mute girl Uma (the caretaker of that donkey) in a village. The 'evil' donkey is held responsible when Uma's stillborn child is found dead outside the temple, and killed. Soon after, while the cremation of the donkey is delayed in order to ensure that the suitable (caste) person is found to light the pyre, miracles occur that lead to the villagers worshipping the donkey. Ultimately, when the donkey is ritually cremated, the fire that spreads engulfs the whole village except for the professor and the girl. The screenwriter Venkat Saminathan criticized the film for its immaturity and unevenness, whereas others endorsed John's political 'cinema of imperfection' (Abraham 16–19). The film incited debates in the media regarding casteist politics. Nonetheless, John's conflation of his leftist politics and the mythos surrounding donkey as an abject figure goes beyond its critique of Brahmanical hegemony as it tries to shake a feudal society out of its slumber by showcasing the absurd universe that its bigots occupy. John's raw and incoherent style was in polarity to the seamless, closed universe of both the classical narratives – responsible for the creation of the MGR myth – and its unthinking/superstitious audience. Aval Appadiththan and Agraharathil Kazhuthai, thus, challenged the classicism of the studio system through their formal innovations and narrative style.

The most enduring influence on Tamil cinema, however, was to come from films that were not so removed from the mainstream. Bharathiraja redefined popular Tamil cinema with his seminal film *16 Vayathiniley[At Age Sixteen]* (d. Bharathiraja, 1977). *Ananda Vikatan*, the popular Tamil weekly, praised the film for representing village life with realism and for avoiding the cliché of (studio) court and police station in its poignant climax (16 Vayathaippatri). Vikatan's technical reviewer, while complimenting cinematographer P.S. Nivas, the Madras film school alumnus, for his framing of the lush green village landscapes, drew attention to the error in focus, advising the assistant/focus-puller to be alert – while the new Arriflex cameras mounted with zoom enabled mobility, the focus-pulling became critical as missing the mark even slightly would lead to a scene that was in soft focus. Besides, the lush green photography was made possible by the availability of cheaper Orwo color stock that favored the green. The reviewer also criticizes the dark scene where the villain asks for beedi (tobacco rolled inside dry leaves) at the kiosk, and wonders whether it was because of underexposure or under-developing in the lab – a criticism that drew attention to the film's aesthetics of location-shooting as well as available-light photography with minimum accessories (like reflectors in the outdoors). Such aesthetics also mirror the mode of production of an independent film with limited resources – the entire film was shot in Karnataka, the neighboring state, to qualify for a subsidy of Rupees 50,000 ($1,200 approx). Further, with reference to editing, the reviewer points to the repetition of shots in the very beginning of the film: when the heroine waits at the railway station with expectation, the train leaves without the expected guest, and instead of a (reaction) shot of her disappointment, the (earlier) shot of her expectation is repeated. The meticulous attention to detail even in reviews within a popular weekly speaks volumes about the informed audiences of the 1970s who were primarily responsible for the success of such films as *Aval Appadiththan* and *16 Vayathiniley*.

Bharathiraja had his training in the industry as an assistant to directors ranging from the arthouse-inclined Babu Nandancode to the veteran director of Kannada mainstream films, Puttanna Kanagal, enabling him to combine the art-cinema sensibilities of location shooting and the use of non-professional actors with the mainstream paradigms of melodrama, romance, songs and action. Thus, he could rework the classical genre of a love triangle, experiment with its possibilities, and render *16 Vayathiniley* in the post-classical mold. While Rudraiah or John also experimented, their films may be more accurately described as anticipating the postmodern in their appeal to an increasingly modernizing and cinematically aware audience in urban cities, whereas Bharathiraja's film catered to a larger audience that had rejected the traditional studio-produced films and were prepared for the reinventions of style and the retelling of stories they were familiar with.

The narrative of *16 Vayathiniley* revolves around the village girl Mayil (Sridevi), her distant and unattractive cousin Chappani (Kamalahasan), who is secretly in love with her, and the village rowdy Parattai (Rajnikanth). Mayil aspires to be a teacher but falls in love with the veterinarian who arrives from the city, and gives up her desire to pursue the teacher-training course in the city. But the veterinarian leaves the village after exploiting her sexually; consequently, Mayil's mother dies of shame. Chappani supports the lonely and despondent Mayil, who begins to appreciate the innocence and commitment behind his appearance and decides to get married to him. When an overjoyed Chappani goes to town to get the *thaali* (*mangalsutra/*sacred thread), Parattai, attracted to her from the beginning, enters her home and tries to rape her. Chappani returns in time to save Mayil but kills Parattai and goes to jail.

This brief sketch informs us of the familiar territory the film treads, but what is unfamiliar is the framing of the entire story in a flashback through Mayil, who is waiting at the railway station for Chappani to return. Unlike such earlier films as *Mother India* (d. Mehboob Khan, 1957) or its Tamil remake *Punniya Bhoomi* (d. K. Vijayan, 1978), there is no closure in the classical sense when the flashback ends, as Mayil is still waiting and we are not informed as to how long her wait will extend, although the (superimposed) title card assures us that Chappani will return and Mayil will be happy. Such a waiting evokes the poignant subjectivity of the ambiguous wait for freedom entailed by the state of Emergency imposed by then-Prime Minister Indira Gandhi from June 1975 till March 1977 – the film went into production immediately after the Emergency. The plot of the classical love triangle is, thus, retooled to address a recent trauma: during the emergency, the MISA – Maintenance of Internal Security Act – could be imposed on anyone (including the Dravidian ideologues or Tamil subnationalists) who voiced disagreement, and invoked to imprison and maim anybody who rebelled (as exemplified by the lame Chappani). Bharathiraja had originally planned the film as a Film Finance Corporation project in black and white during the Emergency.

16 Vaythiniley is today synonymous with color and (outdoor) cinematography. 'Bharathirajaa changed the course of Tamil cinema by taking the camera out of the studios and into the villages and its natural landscapes' (Rao, 227–228). After the classical studio period (from the 1930s till the 1960s) and prior to the invasion of video/MTVstyles in the 1980s, this post-classical period, particularly from the mid-1970s onward (when Bharathiraja visualized his songs through his unique style of repeated entry of faces in close-ups, freeze-frame shots, and symmetrical reversing of movement) marked a unique time in Tamil cinema. Bharathiraja's narration and style of using long takes and improvisations for dramatic scenes instead of the shot/reverse shot technique of the studio-films energized the experimental impulse within mainstream cinema. For instance, addressing the audience directly/frontally through voiceover, improvising with local dialects, and symbolic and contrapuntal sound effects marked his use of sound. Parallel to Bharathiraja's intervention in sound and images was the challenge posed by Elaiyaraja's music to the accepted norms (Chakravarthy, 'Mani Ratnamum', 289–290). Elaiyaraja's training in western classical music enabled him to combine folk melodies with complex orchestral score. His music would soon become the mainstay of the post-classical period – as a dominant star, his inclusion in films would soon enable more effective marketing. Besides, the minimalist use of instruments made him affordable to independent producers, and his ability to draw from composers like Bach to the very specific folk music of the narrative locale contributed to rare melodies and the success of these films.

Above all, *16 Vayathiniley*'s stature as the watershed of the 1970s Tamil cinema lay in the seeking of its audience for a redefinition of Tamil culture and its specificity. During the 1970s, parallel to the waning of hopes surrounding Nehruvian socialism in India, the dreams of an egalitarian Dravidian land alluded by films like *Parasakthi* too vanished in the state, and the audience were searching for ways beyond the empty rhetoric of the politicians to define themselves as Tamilians. Earlier films of the Dravidian ideologues could posit Tamil chauvinism against the Hindi/Congress hegemony, but the 1970s audience were not satisfied by such binaries – the outsider/veterinarian (still) arrives and destroys Mayil's dream, but the focus is on Mayil's readjustment to the realities and her discovery of the heart and spirit of the local/Chappani.

The next landmark film to foreground changing directorial approaches was *Uthirippookkal* (d. Mahendran, 1979) – the top favorite of many directors including Mani Ratnam: 'If I get anywhere near what Mahendran did in (Uthirippookkal), I'll be a happy man' (Sreelalitha). Mahendran, the director of the film was a scriptwriter from the industry, and he adapted Tamil's seminal writer Pudhumaipittan's short story 'Chitrannai' ('Stepmother') for his second film as a director. The film revolves around the family of the administrator of a local school Sundaravadivelu (Vijayan), his wife Lakshmi (Ashvini), and their two kids, his sister-in-law Senbagam (Madhu Malini) and father-in-law (Charuhasan). Sundaravadivelu's character is complex and dark: he is a caring father but a misogynist who lusts after his sister-in-law. His patient wife and her helpless father put up with his schizophrenic persona of dignified calm and threatening turbulence. A new teacher (Sunder) and a health officer (Sarathbabu) arrive at the village, and Sundaravadivelu, growing suspicious about his wife's friendship with the health officer, tortures her. He decides to divorce her and marry his sister-in-law who has already fallen in love with the new teacher. When Sundaravadivelu's sick wife dies, he remarries another woman. Later when his sister-in-law goes to invite him for her marriage with the teacher, he disrobes and molests her. When the village comes to know about this, he is forced to walk – followed by the entire village – to the pond and commit suicide by entering into it. His children wait for him hoping he would swim back.

The characterization of Sundaravadivelu was new to Tamil cinema: although he was an affectionate father and a prideful administrator, he was portrayed unambiguously as flawed, lecherous and scheming, thereby leading the audience into the very heart of darkness of the village. The long shots during the climax wherein the entire village chases him distances the audience, and enables the space to meditate on a weak, conscience-less man juxtaposed with an equally inhumane and rigid society. The visually rendered climax with sparse dialogues recalls Mahendran's authorial style of moving the camera away during key conflictual moments – for example, when Sundaravadivelu's slaps his wife and implores the audience to engage with the visual to interrogate the violence underneath. The absence of lengthy and monotonous dialogues in the film provided Elaiyaraja the space for differential theme music to etch out the characters, especially the laconic

Lakshmi and her profound sorrow and her joyful moments with the children. It was a sign of the times that films like *Uthirippookkal*, which not merely inverted the verbose Tamil cinema on its head but deglamorized the village hero, celebrated silver jubilee (175 days). The synthetic village hero of the studios was replaced by a complex protagonist who propelled the audience to introspect the culture which produced him. Similarly, the Madras film school alumnus and cinematographer Ashok Kumar's predilection for backlit photography to frame the dark hero's journey enabled the juxtaposition of the serenity of the village with its dark unconscious. Released in the same year, *Pasi* (d. Durai, 1979), and *Rosaapu Ravikkaikari* (d. Devaraj-Mohan, 1979), were other milestones in the post-classical period.

All these above films epitomized the empowerment of the technicians and independent producers during a unique period punctuated by the intersection of the changing influence of studios and stars and changing technologies. These post-classical films of the 1970s, marked by unparalleled creativity and experiment, substantially inspired and changed Tamil cinema in the subsequent decades – Mahendran's style of visual rather than verbose storytelling inspired many young filmmakers including Mani Ratnam, particularly his first major success in Tamil, *Mouna Raagam* (1986). Even recently, the critically acclaimed and commercially successful film *Mynaa* (d. Prabu Solomon, 2010) recalled *16 Vayathiniley* in its romance in lush green locales and adventure outdoors ('Myna'). Similarly when *Paruthiveeran* (d. Ameer, 2007) became a landmark success (of the decade), critics invoked the 1970s to map the trajectory of its village backdrop and characterizations.

Conclusion

The 1970s, therefore, was the defining decade of Tamil cinema when the classical era of the studios gave way to the post-classical through a radical reorganization of its modes of production. This was chiefly due to the failure of the studio system and the arrival of new stars – Rajnikanth and Kamalahasan – whose status had yet to be entrenched, thus providing the space for innovative directors for formal and narrative experiments in exploring particular character and thematic traits. This post-classical period, marked by weak and ambiguous protagonists, ambivalence of traditions, realism in dialogues, new subjectivity, avoidance of clichéd and cathartic closures, shooting on locations and subtler melodramas, was driven by the necessity to redefine Tamil/regional specificity in the wake of the unkempt promises of the Dravidian government when it came to and remained in power from 1967 onward. Such a re-articulation of the regional by these post-classical Tamil films which successfully pushed the limits of mainstream cinema not only undermines the collapsing of Tamil cinema with Madras studio productions, but also, through its specificity, haunts the claim of popular Hindi cinema to be representative of all Indians/the nation.

Notes

1. According to Anandan, the number of films produced by the various independent producers with the assistance of the major studios would be much higher than the number of films produced by the studios themselves.
2. All the statistical details in this paper are from Anandan, *Sadhanaigal Padaitha Tamilththiraippada Varalaru.*
3. For Deleuze such 'any-space-whatevers' are singular spaces wherein the homogeneity is lost – in this case our labeling of Manju as a cynical loser.

References

"16 Vayathaippatri Sila Ennangal." *Vikatanpokkisham*, 23 July 2008. Vikatan.com. Web. 7 Mar. 2011.

Abraham, John. "Nerthiyatra Cinemavin Azhagiyal." *Kalagakkaranin Thiraikkathai*. Ed. R.R. Srinivasan. Thiruvannamalai: Vamsi, 2010. 16–19. Print.

Anandan, Film News. *Sadhanaigal Padaitha Tamilththiraippada Varalaru*. Chennai: Sivagami, 2004. Print.

Anandan, Film News. Personal interview. 10 July 2007.

Baskaran, Theodore S. *History Through the Lens: Perspectives on South Indian Cinema*. Hyderabad: BlackSwan, 2009. Print.

Bordwell, David, Janet Staiger, and Kristin Thompson. *The Classical Hollywood Cinema: Film Style and Mode of Production to 1960*. New York: Columbia UP, 1985. Print.

Bordwell, David. *The Way Hollywood Tells It: Story and Style in Modern Movies*. Berkeley: U of California P, 2006. Print.

Chakravarthy, Venkatesh. "Maniratnamum Cinema Arasiyalum." *Chithiram Pesuthadi*. Ed. S. Theodore Baskaran. Chennai: Kalachuvadu, 2004. 284–295. Print.

Chakravarthy, Venkatesh. "Naam Iruvar: We Two." *The Cinema of India*. Ed. Lalitha Gopalan. London: Wallflower, 2009. 46–55. Print.

Chakravarthy, Venkatesh. Personal interview. 11 Apr. 2007.

Deleuze, Gilles. *Cinema 1: The Movement-Image*, Trans. Hugh Tomlinsom and Barbara Habberjam. London: Athlone Press, 1983. Print.

Elsaesser, Thomas and Warren Buckland. *Studying Contemporary American Film: A Guide to Movie Analysis*. London: Arnold and New York: Oxford UP, 2002. Print.

Hariharan, K. "Strokes of a Genius: Sivaji Ganesan." *The Hindu*, 29 July 2001. Cscsarchive.org. Web. 14 March 2010.

Kumar, Amshan. Personal Interview. 20 Aug. 2007.

Lakshmi, C.S. "A Good Woman, a Very Good Woman: Tamil Cinema's Women." *Tamil Cinema: The Cultural Politics of India's Other Film Industry*. Ed. Selvaraj Velayutham. New York: Routledge, 2008. 16–18. Print.

"Myna: Cinema Vimarsanam." Ananda Vikatan. 17 Nov. 2010. *Newvikatan.com*. Web. 31 March 2011.

Rao, Vittal. *Tamil Cinemavin Parimanangal*. Chennai: Nizhal, 2003. Print.

Sreelalitha, W. "The Magic of Mahendran." *The Hindu*, 6 Sept. 2007. Hinduonnet. Web. 14 March 2011.

Subramanian, Narendra. *Ethnicity and Populist Mobilization: Political Parties, Citizens and Democracy in South India*. New Delhi: Oxford UP, 1999. Print.

Subramanian, T.S. "The Celluloid Connection." *Frontline* 21.15 (2004). Hinduonnet. Web. 14 Feb. 2011.

Suryanarayanan, M. President. Tirunelveli/Kanyakumari Distributors' Association. Personal Interview. 14 Apr. 2000.

Venkatasamy, Ra. *Mudhalali: Modern Theatres T.R. Sundaram Avargalin Vazhkai Varalaru*. Chennai: Vanathi, 2003. Print.

Filmography

16 Vayathiniley. Dir. Bharathi Raja. Shri Amman Creations. 1977. Film.

Agraharathil Oru Kazuthai. Dir. John Abraham. Nirmithi Films, 1978. Film.

Alibabavum Narpathu Thirudargalum. Dir. T.R. Sundaram. Modern Theatres, 1956. Film.

Arangetram. Dir. K. Balachander. Kalakendra Movies, 1973. Film.

Au hasard Balthazar. Dir. Robert Bresson. Athos Films, 1966. Film.

Aurat. Dir. S.S. Balan. Gemini Studios, 1967. Film.

Aval Appadiththan. Dir. C. Rudraiah, Kumar Arts, 1978. Film.

Aval Oru Thodarkathai. Dir. K. Balachander. Andal Movies, 1974. Film.

Avan Than Manithan. Dir. A.C. Tirulokachandar. Krishna Pictures, 1975. Film.

Balan. Dir. T.R. Sundaram. Modern Theatres, 1938. Film.

Bharatha Vilas. Dir. A.C. Tirulokachandar, Cine Bharath, 1973. Film.

Chandralekha. Dir. S.S. Vasan. Gemini Studios, 1948. Film.

Die Hard. Dir. John McTiernan. 20th Century Fox, 1988. Film.
Do Aankhen Barah Haath. Dir. V. Shantaram. Rajkamal Kalmandir, 1957. Film.
Insaaniyat. Dir. S.S. Vasan. Gemini Studios, 1955. Film.
Kudisai. Dir. Jayabharathi. Jwala, 1979. Film.
Madurai Veeran. Dir. D. Yoganand. Krishna Pictures, 1956. Film.
Mattukara Velan. Dir. P. Neelakantan. Jayanthi Films, 1970. Film.
Meenava Nanban. Dir. Sridhar. Muthu Enterprises, 1977. Film.
Mouna Raagam. Dir. Mani Ratnam. Sujatha Productions, 1986. Film.
Mynaa. Dir. Prabu Solomon. Shalom Productions, 2010. Film.
Naalai Namathe. Dir. K.S. Sethumadhavan. Gajendra Films, 1975. Film.
Nam Naadu. Dir. Jambulingam. Vijaya International, 1969. Film.
Ninaithathai Mudippavan. Dir. P. Neelakantan, Oriental Pictures, 1974. Film.
Oru Nadigai Natakam Parkiraal. Dir. A. Bhimsingh. Girnar Films, 1978.
Paigham. Dir. S.S. Vasan. Gemini Studios, 1959. Film.
Pallandu Vazhga. Dir. K. Shankar. Udhayam Productions, 1975. Film.
Parasakthi. Dir. Krishnan-Panju. National Pictures, 1952. Film.
Paruthiveeran. Dir. Ameer. Studio Green, 2007. Film.
Pasi. Dir. Durai. Sunitha Cine Arts, 1979. Film.
Piriya Vidai. Dir. Srikanth. Prasad Productions, 1975.
Rajaraja Cholan. Dir. A.P. Nagarajan. Anand Movies, 1973. Film.
Rickshakkaran. Dir. M. Krishnan. Satya Movies, 1971. Film.
Rosaapu Ravikkaikari. Dir. Devaraj-Mohan. Vivekananda Productions, 1979. Film.
Sacha Jhutha. Dir. Manmohan Desai. V.R. Films, 1970. Film.
Sanjog. Dir. S.S. Balan. Gemini Studios, 1971. Film.
Sila Nerangalil Sila Manithargal. Dir. A. Bhimsingh. A.B.S. Productions, 1977. Film.
Thagam. Dir. Babu Nandancode. Kaviya Chitra, 1974. Film.
The Jungle. Dir. William Berke. Modern Theatres, 1952. Film.
Thikkatra Parvathi. Dir. Singeetham Srinivasa Rao. Film Finance Corporation, 1974. Film.
Uthamaputhiran. Dir. T. Prakash Rao. Venus Pictures, 1958. Film.
Uthirippookkal. Dir. Mahendran. Dimple Creations, 1979. Film.
Yaadon Ki Baarat. Dir. Nasir Hussain. Nasir Hussain Films, 1973. Film.

Aesthetic dislocations: A re-take on Malayalam cinema of the 1970s

Ratheesh Radhakrishnan

Rice University, Houston, USA

The centrality of South Indian cinemas in 'New Indian Cinema', one of the many cultural constellations of the turbulent and vibrant 1970s, has been widely acknowledged. Focusing on the aesthetic structuring of select moments from Adoor Gopalakrishnan's *Swayamvaram*, K.P. Kumaran's *Athithi* and P.A. Backer's *Kabaneenadhi Chuvannappol*, this paper investigates the contestations central to the emergence of a realist aesthetic in Malayalam cinema. It unpacks the movement towards the consolidation of realism as a mode of address that generates certain spectatorial responses, as opposed to understanding this turn in Malayalam cinema as foregrounding a new version of the social. The status of popular cinema and cinephilia are at the center of these contestations, as these film texts actively intervene in debates around aesthetics.

Discussions on the legacies of any historical period of cinema necessitate that one bracket off nostalgia and attend to the intricate histories of cinematic practices. Such histories may include narratives of how the retrospective understanding of a given period of cinema crystallized through film journalism, film criticism, and repeated iterations in later film practices. Or, one might attend to the aesthetic practices of films of the time to see how they actively engaged and intervened in debates that imaged a framework for a cinema to come. The 1970s was a turning point in Indian politics and history, and a period of radical shifts in Indian cinema. The emergence of the 'angry young man' films and the 'New Indian cinema' have been read alongside the shifting nature of the Indian state and the emergence of mass politics (Prasad). Following new economic imperatives and the resulting aesthetic shifts,[1] the industry became segmented. A new breed of Film Institute trained filmmakers and actors who brought new concerns and aesthetics to the screen entered the industry during this period. Furthermore, the formation of film societies not only brought cinema from different parts of the world to audiences in different Indian cities and to a wider audience in states such as Kerala, but also provided the space for deliberations and publications on cinema. In the non-Hindi-speaking regions, formation of film societies and active state support for cinema were significant factors behind the shifts in film practices. Around the same time, different language cinemas of the South shifted their base away from Madras (now Chennai). For Malayalam cinema, independence from Madras was at best partial, and shifts were more related to anxieties of authenticity vis-à-vis the influence of Tamil cinema that plagued it since the 1950s. The confluence of an intellectual context provided by the film societies, the economic support from the state and traditionally landed elite, and the pervasive arguments regarding cultural authenticity made Malayalam cinema central in the emergent New Indian cinema.

Malayalam art house cinema of the 1970s has been understood as a turn to realism and a move away from the popular fare that was on offer. I argue that the term realism as opposed to melodrama (the latter term has unproblematically been used to describe the affective economy of popular cinema) was at this point of time newly defined and positioned in a hierarchical order. This paper juxtaposes two relatively unknown films categorized as Malayalam parallel cinema, K.P. Kumaran's *Athithi (1975)* and P.A. Backer's *Kabaneenadhi Chuvannappol (1975*; *Kabanee*, hereafter), with the well-known *Swayamvaram (1972)*, the debut feature of the canonical Adoor Gopalakrishnan (Adoor, hereafter), to analyze the critical historical import of these films as they navigated the terrain of realism and melodrama. After flagging the problematic understanding of realism as the representation of real world issues, one may tease out the definitional struggle that these films participate in – that is, the manner in which an aesthetic of realism as a contract between the screen and the spectator, which allows for the erasure of the act of 'looking' and the apparent materialization of a shared 'real' world, was carefully plotted. Focusing on the aesthetic structuring of select moments from these films, the paper traces the movement towards consolidating realism as a mode of address that generates a certain spectatorial responses, and presents two instances of cinematic practice outside this framework.

The status of popular cinema as the Other of the newly emerging film practice was contested right at its inception. In the case of Malayalam cinema, lineages of popular cinema and its status within the art house provided the arguments for contestations over realism unlike the case of avant-garde in Hindi and Bengali cinema which was in conversation with globally emerging aesthetic and political concerns (Rajadhyaksha 219–230). Film criticism and the monetary structure that allowed for the emergence of parallel cinema provided the conditions of possibility for such a contestation and its discursive resolution, to a large extent in favor of realism. Rather than delineating the social or the historical that is outside the cinematic apparatus, the concerns here are particular to the history and aesthetics of cinema, and this debate is about Malayalam cinema only insofar as such specificities are derived from within its practice. In order to unravel these contestations over realism, I employ the approach outlined in the beginning of the paper, namely, thinking through the participation of film texts in determining the ways in which cinema is understood.

Assembling the spectator

An unexpected narrative development ten minutes into *Swayamvaram* serves as a starting point for the re-examination of the narratives about Malayalam parallel cinema of the 1970s. The film narrates the story of Viswam (Madhu) and Seeta (Sarada), who have eloped in the city. Around the tenth minute, their romance in a hotel room cuts to a fantasy sequence on a beach and in other secluded idyllic spots, accompanied by a romantic score.[2] These spaces of fantasy are familiar scenes from Malayalam popular cinema. The couple performs standard romance routines like walking on rocks, sitting on the beach as Viswam's head rests on Seeta's lap, and holding hands while walking on railway tracks, until a shift happens in the sequence. They are shown spread out on the beach at the edge of water in a visual quotation of the tragic climax of the much-celebrated classic, *Chemmeen* (d. Ramu Kariat, 1965): the romantic couple's union in death. The fact that Pareekutty, the hero of *Chemmeen*, was one of Madhu's most memorable and successful characters adds a layer to the quotation. Seeta wakes up from that posture as Viswam remains still. Devoid of any background score, these extra seconds present a moment of anxiety and a break in the romantic routine. It is followed by another romantic moment in which Viswam playfully keeps his ears to the railway tracks as we hear a train arriving. The innocent prank turns into a moment of anxiety with the noise of the train going up on the soundtrack and the shaky camera lingering on Seeta's face, disallowing spectatorial access to what she is seeing. The couple is then featured in a tight embrace intercut with sketches of iconic Malayalam screen couples Prem Nazir – Sheela, Sathyan – Vijayashree, etc., in similarly amorous embrace. After this montage, Viswam leaves Seeta's embrace and starts running away from her with a mischievous smile. The run suddenly picks up speed, the smile changes into an expression of pain, and he disappears. What follows is a long sequence of Seeta's search for Viswam as she runs through forests and hilly terrains. The background score is replaced with the sound of wild animals. As a tired Seeta stops her search, a hand, presumably Viswam's, enters the frame and grabs her. She screams loudly. In place of the standard romantic resolution, in the next shot we see Viswam and Seeta on the rocks by the beach, far away from each other in a single frame and looking grave and thoughtful. Later we witness Viswam deep in thought, alone in the hotel room.[3] Here a conversation concerning melodrama, represented by acting styles, references to popular cinema, and the promise of the new moment that keeps on interrupting the melodramatic, is initiated. This, as I will demonstrate further in the paper, is the promise of realism. The instability of the couple at the end of the sequence is not the result of a narrative development in their relationship. What is at issue are the aesthetics of couple formation.

In Malayalam film historiography, *Swayamvaram* is read as a film that inaugurated realist cinema by dealing with the 'real' problems of the emerging middle class like modernity, urbanization, and poverty (see Venkiteshwaran 32; Wood 149–154). Within the frame of a national parallel cinema, it is often erroneously seen as one of the many films from the South to deal with 'caste, religion and the decadence of traditional village life' (Kishen 29). Realism is understood here to mean a variant of the earlier prevalent social realism[4] or at least an extension of it, with emphasis on its ability to deal with the real world. The logic of a nationwide thematic for parallel cinema has been challenged on the grounds of the diversity of themes that they dealt with. It has been suggested that unlike its counterparts in other parts of the country, Malayalam parallel cinema was not especially concerned with rural themes given that the urban-rural divide does not obtain in the region (Muraleedharan 194). I argue that the grounds of this debate need to be reexamined. To understand the specific contexts of the emergence of that which is termed the 'realist aesthetic' in Malayalam cinema, one will have to move away from thematic concerns and focus on the disjuncture of the kind that I described within the early moments of *Swayamvaram* – that of aesthetics.

Swayamvaram elaborates an aesthetic argument as opposed to inaugurating new themes. The disjuncture between realism and melodrama is introduced right at its beginning. The title sequence of the film is a five-minute bus ride shot entirely within the space of the bus as the landscape outside changes from rural to urban. Among the passengers of the bus are the protagonists of the film. But rather than being revealed through established techniques of framing and centralization, the first sighting of Viswam and Seeta is effected by a shot in which their backs are to the camera, following a series of shots that show other passengers. We identify them the protagonists by a rather commonplace strategy – casting. Two of the biggest stars of the time, Madhu and Sharada, are seen traveling in the bus. The discordance between the realist strategies of mise-en-scène (the long sequence, the successive shots of the interior of the bus that locate the passengers in clear time and space) and the presence of the stars who are known for their melodramatic acting styles, is one that could easily escape discernment by the spectator who, by the early 1970s, was entrenched in cinematic economies of stardom. This aesthetics dissonance is kept in place through subsequent sequences, including the one discussed earlier in the paper.

In an attempt to publish a novel he has written, Viswam meets with the editor of a journal, played by the well-known novelist Vaikom Chandrasekharan Nair (playing himself). In his office, we are made privy to a discussion on literature in the presence of a number of other writers including G. Sankara Pillai (playing himself), considered to be the founder of modern theater in Kerala. Viswam's novel titled 'Nirvrithi' (Ecstasy) is rejected on the ground that 'it is too sentimental.' The link between the condition that Viswam and Seeta find themselves in, i.e. sentimentality, is linked to cinema in the sequence that follows the rejection of Viswam's novel. As he walks through the city, a sentimental song floats from the cinema theater in the background. The theater that we see is 'New Theater' in Thiruvananthapuram, among the oldest cinema halls in Kerala, established in 1930 by one of the pioneers of Malayalam film industry, P. Subrahmaniam, who established Merryland Studio in 1951 and was accused by film magazines of the 1970s (along with Kunchacko of Udaya Studios) of indulging in crass commercialization. To make matters explicit, the song is sharply cut to a hall into which Viswam enters, where a public speech on the conditions of the working class is underway.

In *Swayamvaram*, interior and exterior landscapes are mapped on to melodrama and realism, respectively. Inside is the space of the couple, of melodrama. As the initial sequence in the bus reveals, it is a well-organized external landscape that frames the inside, occupied by Viswam and Seeta. The space of the couple and the city are neatly divided and separated though intercuts. In a scene after they check into a hotel, a bellboy knocks on their room door, interrupting a moment of intense passion. Rather than romance itself, this moment of transgression of the ordering of the inside and the outside interrupts a particular representation of romance, as exemplified by the melodramatic and excessive, but immensely popular, acting styles of Madhu and Sharada. It is not accidental that the bellboy's entry is on cue to Viswam's dialogue, 'unbelievable, like a dream.' This prefigures the relationship between the melodramatic interior and the realistic exterior that the film carries forward. The world outside is the privileged space of 'reality' – of politics, unemployment, illegal economies, and sex workers – represented by the various characters that the couple encounters in the film. The thematic ingredients that critics misrecognize as constituting realism in *Swayamvaram* and later art house cinema are deployed here to put together a domain (exterior/reality/context) from where an aesthetic argument for realism is launched. This is the space where the spectator – the idealized Metzian abstraction[5] – will be enshrined through the course of the film. In mapping the film in these terms, I differ from the argument that Malayalam art house cinema, and especially *Swayamvaram*, is *about* the middle class nuclear family (Venkiteshwaran 29–30). Rather, it is about the ordering of the outside, which houses the melodramatic domestic, into a spectator position. *Swayamvaram* is also not *about* Viswam and Seeta. It is about the how their world has to be read. Like most of Adoor's heroes, Viswam's tragedy is signaled by a failing system. In this case the system is an aesthetic one – melodrama.[6]

The stark distinction between the inside and the outside gets its elaboration as the status of *the* gaze in the character played by the actor Gopi, the very spectatorial position in question. Gopi, in a striking and memorable cameo, is a disgruntled young man who accuses Viswam of usurping his position as manager in a sawmill factory. In the latter half of the film, Gopi appears a number of times in the margins of the frame (and once as an intense close-up), projecting a look of anger and betrayal at Viswam. In a telling sequence, Viswam gets up from his table at the sawmill, presumably to take a break, only to be stopped by a mere look from Gopi's character. The distinction between the inside and the outside gets coded into spectatorial activity with the narrativization of the look from the outside. Gopi's gaze upon the world of the couple is elevated to the metalanguage of realism as he disappears from the film as abruptly as he appeared.[7] The space of 'reality'/outside is transformed into a spectatorial position through the embodiment and the subsequent relocation of the gaze outside the diegetic space, via this character. Most of the last sequences of the film are shot in the interior as a space that can be fully negotiated, once the relationship between the private and the public is put in place and the gaze externalized as the spectatorial gaze. The last shot of the film presents Seeta after the death of Viswam, alone with her child, looking anxiously at the closed door as some force from the outside pushes at it violently. Her anxious gaze, on which the camera freezes, has been seen as 'raising the question of the viewer's implication in the conditions portrayed in the film' (Rajadhyaksha and Willemen 415). Even while moving away from the standard reading of the last shot as ambiguous (what will Seeta's future be?), film theorists Ashish Rajadhyaksha and Paul Willemen understand this spectatorial ordering as the extra-diegetic opening up of thematic concerns of the film. The end is unambiguous because the narrative burden of the film is to produce a spectator who has to ponder this very question. Anxiety over Seeta's future is the response that signals the culmination of the enshrinement of the new spectator. The spatial structuring of realism as the outside is relocated to spectatorial response – a contract that provides a definition of realism.

The film engenders a subtle slippage between the location of the disgruntled young man played by Gopi and the arrested gaze at the end of the film. The casting of Gopi, already well known as an actor in the modernist *thanathu nataka vedi* ('indigenous theatre,' a response to popular theater) by 1972, as the brief holder of the gaze aids such a slippage. The casting collapses the character's working class location with the actor's middleclass and modernist, though extra cinematic, image, providing a layered location for the gaze.[8] Gopi went on to play the protagonist in Adoor's next film and then to become the face of Malayalam parallel cinema and middlebrow cinema (also acting in Mani Kaul's *Satah Se Uthata Aadmi* and Govind Nihanalani's *Aghaat*), translating the location of the gaze into economies of stardom, as a parallel structure to mainstream stars of the time.

The institutional structure of cinema at the time in regional, national, and international contexts were amenable to the aesthetic positioning engendered by a film such as *Swayamvaram*. In Kerala, the setting up of film societies and the increased state support led to the formation of parallel cinema. The conscious production of the realist position was aided by the financial choices that these films made.[9] The funding came from co-operatives like Chithralekha that produced *Swayamvaram* and later from traditional elites such as Raveendran Nair ('General Pictures' Ravi) at a time when money from the Persian Gulf, as a result the migration that started in the early to mid 1970s, was entering the Malayalam film industry. Support for art house cinema of the realist kind lay among the efforts by the state to relocate film production to Kerala and to save it from dubious economies. By arguing that state support should be given to 'films with a Kerala background and the smell of the Malayalam soil (*sic.*)' ('Malayalacinema Keralamannil Verurakkumo?' 156), Adoor became a significant voice in the attempts to link economics and aesthetics with cultural authenticity. The restructuring of film festival programming across Europe in the wake of political developments of 1968 renewed interest in filmmakers from the 'Third World.' Filmmakers could bypass national governments and directly approach film festivals (de Valck 61–62), giving more leeway to the emerging parallel cinema. In 1982, Adoor's *Elippathayam* (1981) was screened in the 'Un Certain Regard' section at Cannes Film Festival and won the British Film Institute's Sutherland Trophy, marking the triumph of the realist aesthetic framework within Malayalam cinema.

Another site where one could identify the enshrining of the ideal spectator of realism is in the domain of film criticism in Kerala that emerged in the wake of parallel cinema.

In a fascinating introduction to a 1981 collection of screenplays, titled *Yaadhaarthyathinte Naalu Mukahangal* ('Four faces of reality'),[10] philosopher Nissar Ahammad, introducing a new language for film criticism in Malayalam using Barthesian semiotics, makes a distinction between *ithivrutha pradhana cinema* (content based films), *lahari pradhana cinema* (cinema of intoxication), and *rachana pradhana cinema* (writerly cinema). Even though he lumps most of parallel cinema into the last category, he makes a significant classificatory move that reads *Chemmeen*, *Olavaum Theeravum* (d.P.N. Menon, 1969), and *Nirmalyam* (d.M.T. Vasudevan Nair, 1973) together as *ithivrutha pradhana cinema* (14–27). This distinction between *Swayamvaram* and *Nirmalyam* (usually lumped together) provides one axis of differentiation in Malayalam parallel cinema. This useful taxonomy emphasizes that not all films in this category are interested in thematics, but fails provide a description of their concerns in positive terms. About *rachana pradhana cinema*, Ahammad writes: 'Taking *Swayamvaram, Ekakini* and *Athithi* together, we see that there are only moments of passage in them and no moments of arrival' (23). Attempting to provide an account for these distinct films, Ahammad collapses them into one group, and once again falls back on the content, albeit negatively. This argument symptomatically elides the fact that, of the films in the category, *Swayamvaram* (as opposed to *Athithi*, as we will see later) does have a definitive moment of arrival – the production of a new spectator position. Film criticism, from the late 1970s to the present, has been an active participant in the discursive erasure, and further, the naturalization of this point of arrival. *Swayamvaram* is an aesthetic manifesto for realism, founded on the production of a spectator position. Once this elaboration is engendered in *Swayamvaram,* Adoor proceeds to 'become' a realist filmmaker through his later films, starting with *Kodiyettam (1977)*, which, for most commentators and interviewers, constitute his oeuvre.

The rest of the paper attempts to present other aesthetic possibilities that were available within emerging parallel cinema.

Re-take: the not so parallel

While *Swayamvaram* began by locating its own time-space structure in the very first sequence of the bus ride, both *Athithi* and *Kabanee* start by dislocating their frames from such co-ordinates. The dislocation that I mark below is in relation to a hierarchical structure that has been outlined above, which, I suggest, makes possible a recognizable realist aesthetic in Malayalam cinema. These films, with their emphasis on the significance of melodrama and associated cinephilia, are deemed unreadable and hence unaccountable under the privileged realist contract.

Athithi starts with a sequence of a sand dune being mined. The expansive sand dune does not provide any specific codes as to the context of the film, like urban-rural, modern-traditional. The sequence is cut to Karunan (P.J. Antony) who, from behind the window of his house, looks at the sand dune. Even though the structuring of the inside and the outside is central to the film, its elaboration is entirely different from *Swayamvaram*. The inside becomes the space from which the outside is beheld, and the outside is the space of fantasy. The film revolves around the wait for Sekharan, who everyone in the house expects will solve his or her 'problems.' Though everyone has a materially definable problem for himself or herself, the common problem, evident from the early sequences of the film, is the lack of affective bonds between people within the domestic space. Dialogues and actions seem to be at cross-purposes in the tradition of the absurd. Sekharan arrives and leaves, never appearing on screen and not changing anything.

The film employs popular stars like Kottarakkara Sreedharan Nair, P.J. Antony and Sheela in central roles. The use of actors with melodramatic acting styles is radically different in *Athithi* compared to *Swayamvaram*, where it is circumscribed by the 'outside' and made visibly excessive. Melodrama is employed in its fullest in *Athithi*. Within such a structure, the distinction between the inside and outside cannot be mapped onto melodrama and realism. In a telling sequence, we see Ramani (Karunan's wife, played by Sheela) observing her sister Latha and Raghavan (Balan K. Nair) in a moment of passion under a tree next to the sand dunes. Both Ramani and the couple are placed in the public. Later, we see Ramani observing herself dancing amorously with a man, from the same location. At the end of the film, after the father (Kottarakkara) announces that Sekharan has disappeared and all the characters realize that their plans are shattered, the shot is cut once again to the sand dunes. We see Ramani running away, followed by Raghavan. The fantasy-like resolution of the film has the two of them in a passionate embrace. With the splintering of the melodrama/realism, inside/outside oppositions, the film proposes a third location from which we may theorize spectatorship.

I propose that the unseen Sekharan is that location for the spectator. I will point to two sequences in the film. In a flashback featuring a romantic song, we see Ramani's unfulfilled past romance with Sekharan. Shekharan is absent in the sequence. But the song is shot in a way that presents the camera, i.e. the spectator, as Sekharan. In a series of frontal shots, Ramani literally romances the camera. The second sequence is also a flashback. Ramani and Karunan, after their marriage, visit the fair. Ramani watches six clowns dancing to a song. The voice claims the position of the enlightened one and sings: '*Aham Brahmasmi*/ the fantasies of a blind man who looks for the non-existent cat in the sack of darkness/ . . . .' At one point Ramani starts to believe that one of the clowns is Sekharan. But before she can check, the clown disappears. While this sequence positions Sekharan as an absent presence (by the time we know it might be him, he disappears) who can make a judgment, the former aligns him along with the camera, thus establishing the position of the spectator. If the sequences in the fair narratively privilege Sekharan as the moral centre of the film, the romance sequence transforms him into the position of the spectator. The absent gaze of Sekaharan then is the central problem in the film. In another moment in *Athithi* we see Latha performing classical dance on stage. She is a bad dancer, her dance almost comical. She ends the dance and bows to the audience, to the camera. The shot is cut to the diegetic audience to whom she bows, but what we see is an empty auditorium. The position of the spectator, capable of aesthetic judgment and critical of this comical performance, is once again rendered empty.

When, at the end of the film, the old man announces Sekharan's disappearance, we have two shots in film negative, so as to indicate the visual nature of the issue at hand. Sekharan, I argue, is not a character that is awaited in the film, but the location of spectatorship that will render the disorganized world intelligible in realist terms. The promise of realism lies shattered as it shifts from being a moral placeholder to that of greed and desire for wealth represented by Sekharan who represents an economy that is founded on migration (he ran away to Bombay, we are told) to the corruptible outside. With the film collapsing the desire for Sekharan into the desire for realism, the latter is deemed obscene, a lost promise. This collapse shows up the class positioning of the realist gaze, i.e. as that of the emerging middle classes in Kerala. The moment of tragedy in the film is the realization that the agency of order, the realist gaze, is both impossible and probably undesirable. What is usually seen as the problem with *Athithi* is its central concern – the impossibility of a realist ordering of time and space. What remains is the fantastic, apparently conventional popular resolution on the sand dunes.

Issues of dislocation in *Kabanee* begin with the fact that the film is shot on location in the city of Bangalore (Karnataka), outside Kerala. This is unique because parallel cinema was shot on location in Kerala, while popular cinema that was shot outside Kerala used mostly studio floors. The space of the city, outside Kerala, allows the film to sidestep the space of the domestic and cultural located-ness completely. Even though most of the action in the film happens inside the house of Shari (Shalini), there is no attempt to structure it as the domestic – the space of the couple/the family. Gopi (Chandran), a Naxalite on the run after being involved in a political murder, has come to meet his girlfriend Shari for one last time. Unlike both the films that were discussed earlier, *Kabanee* starts, after two shots – one of burning torch and of a moving train, in a long tight shot of the interior, with a conversation between the couple in the background. Once the slow-moving tightly framed camera rests on Shari, it cuts a close-up on Gopi. To Gopi, who is now looking straight at the camera, Shari poses a question on behalf of the spectator: 'Can the world be changed with murder?' Dispensing with realism, the film is shot in a series of frontal shots as characters either ask questions or proclaim revolutionary ideals to the camera, producing an alienated spectator. With a clear pedagogic intent, the film does not attempt to locate itself either within a cultural frame or realism/melodrama debate.

Cinema is a recurring presence in the film. Interestingly, because of its geographical dislocation, these are neither references to Malayalam cinema, nor indexical references to a condensed version of melodrama as in *Swayamvaram*. An amateurish rendering of the song '*Chingaari koi bhadke . . .*' from the Hindi film *Amar Prem* (d. Shakti Samanta, 1971) ensues in the background while the protagonists are discussing their relationship. The incorrect and incomplete lyrics of the song point to the fact that it is not used here as a framing device but as a marker of youth culture, where the protagonists (and the film itself) can be located. The second prominent image of cinema is the shot of the poster of *Sholay* (d. Ramesh Sippy, 1975), released in the same year as *Kabanee*.[11] Rather than being a statement of the aesthetics, *Kabanee*'s invocation of cinema is part of its landscape and points to its cinephilia. This is not surprising as P.A. Backer has been associated with Malayalam cinema from as early as 1957 when he became assistant director to Ramu Kariat, then the production in-charge of *Chemmeen* and later producer for *Olavum Theeravum*. G. Devarajan, known for his music for stage and film melodramas associated with the Communist party, composed the background score of the film. Parts of *Kabanee* were initially shot with mainstream stars like Sudheer and Usha Nandini, but later abandoned. A number of individuals associated with the film, including the producer Pavithran, the hero T.V. Chandran, and actor Raveendran, went on to become directors in their own right.

The city as constituted by the images of cinema is seen as contiguous with the space of the house where Shari lives. There is no attempt to elaborate the outside just as the inside is shot mostly in tight frames. The sequences of romance are located within the memory of the protagonists and thus in the past, as that which is lost, unlike in *Swayamvaram* where romance is not temporally, but aesthetically, distanced. With its radical re-figuring of the inside/outside, *Kabanee* is a film about the impossibility of authenticity, describing a world that is dislocated both in space (migration to the city) and in terms of politics.

It is erroneous to think of *Kabanee* as a politically radical film though the period of Naxalite politics forms its background.[12] Backer himself suggested that it is a film about Shari and not about Gopi, the revolutionary (Krishnakumar 64).[13] The film successfully stages a pedagogic intervention by making Shari its protagonist, right from the first sequence where Shari vocalizes a question on behalf of the spectator. In another sequence, Gopi is seen looking at a mirror and saying that he hasn't seen himself for a long time. Shari enters the frame of the mirror to complete the circle of looking and ingrain the spectator into his field of vision, with Gopi now looking at Shari's reflection instead of his own. The film is more or less devoid of moments where the looks of the characters can be worked into an aesthetic of realism. The film's central concern is a flattened out world of desire where the connection between individuals can only be built through static frontal shots and addresses. The space-time co-ordinates of the diegetic world become legible only through the affective intervention of the politically radical viewer via the character of Shari.

In the final shot of the film we see Shari, after she knows that Gopi has been killed by the police, looking straight into the camera with Gopi's voice in background: 'I am sure that the time when human beings love each other and will listen to each other's words like music, will definitely arrive' – a line we hear him say earlier in the film. Gopi's presence in the film – with Chandran's plain style of acting – is spectral. Within the pedagogic economy of the film, the spectator is aligned with Shari, as the one who is to be guided by this voice. In an early sequence in the film, we see Gopi in the foreground of the frame, arms spread, reminding us of Christ. In another sequence towards the end of the film, Shari is seen dragging Gopi on the ground a la Christ carrying the cross. An interesting character in the film is that of the worker, played by Raveendran. Silent through the film, his purported role is that of a messenger and a go between for Shari and Gopi once the latter moves out of her house. It is implicit that Gopi's politics are played out on his behalf. The film operates in between his mysterious silence and Gopi's constant revolutionary rhetoric. The film never attempts to imbue the figure of the worker with moral authority, as we see in *Swayamvaram*.

Different strategies of dislocation are central to the two films discussed above. Of the two films, the mode of address employed by *Kabanee* has had a staying power in Malayalam cinema, with Backer following up with the more absurd political film *Sanghaganam (1979)* and John Abraham achieving a more striking aesthetic elaboration in *Amma Ariyaan (1986)*. On the other hand the modes by which *Athithi* dislocates the hegemonic presence of realism were never followed upon, even by Kumaran in any fruitful sense, making it a singular film.

Waiting for realism?

Looking back at the decade, one is surprised to see how realist aesthetics, which were put together in *Swayamvaram* and came to dominate the imagination of 'good cinema,' were marginal to the cinematic practices of Kerala in the 1970s. A number of films – especially those of Pavithran, Raveendran and G.S. Panicker – complicate the narrative of realism. So do the films of G. Aravindan who, after his first film, attempted to delineate the spaces of cultural and aesthetic authenticity on grounds distinct from realism through the use of myth and by bringing cinema closer to practices of visual art and music, especially in *Esthappan (1980)* and *Pokkuveyil (1981)*.

Salaam Karasseri, producer and an actor in *Kabanee*, remembers an incident after the preview of the film at Ajanata Theater in Thiruvananthapuram. After the screening, Kulathoor Bhaskaran Nair, the co-founder of Chithralekha, which produced *Swayamvaram* and *Kodiyettam*, asked Backer if the film had problems with postproduction. Adoor followed by asking whether there were problems with editing. Though Karasseri remembers Backer retorting sarcastically, 'Once the two of you decide between yourselves, let me know,' he agrees with the criticism of the film's formal incompetence (Krishnakumar 105). The criticism of *Kabanee* was being made from a realist standpoint. Film criticism, institutional structures, and the discourse of cinema had quickly accepted realism as the yardstick foregrounding a consensus on it as the teleological goal for these films. This allows for the dominant account of all the films I discussed here, including *Swayamvaram*, as flawed and as awaiting, like the characters in *Athithi*, a realist future. Refiguring these indefinite waits as aesthetic statements in themselves and as constituting definitive arguments about film form is imperative for a more critical retake on the 1970s.

Post-script

In the early 1980s, a third strand of Malayalam cinema, called *madhyavarthi cinema* (middlebrow cinema) and sandwiched between realism and the melodramatic popular, emerged. In film criticism and popular understanding, these commercially viable realist films constitute Malayalam cinema's lost golden age. These films mark the triumph of the realist contract, as it oversaw the deployment of melodrama in these films. If Gopi was the star of the early films of this compromise, the two superstars of contemporary Malayalam cinema – Mammootty and Mohanlal – emerged within this matrix. Under the aegis of realism as spectatorial contract, the challenges posed to the hierarchical ordering of realism and melodrama by a number of films, including those discussed above, were reduced to mere footnotes in the linear story of Malayalam cinema's movement towards a realist destiny.

Notes

1. Film theorist Madhava Prasad describes the 1970s as the time of the disintegration of the 'feudal family romance' with the emergence of what he calls 'the aesthetics of mobilization,' 'development aesthetic' in the films of Shyam Benegal and the middle cinema exemplified by Basu Chatterjee (Prasad 117–216).
2. Film historian John W. Wood identifies this sequence as a flashback (149–150). This reading, based on no textual evidence, is an attempt to account for these sequences in terms of a linear story – a reading that I argue against.
3. Venkiteshwaran, prominent film critic, lists the references to cinema in *Swayamvaram* and identifies the statement about aesthetics. I differ from him on one significant count. He presents this argument about aesthetics as 'self-referential and [as pointing] towards notions about creativity and "art" inherent to the new wave project' (Venkiteshwaran 31). For me this set of references is the central project of the film and not just a matter of self-referentiality. This is the meta-narrative of the film – one that ties different aspects of it together.
4. In the context of Malayalam cinema, social realism refers to an emphasis on social conflicts even as they deployed melodramatic tropes. Films of the mid-1950s that dealt with issues of the working class and the lower castes are popularly seen as representing the singularity of Malayalam cinema.
5. In his *The Imaginary Signifier* (1986), film theorist Chritian Metz argues that the viewer in the cinema hall identifies with himself as a narrativized and abstracted subject position put together by the filmic text (97, 42–57). As has been noted by many, the suturing of the actual viewers with the abstract spectator is never complete.This has implications in understanding the viewers of Malayalam parallel cinema, a discussion that is outside the scope of this paper.
6. In other films, the systems that are in crisis inlcude matriliny (*Elipathayam*, 1982), Communism (*Mukahamukham, 1984*), and feudalism (*Vidheyan, 1994*).
7. Madhava Prasad describes the structuring of realism as metalanguage thus:

   > ... a contractual link [is established] between the members of the audience, including the film-makers, thanks to which the object-world can be represented in its there-ness. It is this latter contract that is at the base of the metalanguage of realism and it is because of the operation of this contract that it is possible for the metalanguage to effectively disappear in its material aspect without eliminating any of its effects. (73)

   Reality in these articulations is contractually produced. Realism is then the way of apprehending this contractually formed 'reality,' a specific way of 'looking.' See also Rajadhyaksha (124–126).
8. The presence (in a sequence discussed earlier) of G. Sankara Pillai, one of the founders of the *thanathu nataka vedi*, provides us with another clue to the salience of modernist theatre in articulating realism in this film.
9. For a detailed discussion of the economic context and the emergence of parallel cinema in Kerala, see Radhakrishnan (219–231).
10. This book, along with the path breaking *Kalaavimarsham: Marxist Maanadhandam* (Art Critique: Marxist Yardsticks, 1983) edited by Raveendran, consolidated a form of art/film criticism that was influenced by Antonio Gramsci and Frankfurt School and anticipated the emergence of film studies in the 1990s.

11. A third film reference is the poster of a film titled *Aa Maze Lelo* ('Come, have fun'), possibly a B-movie, on the back of an auto rickshaw. This is the only reference that could be a direct comment on popular cinema, but I guess that, even if it were, it would have completely missed the audience in Kerala.
12. The film, made during the Internal Emergency between 1975 and 1977, could secure a release only after being subjected to a number of deletions by the Censor Board, which was more powerful than ever. Because of the precarious conditions under which it was screened, *Kabanee* became, much like Mrinal Sen's *Calcutta '71* (1972), a locus for political mobilization.
13. Perhaps as a testament to the ambiguity of its politics, at the height of Internal Emergency in 1975, *Kabanee* was selected as the Second Best Film and Backer was selected as the Best Director by the State Film Awards. Backer accepted the award from the hands of the then Home Minister of Kerala, K Karunakaran who spearheaded the hunt, and in many cases murder, of Naxalites. Backer writes that Karunakaran had said to a journalist that *Kabanee* carried the message that if you indulge in anti-State activities, you could be killed (Krishnakumar 42).

References

Ahammad, Nissar. "Preface." *Yadharthyathinte Naalu Mukahngal.* Ed. Nissar Ahammad. Cochin: Nila Publishers, 1981. 7–38 Print.

de Valck, Marijke. *Film Festivals: From European Geopolitics to Global Cinephilia.* Amsterdam: Amsterdam UP, 2007. Print.

Kishen, Pradip. "Knocking at the Doors of Public Culture: India's Parallel Cinema." *Public Culture* 4.1 (1991): 25–41. Print.

Krishnakumar, S., ed. *P.A. Backer: Ekakiyude Sanghaganam.* Thiruvananthapuram: Souparnika Movie Arts, 1998. Print.

"Malayalacinema Keralamannil Verurakkumo?", *Kumkumam Weekly,* Onam Special Issue (1981): 141–51, 156. Print.

Metz, Christian. *The Imaginary Signifier: Psychoanalysis and the Cinema.* Bloomington: Indiana UP, 1982. Print.

Muraleedharan, T. "Elippathayam/Rat Trap." *The Cinema of India.* Ed. Lalitha Gopalan. London and New York: Wallflower Press, 2009. 190–9 Print.

Prasad, M. Madhava. *The Ideology of the Hindi Film: A Historical Construction.* New Delhi: Oxford UP, 1998. Print.

Radhakrishnan, Ratheesh. "The Gulf in the Imagination: Migration, Malayalam Cinema and Regional Identity." *Contributions to Indian Sociology* 43.2 (2009): 217–45. Print.

Rajadhyaksha, Ashish. *Indian Cinema in the Time of Celluloid: From Bollywood to the Emergency.* New Delhi: Tulika, 2009. Print.

Rajadhyaksha, Ashish and Paul Willemen. *Encyclopedia of Indian Cinema.* New Delhi: Oxford UP, 1999. Print.

Raveendran, ed. *Kalavimarsham: Marxist Maanadhandam.* Cochin: Nila Publishers, 1983. Print.

Venkiteshwaran, C.S. "Swayamvaram: Classic Prophesies." *A Door to Adoor.* Ed. Lalit Mohan Joshi and C.S. Venkiteshwaran. London: South Asian Cinema Foundation, 2006. 27–32 Print.

Wood, John W. *The Essential Mystery: The Major Filmmakers of Indian Art Cinema.* New Delhi: Orient Longman, 2000. Print.

Filmography

Aa Maze Lelo (details unknown). Film.
Aghaat. Dir. Govind Nihanalani. Neo Films, 1985. Film.
Amar Prem. Dir. Shakti Samanta. Shakti Films, 1971. Film.
Amma Ariyaan. Dir. John Abraham. Odessa Movies, 1986. Film.

Athithi. Dir. K.P. Kumaran. Rachana Films, 1975. Film.
Calcutta '71. Dir. Mrinal Sen. DS Pics, 1972. Film.
Elipathayam. Dir. Adoor Gopalakrishnan. General Pictures, 1981. Film.
Esthappan. Dir. G. Aravindan. General Pictures, 1980. Film.
Kabaneenadhi Chuvannappol. Dir. P.A. Backer. Saga Movies, 1975. Film.
Kodiyettam. Dir. Adoor Gopalakrishnan. Chithralekha Film Society, 1977. Film.
Mukahamukham. Dir. Adoor Gopalakrishnan. General Pictures, 1984. Film.
Nirmalyam. Dir. M.T. Vasudevan Nair. Novel Films, 1973. Film.
Olavaum Theeravum. Dir. P.N. Menon. Asha Films,1969. Film.
Pokkuveyil. Dir. G Aravindan. General Pictures, 1981. Film.
Sanghaganam. Dir. P.A. Backer. Navadhara Movie Makers, 1979. Film.
Satah Se Uthata Aadmi. Dir. Mani Kaul. Infrakino Film & Madhya Pradesh Kala Parishad, 1980. Film.
Sholay. Dir. Ramesh Sippy. United Producers & Sippy Films, 1975. Film.
Swayamvaram. Dir: Adoor Gopalakrishnan. Chithralekha Film Society, 1972. Film.
Vidheyan. Dir. Adoor Gopalakrishnan. General Pictures, 1994. Film.

The retro noughties: 1970s Hindi films in 2000s Bollywood cinema

Rajinder Dudrah

The 2000s saw an increased interest in Bollywood films that made explicit reference to, or were set in, the 1970s. In some cases a few of these films were remakes, in part or full, of 1970s hits and some of these noughties films achieved global box office and critical success. A select list reveals films such as *Main Hoon Na* (d. Farah Khan, 2004); *Jaan-E-Mann* (d. Shirish Kunder, 2006), *Don* (d. Farhan Akhtar, 2006); *Om Shanti Om* (d. Farah Khan, 2007); *Ram Gopal Varma Ki Aag* (d. R.G. Varma, 2007); *Bachna Ae Haseeno* (d. Siddharth Anand, 2008); *Action Replayy* (d. Vipul Shah, 2010); *Once Upon a Time in Mumbai* (d. Milan Luthria, 2010); and *Delhi Belly* (d. Abhinay Deo, 2011).[1] What was it about the 1970s – in terms of aesthetic style and its meanings - and why was there a recurrent fascination for this decade in contemporary 2000s Bollywood cinema? Pursuing this question further, when was the 1970s in cinematic terms? Is it possible to neatly locate the 1970s in ten compact years, or is it more productive to consider the years leading up to and after, either side of the 1970s, in terms of porous socio-cultural boundaries? If so, in what audio-visual forms did the 1970s manifest itself, and how have these forms been recreated in contemporary Bollywood cinema? This chapter is concerned with making sense of the aesthetic legacies of 1970s Hindi films in select recent Bollywood cinema and how they have been used and re-used. To read these latter day texts through close film analysis will allow us to decipher their audio-visual forms and content. Reading them closely also invites a scrutiny of how they were composed with possible intended meanings for pleasure and profit through the act of consumption by its film audiences. In one sense, then, the 2000s may be considered as the retro noughties of Bollywood cinema, looking back to and creating anew the 1970s.[2]

The idea of the 'retro' in my examination of 'retro noughties Bollywood cinema' is inspired by the scholarship of Elizabeth Guffey. In her 2006 critically acclaimed book, *Retro: The Culture of Revival*, Guffey draws on intellectual traditions across the humanities, particularly from cultural theory, popular cultural studies and design history and criticism, to bring into relief a useful sense of the term 'retro'. Even as it is difficult to pin down as a phrase, Guffey argues for it as an overlooked methodological concept that allows us to come to terms with the modern past (Guffey 9). Drawing on Frederic Jameson's (Jameson 283) interrogation of nostalgia in a postmodern context, Guffey reminds us that retro as a cultural device is often deployed in societies to tell their histories in new ways; even as history is being worked upon by different and successive social actors who posit a slightly different version of events from within it. As she puts it:

> Retro carries a pervasive, if somewhat imprecise, meaning; gradually creeping into daily usage over the past thirty years, there have been few attempts to define it. Used to describe cultural predisposition and personal taste, technological obsolescence and mid-century style, 'retro's' neologism rolls off the tongue with an ease that transcends slang. ... While words like 'fad', 'fashion' and 'revival' swirled around the resurrected Art Nouveau style, 'retro' acquired its current connotations in the early 1970s. Although retro is easily dismissed as a backward glance at the past, the nuances underlying its appeal are often overlooked. (Guffey 9)

Rather than simply being about period goods, materials, and aspects of culture that are then simply replicated in a new era, 'retro' can also be usefully understood as an outlook on life. On the one hand this could include a kind of longing for the past with a suspicion of the new and the current, and on the other hand it can suggest a fundamental shift in the popular relationship with the past by being half-ironic and half-longing, as 'retro' considers the recent past with an unsentimental yearning (Guffey 9-10). In this latter mode, "retro' is unconcerned with the sanctity of tradition or reinforcing social values; indeed, it often insinuates a form of social subversion while side-stepping historical accuracy' (Guffey 11). Guffey goes on to outline a range of social and cultural examples from post-war Western popular culture that use 'retro' in one of these two ways including, amongst others, popular press ads that promoted home schooling and reinforced traditional gender roles in the US, to the work of a coterie of Parisian film critics, writers and fashion designers who engaged with a genre of films and literature dubbed as '*la mode retro*' that examined themes of resistance to, as well as collaboration with, the Nazis during World War two (Guffey 14–17). 'Retro,' then, can also be considered as demonstrating or being interchangeable with postmodern characteristics: it is self-reflexive, has an ironic reinterpretation of the past, and has a disregard for the kinds of traditional boundaries that had separated high and low art, all found in the theory of Postmodernism (Guffey 21). In this sense retro asks us to take stock of our move forwards in space and time, inviting us to pause to consider what has gone before and how it is sometimes re-used, sometimes fabricated, and is sometimes critically effervescent in the contemporary present. To this effect, what kinds of 1970s retro can be found in 2000s Bollywood and how are they being used in specific instances?

The two noughties films that are taken up to illustrate and answer the above questions are *Om Shanti Om* (d. Farah Khan, 2007) and *Delhi Belly* (d. Abhinay Deol, 2011). Both were popular and critical successes of the 2000s that were also explicitly retro in their use of the 1970s. They are also two very different films of the Bollywood cinematic spectrum in the 2000s. *Om Shanti Om*, with an A-list star cast, was a big budget song and dance melodrama spectacular, featuring Bollywood's current global box office hero, Shah Rukh Khan, with Deepika Padukone, a newcomer, as female lead. The film is deliberately postmodern and tongue in cheek in its use of prior

Bollywood genres and draws on and re-uses liberally from the 1970s of Hindi cinema. It was successful and remembered for its use of a star-studded song and dance sequence, 'Deewangi Deewangi,' which included 31 renowned Bollywood stars and supporting actors from the 1960s to the present.[3] Made on a budget of US$7.2 million, *Om Shanti Om* went on to achieve a box office total of over US$24 million.[4] *Delhi Belly*, on the other hand, featured the up-and-coming actor Imran Khan in a multi-starrer with a young and relatively unknown cast of actors and actresses in the other lead and supporting roles. It was not conventional mainstream Bollywood fare – neither a romantic film, nor a family melodrama, and neither a predominantly *masala* film. Instead it was aimed at the emerging multiplex audiences of India and the diaspora, with an attempt at trying to appeal to a crossover non-South Asian global audience.[5] Its material was risqué, dealing with male adult toilet and black humour (it features a subplot literally dealing with faeces that are swapped and mistaken for stolen diamonds), prostitution, and explicit sexual references and coarse swearing. The film was not what one might call a traditional Bollywood family entertainer, but rather one primarily catering to an urban youth audience with its Indie look and feel. Produced on a budget of US$4 million, *Delhi Belly* went on to make over US$15 million at the box office.[6] *Delhi Belly* also makes retro use of the 1970s in its own distinctive way. Let us turn to each of these films to consider their respective retro inflections.

Om Shanti Om

Directed and choreographed by female filmmaker Farah Khan and co-produced by Shah Rukh Khan and his wife Gauri Khan's production house, Red Chillies Entertainment, *Om Shanti Om* is predominantly a romantic film that deals with the theme of reincarnation inspired by, and a tribute to, the film *Karz/Debt* (d. Subhash Ghai, 1980). On the DVD bonus content and the director's audio track commentary, Farah Khan acknowledges her and Shah Rukh Khan's debt to the 1970s era for being one of their most favourite periods of Hindi cinema. The film features Shah Rukh Khan as Om Makhija Kapoor in the first half of the film as a struggling junior artist who is trying to become a star in the 1970s Hindi film industry. He meets and falls in love with the leading actress of the time, Shantipriya/Shanti, played by newcomer Deepika Padukone, but that love is never reciprocated in the same way. Shanti is in love with and is pregnant by a film producer, the film's villain Mukesh Mehra (Arjun Rampal). Mukesh arranges for Shanti to be murdered and as Om Makhija tries to save her, he too ends up dying. In the second half of the film, set twenty five years later, Om Makhija has been reborn as Om Kapoor who is a leading, yet irritating, A-list Bollywood star. Through a series of events, his past life and friends and family all begin to come back to him and he sets about seeking revenge on Mukesh. Along the way he meets and enlists the help of Sandhya/Sandy, also played by Deepika Padukone, who bears an uncanny resemblance to Shantipriya, though she is not a reincarnated soul in the same way that Om Kapoor is. Being set in both the 1970s and 2000s in the pre- and post-intermission respectively, the film also pays homage to and makes fun of the Indian film industry of both these periods. Released during the Diwali festival of November 2007, one of the biggest cinema weekends in the Indian film calendar, the film went on to become the highest-grossing Hindi film of all time during its release.[7]

Figure 1. *Om Shanti Om's* DVD menu screen depicting the film's 1970s retro look.

Source: DVD image grab, copyright of Red Chillies Entertainment, India.

To mark the popularity of the film, a full colour memorabilia book on its making was released some months later in 2008 by author Mushtaq Shiekh. Shiekh has been a film reporter for press and magazines on Indian cinema and then moved into script-writing and media production for TV serials and films. He is known to be a personal friend of Farah Khan and Shah Rukh Khan and appears in a minor role in the film, which might account for his access to the information he presents. As Shiekh comments on the enduring appeal of the 1970s mixture of genres which are pastiched, parodied and re-created in *Om Shanti Om*:

> Hope. Dream. Revenge. Reincarnation. Those were the days. Back in the seventies when everything was in Eastman movie colour. Dialogues, characters, scenes that have become a part of our cultural psyche. These were the trendsetters, now reveled as clichés, but back then they had created a definitive genre – the masala movie, with improbable plots, heavy doses of melodrama, unforgettable dialogues, and superlative music and at times legendary and over the top histrionics. … Bollywood in the seventies had become a genre itself. (Shiekh 8)

Shiekh's claim of Bollywood in the 1970s as a genre deserves attention. Whereas there has been some debate as to when the term 'Bollywood' became meaningful and to what it refers, it did not actually exist as a popular term of reference to the Hindi film industry in the 1970s in quite the same way that it is now commonly used (see footnote 2). Nonetheless, as a chronicler of popular Hindi cinema, Shiekh is retrospectively locating understandings of the term 'Bollywood' as a multi-generic cinema which included technical film production processes such as Eastman colour in the 1970s Indian film industry, that it is then interpreted and developed in the 2007 film.

In the first half of *Om Shanti Om*, the *mise en scène* replicates working studio sets of the 1970s on a grand scale. Shiekh illuminates the period setting as:

> … a working studio in the 70s. Junior artistes fill every frame, men with long sideburns and colourful bell bottoms and women with bouffant hair. Mock shoots happening everywhere, so you had girls in cabaret outfits sitting having a beedi, Lord Krishna going on a scooter, goons beating up each other, heroines chatting up their directors, a big ass moon with sparkles on it coming into the shot. It's not easy to nail down a sense of place but that's exactly what Farah has done. Art nouveau studio sets, carefully selected props, natty costumes of the disco age and the magic of twenty-first century digital effects, all working together to create this world of Bollywood in the 70s. This is where the film lives in its first half. This is Farah's world; every brick has been layered in with her imagination. (Shiekh 81)

In conjunction with the Art Director, Sabu Cyril, who was in charge of the production design of the sets, director Farah Khan was insistent on the look and feel of the 1970s studio that she recalls from her childhood and wanted to recreate in her 2007 film. From Indian mythologicals, to period fashion, including aesthetic quotations from earlier western art styles of the early 1900s, the first half of *Om Shanti Om* also includes references to 1970s big blockbuster Hindi *masala* movies such as in the song 'Dhoom Tana,' with a pirate dance sequence that makes references to both the film *Dharam Veer* (d. Manmohan Desai, 1977) and Gene Kelly in *The Pirate* (d. Vincente Minnelli, 1948).

Prior to the start of filming, the director employed two research assistants who undertook research over three months in 2006 which included watching over 250 films, with some being scanned thirty times. Following this research, the senior costume designer, Sanjeev Mulchandani, was handed a 500 page file with references from 1970s films (Shiekh 26). The film deployed filmmaking techniques from the 1970s in order to recreate a period look:

> Certain production techniques of the past were used on the sets to authenticate the seventies look. … They even used 70s lighting – more of hard light, flat lighting making the heroines like goddesses. Stuff like [the actor] Rajesh Khanna turning to the camera and talking for no reason – people would non stop turn into the camera in the seventies, the typical zooming into the dear departed father's picture and all of that, the actor's hamming away to glory. (Shiekh 95, [ ] my insertion)

The retro feel was further achieved through the use of contemporary CGI technology alongside practices from the 1970s, particularly where large numbers of hundreds or a thousand were needed as fans, crowds, and extras at film sets or at the premier of the film *Dreamy Girl* within *Om Shanti Om*. During the 1970s, extras were available *en masse* inexpensively or for free, while in the 2000s computer special effects assist in creating the illusion of numbers according to Shiekh:

> … mylo shot motion control camera was used. They had 200 people on the set but they needed to show a crowd of 1000. That's where Mylo steps in, you can multiply. What happens with mylo, once you decide your movement, you can redo the movement any number of times. Mylo is motion control computerized, you control

> it with a laptop shift, then make them, sit, or move them and then you can shoot it with the camera. FX is tough, it's done after the editing, because then the guys know which shot they have to work on. Once the editing is done, they don't get more than 2 to 3 months on each movie. So the work is not just painstaking but needs to be flawless. In this movie, the FX guys would make a low quality print, show it to Farah for approval and then make the final copy in full resolution. How does this happen. Well, the scene is shot and edited, and sent to the FX guys, then it is scanned from film to digital, which makes it fodder for the computer whiz to work on. Once the magic is added, then again you have to put it back on film. You really need to know where to use the special effects in the story. (Shiekh 94)

The retro use of the 1970s is partly crafted from motion-picture practices from the seventies itself and partly generated through actual actors and state of the art computer assisted technology. The retro 1970s are not just simply copy and pasted into the 2000s but mediated and worked on, sometimes painstakingly over weeks and months, in the contemporary present of the noughties.

Throughout the film, the 1970s is regarded as a period more than a decade long. It is posited as much broader, taking its cues and references from other cinemas and other periods too. For instance, in the 'Main Agar Kahoon' song (If I Say Something, sung by Sonu Nigam and Shreya Ghoshal), the filmmaking processes of the 1960s and 1970s are displayed as part of the diegesis and of the story telling itself. Om Makhija is trying to woo Shantipriya with the assistance of his best friend Pappu Master (Shreya Talpade). Om Makhija comes across as nothing less than a caring gentleman in this song, as he is throughout the first part of the film before his untimely demise; and his heroic endeavours are referenced throughout this song not only from 1970s Hindi cinema but also from 1950s Hollywood. The song is inspired from the romantic sequence in *Singin' in the Rain* (d. Stanley Donen and Gene Kelly, 1951), particularly during the song 'You Were Meant For Me' where Gene Kelly's character displays his affection towards Debbie Reynolds's in the film studio using in-house sets and equipments (Shiekh 83). The purple and pink hues that are present in the 1950s Hollywood film have been lovingly coloured into a deep purple. Rear projection technology, used from the 1930s and widely throughout the 1950s in Hollywood, is used in this song during one of its verses as Om Makhija and Shantipriya are seen getting into a stationary vehicle, after which Pappu Master switches on the projection on to the back screen. Pappu turns on a large fan that acts as the gentle wind which breezes through Shantipriya's and Om Makhija's hair. Not too dissimilar to the 1950s Hollywood studio system, the backlight, rear projection and wind give the two performers an aura that enhances their onscreen presence not just as actors but also as the hero and heroine.

Om Shanti Om draws on a feature common throughout the *masala* films of the 1970s where trinkets, lockets and small objects that were exchanged between the protagonists as young children, who then become separated and cross paths as adults. The presence of the material icons reminds the parted friends of their past in order to be reconnected again. Similar props include Om Makhija wearing a necklace with a medallion that comprises the three signs of three of the major faiths in India – those of Hinduism, Islam and Christianity. This gesture to a secular community harks back to the post-independence 'all India' films that attempted to cater for all of India's major religious groups in a salute to Nehruvian idealism (Chakravarty). *Amar Akbar Anthony* (d.

Manmohan Desai, 1977) remains one of the more popular blockbusters of the 1970s that deals with this preoccupation.

The large hand-painted hoardings at the Kamlistan Bridge set seen throughout the film during three sequences further recall the 1970s. The first sequence occurs when Om Makhija is seen talking to the large poster of Shantipriya, as if she were actually in front of him; the second time when he is heartbroken realising that Shantipriya is in love with Mukesh Mehra and he again speaks to her poster, this time tearfully, in order to let her go; and the third time is in the post-intermission when the hand-painted hoardings have become mass produced printed billboards relating to the images and goods around Om Kapoor as a star. The hoardings used in the pre-intermission consist of advertisements for Exide battery, Ovaltine and the *masala* hit film *Sholay* (d. Ramesh Sippy, 1975), amongst others. The hoardings do more than just create a look and feel for the period within the diegesis. They draw attention to the artisan craft of sketching and hand painting large posters that were a key feature of film promotion throughout the period and before.[8] Implicitly some ads that are used in the first part of the film cheekily remind us of the political situation and comment on it. As Shiekh notes:

> To complete the feel, film posters of Deepika as Shantipriya and other 70s commercials are put up at the Kamlistan Bridge set. The Amul ads that were put up were the original 70s ones. One was a take off on the Maintenance of Internal Security Act introduced during emergency and the other one was on compulsory sterilisation introduced during Indira Gandhi regime. (Shiekh 85-87)

By the second half of the film, the ads and posters are still larger than life, only this time we see them in the post-2000s and in the age of 24/7 media, stardom, and digitally reproduced mass hoardings which feature actual products that Shah Rukh Khan endorses. Prominent in the centre is a Tag Heuer advertisement featuring Shah Rukh Khan himself that doubles as a sign of Om Kapoor's rise as a star in *Om Shanti Om*. The ad alludes to and plays with Khan's actual stardom by cannily product placing the high-end wristwatch in the film. The craft of hand painted hoardings has been superseded by the technology of the digitally reproduced, and we are reminded of a very different milieu in Hindi cinema. We are now present in a globalised Bollywood cinema industry but one that owes a debt of aesthetic and industrial gratitude to the broader 1970s.

Figure 2. Om Makhijia talks to the hadn painted poster of Shantipriya on the Kamlistan Bridge set in the first half of *Om Shanti Om*

Source: DVD image grab and copyright of Red Chillies Entertainment, India.

Figure 3. Om Kapoor and Pappu talk on the Kamlistan Bridge set in the second half of *Om Shanti Om* in front of an actual Tag Heuer poster that SRK endorses in real life.

Source: DVD image grab and copyright of Red Chillies Entertainment, India.

The shift between the 1970s and the 2000s is also marked with the entry of the villain, Mukesh Mehra, during pre- and post-intermission. In the first part of the film Mukesh appears as the stylishly dressed 1970s producer who enters the studio in his chauffeur driven car, arriving with a briefcase of money. The connotations to illicit or black money and dubious filmmaking practices is unmistakeable, not least around film finance, where allegations of money laundering were regularly made in the film trade press, allegedly involving sections of the criminal underworld in Hindi filmmaking.[9]

In the second half of the film Mukesh Mehra returns as an older film producer who has left India and is now resettled in the USA working in the Hollywood film industry. His name has changed from Mukesh to Mike/Mikey and he wears a long and silver-greying pony tail. He re-enters the film frame towards the second half of the film with lit cigarette in hand and puffing smoke during the 'Deewangi Deewangi' song. His western attire and smoking clearly re-establishes him as the villain and acts as a further memory trigger setting off Om Kapoor's recollections of his past life and interactions with this negative character. The actor's costume has been carefully chosen to create the effect of a masquerade underneath the veneer of high class respectability:

> Arjun Rampal's entire wardrobe is pretty stylish in the film. Not Bollywood at all actually. He's really cutting edge chic, though even Arjun had an issue about the high waist but we took it down a bit for him. He looked good like a young Vinod Khanna with those leather jackets, he looked the part. (Shiekh 91)

On the one hand, then, Mukesh is a stylish producer with access to funds and networks but this is only his surface appearance. The sartorial likeness to a suave hero of the 1970s – actor Vinod Khanna – also creates this effect. One the other hand, however, Mukesh's exterior fashion conceals a dark villainy that works to place his costume in the context of informal and illicit trade regimes of the 1970s and 80s; and then again with his re-entry in the second half, he is marked as the coming of foreign and global capital (namely via Hollywood), which is to be cautiously dealt with and examined due to the character's dubious past and his lecherous intentions in the 2000s (in the post-intermission Mikey lustfully pursues a younger Indian actress for sexual gratification). There is a self-conscious play in the exchanges over lunch between Om Kapoor and Mikey as to why Hollywood is now interested in Bollywood as a new market possibility, and why and how Bollywood should respond to this. Mikey appears interested in funding a new Bollywood venture for maximum profit, and Om Kapoor presents the idea of resurrecting the abandoned 1970s film that was being made in the first half of the film prior to his and Shanti's death. The 2000s film Om Shanti Om references itself as a possible answer to this exchange between Bollywood and Hollywood – Om Kapoor proposes to Mikey that his incomplete Bollywood film will work best if it is left in the creative hands of the Indian film makers and with co-production and negotiated involvement from US backers. The exchange over re-visioning an older film in a more recent historical moment thematizes a core preoccupation of the retro: namely, a critical pause that takes stock of antecedent moments and their future possibilities. *Om Shanti Om's* retro gestures include a longing for a different audio-visual past, for a different industrial structure of stars and audiences, for a different economic logic, along with a suspicion on the new industrial structures, logics, and stars that have come into being. Somewhat paradoxically, *Om Shanti Om* crafts these desires in a manner that invokes nostalgia for the past while also being half-ironic about it. In this way the 2000s is posited in a dialogic relationship with the 1970s and vice versa, that re-creates and re-imagines both periods anew. Having considered some retro uses in *Om Shanti Om* let us consider the same in *Delhi Belly.*

Delhi Belly

In our second film, it can be argued that the retro uses of the 1970s undermine present-day conservative social ideologies and promote retro aesthetics as social subversion. With the tagline 'S#IT HAPPENS,' *Delhi Belly* deliberately plays with and caters to a young urban crowd. The plot revolves around three male leads who share a cramped and untidy apartment together – journalist Tashi (Imran Khan), photographer Nitin (Kunaal Roy Kapur) and cartoonist Arup (Vir Das). The trio also have very little money between them and lead sexually promiscuous lives. Through a series of mishaps and misdemeanours, one of them, Nitin, suffers food poisoning leading to diarrhoea; his friend Arup swaps his stool sample, meant for testing by a medical lab, with stolen diamonds that have been unknowingly smuggled into the country via Taashi's scatter-brain stewardess girlfriend Sonia (Shenaz Treasurywala). The three friends become embroiled with an underworld gang hungry for their blood and out to reclaim the diamonds.

Delhi Belly, directed by Abhinay Deo, was co-produced by the Bollywood actor Aamir Khan, his wife the filmmaker Kiran Rao, and American producer Jim Furgele.[10] The screenplay was written by Los Angeles based Akshat Verma, penned initially while he was still a student at UCLA.[11] It was also part-financed and distributed by the Indian studio UTV Motion Pictures, which in recent years has diversified its media-making practices with a view to producing Indian films with a potential cross-over global audience.[12] This conglomeration of filmmakers with both Indian and international tastes and inspirations, ranging from commercial Bollywood cinema, to art house fare, adult dark humour, to British and US gangster movies, helps locate the mélange that is *Delhi Belly.* It is an unconventional Bollywood feature film (also running at around 100 minutes, well under the usual two and half hour plus fare), that deploys and plays with the 1970s of Hindi cinema in a knowing retro and subversive manner that questions the contemporary in urban Indian life, including aspirations for upward class mobility.

Figure 4. *Delhi Belly's* DVD menu screen depicting genre motifs associated with young adult issues, action and dark comedy through a comic book layout.

Source: DVD image grab, copyright of UTV Motion Pictures and Aamir Khan Productions, India.

The title credits of *Delhi Belly* begin with an airline captain announcing the arrival of his aircraft into New Delhi's international airport. A cut takes us to a ground level shot, angled and looking up at a relatively clear blue sky. Within the frame of the shot a lamppost is in view canted on the right side of the screen with mangled electric cables, and a red and white kite stuck in between the wiring. Another cut shows us the same lamppost, this time from a slightly different angle from below. In the frame now are three young boys, who appear to be in their early teens, one standing and the other two sitting on a wall next to the street light. They appear to be dressed in basic clothes, possibly suggesting their lowly class status with only two in short pants and the other in a short pant and vest. They are positioned underneath the direct flight path into New Delhi International Airport. They look onwards as fascinated young boys, off screen and towards the sound of an arriving plane as it makes its descent – the same plane that the Captain has announced will soon be landing. Within a few seconds the aircraft zooms overhead towards the landing strip.

As the jet touches down, trumpet notes begin to play as non-diegetic music, marking the opening of the 1970s 'Wakao Theme,' the song and dance competition music medley from the film *Hum Kisise Kum Naheen/We Are Equal to All* (d. Nasir Hussain, 1977). This is a 1970s JazzFunk track with an upbeat drum with its signature call of 'Wakao!' – a part Hong Kong Kung Fu-esque and a part Disco glee shout out - composed by Rahul Dev Burman, who was popularly and critically acclaimed for his production of numerous 1960s and 1970s Hindi film music scores. This music sequence is played over the walking footsteps of one of the criminal characters from the film, Vladimir Dragunsky (Kim Bodnia), as he arrives in the landing hall to reclaim his travel luggage. He is initially filmed walking in medium close-up, with the camera focussing on his legs beneath knee height, giving the opening a gangster-esque genre feel.

As one would expect with a carefully crafted film, the opening takes us into the different textual layers through which this film operates. The initial sounds and images mark a newly modernising India, literally placing us en-route to the capital's New Delhi International Airport. With the arrival of the aircraft, as a marker of modernity through the idea of world travel, the reference to globalisation in India and as India globalises around the world is made. But alongside global aspirations the grounded reality of everyday India and its multiplicity of lived experiences at the street level are also referenced via the messy-wired street lamp, the three young teenage boys, apparently with nowhere to go, with their pre-adolescent fascination of a flying machine in the sky, the mangled kite that was flown but got caught up in the lines of electric cables, the confusion of crossed wires, and the boys' dress code which suggests urban development and aspirations of the less well off: all entangled as part of the same story. The international and national are at once brought into relief as the global travels to and meets with Indian urbanites in the metropolis of New Delhi. This is the first implicit reference to Hindi cinema of yesteryear, not just the 1970s but also earlier and immediate pre-Independence films which included themes of rich and poor, as India strove towards its new found post-colonialism (see Joshi, and Anjaria this collection). The three young boys on the wall also act as precursor characters to the young twenty-something heroes/anti-heroes of our film; with the film's content of blackmail, cheap jokes, toilet humour, sexual awakening, life really going nowhere after a University education, and a desire for upward class mobility and material aspirations which the three young leads come to personify in their different ways. With the onset of the 'Wakao Theme' music we are reminded of the 1970s original *masala* film from which it is taken and transported to the genre of gangster films. The teenage boys/youth film meets with another genre and is mixed together – coming of age in noughties India, even with its state professed ideology of itself as a rising power part of the BRICS economies, is not without its dark undertones and problems as criss-crossed with the underworld in this film.[13] The use of the music is also part direct homage not just to 1970s *masala* filmmaking, but also specifically to the 1977 film director, producer and screenwriter of the 1950s to 1980s, Nasir Hussain (uncle of actor Aamir Khan and co-producer of *Delhi Belly*), and also to music composer R.D. Burman for their lasting impact on popular Hindi filmmaking.

Just as in *Om Shanti Om*, but quite differently too, *Delhi Belly* also makes use of the 1970s of Hindi cinema in complex ways. As part of the *mise en scène* in the young men's flat a poster of a fictitious 1980s movie adorns one of the walls (see figure 4). From the top to the middle of the poster reads: 'Jimmy Arts Presents. SUPERHIT OF THE NAUGHTY 80's!! Daredevil Aamir as and in DISCO FIGHTER. He's a lover and a fighter'. The character of the Disco Fighter is played by Aamir Khan, maternal uncle of the male lead of *Delhi Belly*, Imran Khan, and the film's co-producer. He stands action poised in the centre of the poster, brandishing a pistol with a female in a sexually suggestive pose standing behind him. The poster is a loud 1970s and 1980s mix of the action and disco genres. The character is donned in wardrobe references from both western popular culture of the period and Hindi cinema ones too. The Disco Fighter is a cheeky yet serious chap who is an amalgamation of character types across Bollywood and Hollywood as a cowboy and medallion man-type figure, dressed in white with striped large spectacles. He stands ready for action – fighting, dancing, camp sexual energy – through a costume, hairstyle and dance pose that references Mithun Chakraborty, Rishi Kapoor and Amitabh Bachchan, a performing Elton John and dancing John Travolta almost simultaneously. The Disco Fighter theme runs throughout the film as a postmodern filmic quotation within a film. It is referenced as part of the popular cultural make-up of our three young men and features at two key stages in the film as inter-textual reference.

The first time in which the character of the Disco Fighter is elaborately used and brought to life is via a fantasy dream sequence in which Arup, his ex-girlfriend, Ritu, and her Canadian IT Engineer fiancé, Vivek, feature. Ritu abruptly ditches Arup for an overseas suitor who can offer her better material prospects and Arup is quiet but clearly upset. Arup as a cartoonist is depicted as a geeky and docile character throughout the film; he is creative with his artwork, albeit exploited at work in an advertising company by a bullying manager. At strategic moments his creative streak is allowed to surface in the film, sometimes through an on-screen cinematic explosion, and this is one such moment. After Ritu's selfish rejection, Arup retreats into his private thoughts and fantasizes revenge where he appears as the Disco Fighter character at her Hindu wedding ceremony. Ritu and Vivek's family and guests – all well to do middle-class signified Indians – are gathered at a wedding palace where a priest is reciting the ceremonial scriptures. Just as the couple are about to place a garland over each other to finalise the ceremony, off-screen a character yells 'Wait! This wedding cannot take place'. Three pistol shots are heard fired and these are interlaced with three sweeping camera cuts which move across the groom, his father, and the bride's mother in medium shots looking perplexed towards the shout of the call. The shocked and frightened wedding guests huddle together. The camera begins to pan back through the arched legs of the shouting character, who is none other than the Disco Fighter played by Arup. He stands like a cowboy hero, legs apart, poised for action, and as he comes into full view from behind, he puts the pistols back into their holsters at the side of his hips. An off-screen non-diegetic elongated introduction is heard formally revealing him to the wedding guests and the viewers as 'Disco Fighteeeer!' As the scene reveals him from the front, a waft of smoke clears away from him, super-hero like. A music interlude that draws on string and guitar references from the 1970s and 1980s Hindi films, that themselves drew on global cowboy and action aesthetics, is used over this character's entry, signifying his coolness and comedy at the same time. He goes on to say: 'This girl has given me oral sex!' which echoes a further three times as cuts move between and zoom towards the groom, his father who covers his mouth in disbelief, and the bride's mother who places her hands over her ears while she cries a very filmy 'Naheen!/No!'. The Disco Fighter goes on to declare: 'And because I am a man of the twenty-first century, I have also given her oral pleasure.' Further edit swipes take place over the family members present, with the groom's father clutching at his chest as if to signal a shock to the system and the guests all mutter in melodramatic mode. The soundtrack accompanies these actions only to exaggerate them further – there is a mixture here of film genres and a parody of Indian TV melodramas. The bride's mother turns to her and publically scolds her for bringing shame to the family and orders her to leave her own wedding with a slap across the face. From this smack Ritu twirls across the room and falls at the feet of the Disco Fighter Arup, who then begins to sing the song '*Jaa Chudail*/Go to Hell Witch' – a tabla-sitar-cock-rock fest where he publically berates her and enacts his revenge. The wider 1970s, then, are a viable cultural resource not only to retreat into as a private revenge fantasy, but they also offer the possibility of dealing with present troubles head-on, through character types that have shown an enduring action appeal and rebuttal to conservative societal norms and conventions, used here in ironic and retro subversive ways.

The second sequence in which the Disco Fighter features is enacted in the following way. VJ Sohaya, played by real life MTV Video Jockey Anusha Dhandekar, is depicted as a bit of an airhead, a glamorous wannabe actress in the film, who Taashi has to interview for a magazine as she has released her latest song, 'I Hate You (Like I Love You).' This song plays towards the end of the film as Taashi is compelled into action to declare his real love interest in Menaka (Poorna Jagannathan), after parting with his former girlfriend Sonia. As Menaka slowly reverses her car while looking over her shoulder, Taashi jumps into the driver's side through the full open window and kisses her, with his friend's Nitin and Arup looking on. Menaka is momentarily surprised and then reciprocates and they both become lost in the full-on kissing, while the car continues to roll back; as it does, it collides with Nitin's scooter and comes to a halt. Off-screen Nitin yells 'Bastard! You're gonna pay for that.' A quick blackout cuts to the end of the diegetic story and on the other side of the edit we are taken to the finale song, the colourful item number in which we meet again the Disco Fighter; only this time it takes us into the film within the film territory of the actual *Disco Fighter* film, which stars Aamir Khan as the named protagonist. The actress playing VJ Sohaya appears as the Disco Fighter's female sidekick and lover and the *mise-en-scène* is adorned in loud disco colours consisting of purples, blues, whites and silver with flashing lights.

The aforementioned film poster that we saw in the young men's apartment earlier in the film comes to life, and all the 1970s and 1980s references, with some from even before, are writ large in this song and dance number. A compact and very colourful history is presented, as it were, of the 1970s and 1980s cinematic references that have been used and re-used in Hindi cinema, and as it leads up to and becomes Bollywood in its noughties incarnation as *Delhi Belly.* From generic post-war British and Hollywood films that have represented airplane fighter scenes, to 1970s Blaxploitation, to Kung Fu Cinema, and even references to the disco films of the 1970s and 1980s in Hollywood and Hindi cinema, this item number is an elaborate piece of pastiche and popular culture.[14] Different sets co-mingle the different cinematic and popular culture references that are cited throughout the song and are placed across either side of each stanza. The disco set is comprised of numerous backing dancers, both male and female, wearing throughout the song golden boots, golden hot pants, purple and gold tight-fitting *cholis*/bras with western outfits. The backing dancers also fake play several trumpets together as part of the spectacle and draw attention to the artificiality of the set, while adding to the play and cheekiness of the disco context.

Aamir Khan as the Disco Fighter and lead dancer is often in the centre of the set with his female love interest, swooning around him. He wears white platform heel shoes, a white trousers with a red and yellow flame pattern rising from his ankles to his knees, a colourful striped belt with a heart shaped buckle placed in the centre of his waist. He also dons a red shirt with a white jacket. His shirt buttons are undone, revealing his very fake and hairy chest embellished with a gold medallion centrepiece that hangs on a thick chain around his neck. To top it all off he wears large dark sunglasses and his hair is styled full on with a centre-left parting, almost male bouffant-esque. At other times in the song, he also wears a very long red and black scarf around his collar which drapes down to the floor, almost akin to Tom Baker's Dr Who scarf from the 1970s and early 1980s British sci-fi TV series.

Figure 5. Aamir Khan as the flamboyant Disco Fighter as he appears in *Delhi Belly*.

Source: DVD image grab, copyright of UTV Motion Pictures and Aamir Khan Productions, India.

After the first chorus refrain - 'I hate you, Like I love you. I hate you, like I love you, love you, love you' sung twice by the female lead, with a response from the male voice as 'Your love has turned me mad. This pain has turned me mad. Your love has turned me mad' – a diamond shaped edit swipe moves across the screen and transports us to 1970s London via the Blaxploitation genre. The Disco Fighter and his female lead are in the front seats of a red open top Cadillac. The camera is mounted at the front of the car's bonnet giving us a full wide angled view of the car and its inhabitants. Accompanying our couple and sat on the top of the back seats are six women in zebra print body-hugging outfits, with Foxy Brown-esque style Afros. The Disco Fighter character is blacked-up playing a smooth 'brotha' of the period, donning a black leather jacket and hair in Afro style too. Through the use of rear projection technology the central and busy night time streets of London are on display with black Cabs seen being driven. The six women sitting at the back are holding 1950s Unidyne Fatboy microphones and repeat their lines after the lead female. At times the Disco Fighter appears distracted by the sexual advances and show of affection by his female consort, almost pushing her away as if to say 'do not distract me from my action – there is work to be done', and at other times he plays and teases with her, caressing her sexually and keeping her at bay for any potential sexual action. This mixture of the 1960s and 1970s, then, is a direct homage to the action, style and gender politics of the black brothas and sistas as characters in Blaxploitation cinema.

The end of this verse takes us back to the chorus which is picturised at the disco club set. Here the Disco Fighter dances whilst performing Kung Fu fight moves. Then, through another wipe edit, we are transported to an airplane dog fight sequence where the Disco Fighter is in the pilot seat, his lover behind him, and the six female backing singers and dancers sit on the wings. Through the use of rear projection, black and white filmed footage of dog fights are taking place in the background. The Disco Fighter is dressed in 1950s fighter pilot gear and the females are dressed in regalia that quote inter-war Americana. After this verse we are located back in the disco for the chorus, at the end of which there is a crescendo and an edit shift to a black screen with the advert for the film appearing in illuminous pink type font: 'Aamir Khan in and as Disco Fighter in theatres Christmas 2011.' A fade to black leads to a screen split into three segments. On the left and right appear two screens with the Disco Fighter character mirrored in each screen, and the song continues playing over his movements. In the centre of the two screens the credits begin to roll, marking the film's coming to an end. The Disco Fighter pulls out two large pistols and fires them and begins to dance by circling the guns in the air, shrugging his shoulders and gyrating his hips, thrusting his pelvis towards the camera. This is done to a *qawwali*-esque-rock-pop-rnb infused rhythm and lyrics that gather apace. The lyrics sing, 'I have lost all in the market of your love my companion' and these are a direct reference to the 1984 film *Sharaabi*/ Drunkard, starring Amitabh Bachchan. The Disco Fighter continues to dance and gyrate over these lyrics with his guns in the air as Sufi-esque *qawwals*/calls are let out by the male voice in the song. The images fade to black and the song gathers apace to *tabla* beats as the formal credits take over the entire screen, moving upwards. The 2011 film *Delhi Belly* ends to a retro and postmodernist use of the film within a film via *Disco Fighter*, which itself is set in the popular culture and cinematic references of the wider 1970s.

Conclusion

In response to the questions posed at the outset of this chapter, the retro noughties in Bollywood cinema are as much about the 1970s as they are about the 2000s. The aesthetic legacies of 1970s Hindi films are extant through rich and diverse use and re-interpretation in the 2000s. The two films used in this chapter are illustrative of a wider range of films from the noughties that engaged with the 1970s in a number of ways. They help to widen a critical lens in locating and making sense of the 1970s as a cultural and historical marker. This timeframe did not just simply occur in a neat cinematic ten years, but as has been argued and demonstrated from the composition of key sequences in both films, the 1970s of Hindi cinema itself drew on international films and popular cultural references that spanned much broader periods and aesthetics from the early 1900s to the 1960s, with its socio-cultural and aesthetic afterlives blending over into the 1980s and beyond.

One of the distinctive genres with its mixture of styles that took shape and became popular in the 1970s was the *masala* film, and it has been invariably and partially reconstituted in the 2000s as latter day Bollywood. In *Om Shanti Om*, the filmmaking practices of the 1970s and of this multi-genre are used (including large on-set filming, loud and accentuated colours and lighting, and the use of hundreds of extras to create a larger than life effect), and further amalgamated with noughties technologies such as CGI. The effect and affects result in self-conscious aesthetics that not only re-create a period look and feel but also re-emphasise and amplify the aesthetic legacies of the 1970s. In *Delhi Belly* aspects of the *masala* genre are used by setting the coming of age black comedy film alongside the gangster genre. This enables for a feisty mix of audio-visual storytelling that pokes as much fun at contemporary conservative social mores as it does at itself via retro devices.

The notion of 'retro' usefully elaborated by Elizabeth Guffey allows us to come to terms with the modern past. As a methodological device it allows us to analyse the use of the past in the present beyond mere notions of nostalgia and to consider more carefully the representation of cultural histories that are at stake in such an enterprise. The modern past, as it is sourced from and used to tell stories and create histories anew in noughties Bollywood cinema, is partly about the use of prior artistic styles and performative gestures as a way to respectfully mark what went before and to acknowledge their enduring appeal. For instance, at the beginning of *Delhi Belly*, the 1970s are explicitly marked by way of homage via the 'Wakao Theme' from the original soundtrack of the 1977 film, *Hum Kisise Kum Naheen*, which audibly embellishes meaning on to contemporary 2000s New Delhi. Such references are more than just a series of reflexive stylistic gestures. They can also be seen as representing a useful pause and critical reflection, in which Bollywood cinema as a cultural vanguard, of sorts, in Indian and related popular cultures can look backwards in order to go forward.

Two of the key filmmakers associated with the films in this essay can be considered as being important in promoting such a reflexive understanding - Farah Khan for *Om Shanti Om* and Aamir Khan for *Delhi Belly*. Both were children and then teenagers during the 1970s and 1980s and equally fascinated by and indebted to these broader cinematic periods. Their films re-insert Farah and Aamir into the 1970s through their respective filmmaking practices, homage, and specific uses of retro. Farah Khan literally appears in a minor cameo at the start of her film where she is a dancing extra who fights with Om Makhija during a rendition of the 'Om Shanti Om' song from the 1980 film *Karz*/Debt, and also in the end credits where she walks on as herself as the director alongside the other cast and crew. Hers, then, is a multi-coloured and boisterous part-ironic and part-longing use of the period that is refashioned for a 2000s audience; one that is itself made up of patrons who grew up in the 1970s as well as younger and newer cinema-goers for who the 1970s are re-presented. Aamir Khan appears pictorially in the poster for *Disco Fighter*, as the actual Disco Fighter at the end of *Delhi Belly*, and he also actively promoted the film using his A-list star status as a draw towards the film in promos, and during press conferences ahead of its release. His deployment of the Disco Fighter character as a melange of the characters from the 1970s and earlier (i.e. the angry young man, the cowboy figure, the disco lover, the blaxploitation brotha, the pre-1950s fighter aircraft pilot amongst others), accentuate a male adolescent fascination for coming of age issues that articulate action, taking on the system, camp energy and fun, and sexual awakening all in one. The 1970s as a critical era in Hindi cinema where crime, corruption and the aftermath of Indira Gandhi's Emergency are dealt with on-screen is implicitly re-instated for the noughties. However, the contemporary 2000s period is one where the nation is allegedly on the rise as a global economic player but it is also a time where not all have access to this wealth equally, not least in the urban playground of the metropolis. As a result, the retro character of the Disco Fighter emerges as a postmodern figure - articulated between the 2000s and the 1970s – who plays equally with notions of time and place by askewing them (i.e. he is not from one time or place or film alone), and plays equally with the purposes for which he is invoked (he is used to show up and challenge conservative social ideologies but also through parody as well as pastiche).

The 2000s have been discussed as the rise of Bollywood cinema on the international film, media and popular cultural landscapes in different ways (see for instance Rajadhyaksha; Desai 40-69; and Dudrah *Sociology Goes to the Movies* 16–18, as contributing to this debate). Some of the issues that have been raised in this scholarship include the global resonance of this cinema that spans beyond South Asia and its diasporas, whilst other issues include the uncritical celebration in some parts of the global mainstream media about the rise of Bollywood as not having moved further beyond its stereotypes of being simple kitsch song and dance movies. *Om Shanti Om* and *Delhi Belly* are two contemporary Bollywood films that reflexively and knowingly look back to the 1970s as an important historical and precursor era assisting in the formation of post-1990s and 2000s Bollywood. These noughties films help to generate further interest in Bollywood globally, not least to recent investors such as Hollywood production houses who are increasingly vying for Indian and South Asian audiences as economic markets. As such, the retro pause and reflection that these noughties films offer is a welcome reminder of Bollywood's present as articulated from its continuing past.

Acknowledgements

With thanks to Priya Joshi for her exceptional editorial eye and insightful comments on an earlier draft of this chapter. Thanks are also due to Sue Harper and Moti Gokulsing for their respective inspirational support and comments during the research and writing of this piece.

Notes

1 Of this list *Ram Gopal Varma Ki Aag*, a remake of the hugely successful *masala* film *Sholay* (d. Ramesh Sippy, 1975), was a commercial and critical failure.

2 Methodologically, I make a distinction in this chapter between 'Bollywood' as a term to refer to the popular Hindi cinema and cultural and entertainment industry that gained widespread common and academic currency from the 1990s onwards, and '1970s Hindi films' as a way to delineate and shift between the two, and to argue and demonstrate how the retro Bollywood noughties draw on and make use of 1970s Hindi films. For debates on the term 'Bollywood' and its academic use since the 1990s see Prasad; Rajadhyaksha 'The "Bollywoodization" of the Indian Cinema' and *Indian Cinema in the Time of Celluloid*; Mishra; and Dudrah *Sociology Goes to the Movies* and *Bollywood Travels*).

3 This song and dance sequence was a homage to and retro deployment of the highly popular track of 'John, Johnny Janardan' from the film *Naseeb/Destiny* (1981) produced and directed by one of the 1970s and 1980s most successful *masala* filmmakers, Manmohan Desai. The 'John Johnny Janardan' song originally featured over a dozen stars from the 1980s and earlier of Hindi cinema.

4 See: http://www.boxofficeindia.com/arounddetail.php?page=- shownews&articleid=4409&nCat=, date last accessed 19 September 2013.

5 On the emerging socio-cultural and political economies of the multiplex cinemas in India see for instance Rai; Athique and Hill; and Kumar.

6 See: http://articles.timesofindia.indiatimes.com/2011-07-05/box-office/29738241_1_opening-weekend-crores-profitable-venture, date last accessed 19 September 2013.

7 See: http://boxofficeindia.com/arounddetail.php?page=shownews&articleid=3997&nCat==, date last accessed 19 September 2013.

8 On Bollywood posters see for instance Dwyer and Patel; and Pinto and Sippy.

9 See for instance Tejaswini Ganti (Ganti Chapter 2); and Sanjeev Srivastava, 'Analysis: Bollywood and the mafia', *BBC News Online*, 1 October 2003, http://news.bbc.co.uk/1/hi/world/south_asia/3152662.stm, date last accessed 19 September 2013.

10 See the film's official Facebook page at: https://www.facebook.com/delhibelly, date last accessed 19 September 2013.

11 See 'Shit happens! Or my adventures with Delhi Belly'. *Tehelka* Magazine. Vol. 8, Issue 30, 30 July 2011, http://archive.tehelka.com/story_main50.asp?filename=hub300711cinema.asp, date last accessed 19 September 2013.

12 See UTVs official website at: http://www.utvgroup.com/motion-pictures.html and also its official YouTube channel at: http://www.youtube.com/user/UTVMotionPictures, both sites last accessed on 19 September 2013.

13 BRICS = Brazil, Russia, India, China, and South Africa. For a critique of the possibilities and problems involved in the rise of the BRICS, including the challenges and obstacles of corruption, see the collection of essays in Jain, especially in 'Part V' of the book.

14 The pastiche here is very much in line with the use of the term as outlined in Richard Dyer's illuminating book on the subject, where he argues for and illustrates pastiche as being more than about simple stylistic imitation but as a significant means of representing historicity in terms of feeling.

References

Athique, Adrian and Douglas Hill. *The Multiplex in India*. London: Routledge, 2010.

Chakravarty, Sumita. *National Identity in Indian Popular Cinema: 1947-1987*. New Delhi: Oxford University Press, 1993.

Desai, Jigna. *Beyond Bollywood: The Cultural Politics of South Asian Diasporic Film*. New York: Routledge, 2004.

Dudrah, Rajinder. *Bollywood: Sociology Goes to the Movies*. London and New Delhi: Sage Publications, 2006.

Dudrah, Rajinder. *Bollywood Travels: Culture, Diaspora and Border Crossings in Popular Hindi Cinema*. London: Routledge, 2012.

Dwyer, Rachel and Divya Patel. *Cinema India: The Visual Culture of Hindi Film*. London: Reaktion Books, 2002.

Dyer, Richard. *Pastiche*. London and New York: Routledge, 2007.

Ganti, Tejaswini. *Bollywood: A Guidebook to Popular Hindi Cinema*. New York: Routledge, 2013. 2nd edition.

Guffey, Elizabeth. *Retro: The Culture of Revival*. London: Reaktion Books, 2006.

Jain, Subash ed. *Emerging Economies and the Transformation of International Business*. Cheltenham, UK: Edward Elgar Publishing, Inc. 2006.

Jameson, Fredric. *Postmodern, Or, the Cultural Logic of Late Capitalism*. Durham, North Carolina: Duke University Press, 1991.

Kumar, Akshaya. 'Provincialising Bollywood? Cultural economy of north-Indian small-town nostalgia in the Indian multiplex', *South Asian Popular Culture* 11.1 (2013): 61-74.

Mishra, Vijay. *Bollywood Cinema: A Critical Genealogy*. Pdf print edition. Wellington, New Zealand: Asian Studies Institute, 2008. Available at: http://www.victoria.ac.nz/slc/asi/publications/17-bollywood.pdf

Pinto, Jerry and Sheena Sippy. *Bollywood Posters*. London: Thames and Hudson Publishers, 2008.

Prasad, Madhava. 'This thing called Bollywood' *Seminar Magazine* 525, http://www.india-seminar.com/2003/525/525%20madhava%20prasad.htm, originally published May 2003.

Rai, Amit. *Untimely Bollywood. Globalization and India's New Media Assemblage*. North Carolina: Duke University Press, 2009.

Rajadhyaksha, Ashish. 'The "Bollywoodization" of the Indian Cinema: Cultural Nationalism in a Global Arena', *Inter-Asia Cultural Studies*, 4.1 (2003): 25-39.
Rajadhyaksha, Ashish. *Indian Cinema in the Time of Celluloid. From Bollywood to the Emergency.* Bloomington and Indianapolis: Indiana University Press, 2009.
Shiekh, Mushtaq. *The Making of Om Shanti Om.* New Delhi: Om Books International, 2008.

Filmography

Action Replayy. Dir. Vipul Shah, 2010. PVR Pictures. Film.
Amar Akbar Anthony. Dir. Manmohan Desai. 1977. Tip Top. Film.
Bachna Ae Haseeno. Dir. Siddharth Anand. 2008. Yash Raj Films. Film.
Delhi Belly. Dir. Abhinay Deo. 2011. UTV Motion Pictures and Aamir Khan Productions. Film.
Dharam Veer. Dir. Manmohan Desai. 1977. S.S. Movietone. Film.
Don. Dir. Farhan Akhtar. 2006. Excel Entertainment. Film.
Hum Kisise Kum Naheen. Dir. Nasir Hussain. 1977. Eros Entertainment. Film.
Jaan-E-Mann. Dir. Shirish Kunder. 2006. Nadiadwala Grandson Entertainment. Film.
Karz. Dir. Subhash Ghai. 1980. Mukta Arts Ltd. Film.
Main Hoon Na. Dir. Farah Khan. 2004. Red Chillies Entertainment and Eros International. Film.
Naseeb. Dir. Manmohan Desai. 1981. Aasia Films Pvt. Ltd. Film.
Om Shanti Om. Dir. Farah Khan. 2007. Red Chillies Entertainment. Film.
Once Upon a Time in Mumbai. Dir. Milan Luthria. 2010. Balaji Motion Pictures. Film.
Ram Gopal Varma Ki Aag. Dir. R.G. Varma. 2007. Adlabs and K Sera Sera. Film.
Singin' in the Rain. Dir. Stanley Donen and Gene Kelly. 1951. Metro-Goldwyn-Mayer. Film.
The Pirate. Dir. Vincente Minnelli. 1948. Metro-Goldwyn-Mayer. Film.

The afterlives of 1970s Hindi cinema

Sangita Gopal

Indie extreme

A recent and acclaimed documentary, *Supermen of Malegaon* (d. Faiza Ahmad Khan, 2008),[1] outlines, in a mode that is simultaneously witty and heartfelt, the rise of a very local, ultra-artisanal film 'industry' based in Malegaon, a small town about 300 kilometers from Mumbai. Shaikh Nasir, playfully referred to as the 'Dadasaheb Phalke' (Joshi, 2009) of Malegaon, got this show on the road when he made a film entitled *Malegaon ke Sholay* (2000), shot on a handycam and starring locals who resembled the megastars of the classic. It was clearly a spoof: the villain was called Rubber *pace* Gabbar and *Sholay*'s (Ramesh Sippy, 1975) Basanti turned into Basmati. At the same time, the spoof was also a loving homage to what is probably *the* defining film of the 1970s. It became an instant classic as the residents of Malegaon poured into the video parlor to watch their own *Sholay,* and Nasir doubled his investment and went on to make many more such 'remakes.' More recently Nasir has turned his sights to Hollywood and made his most expensive film to date, *Superman* (2008), where the eponymous hero played by Shafique is Malegaon's version of the caped crusader out to fight the local gutka-king who is turning the town into tobacco addicts.

As the documentary points out, the film industry in Malegaon thrives on remakes, turning out local versions of not only 1970s classics like *Sholay* and *Don* (d. Chandra Barot, 1978) but also New Bollywood hits such as *Rangeela* (d. Ram Gopal Verma, 1995), *Lagaan* (d. Ashutosh Gowarikar, 2001) and *Ghajini* (d. A.R. Murugadoss, 2008). Part-fanvid and part-parody, these Malegaon films (many circulating on youtube) are a hyper-local cinema enabled by inexpensive global technologies such as the VCR, DVD, handycams, chroma green-screen, CGI, editing options ranging from two VCRs to AVID software. Malegaon represents an instance of what one may call 'indie extreme' and it must be viewed as part of the many mutations and expansions that the Hindi cinema is witnessing at the moment as new media and multi-platform technologies are re-orienting the industrial basis of cinema, its production, distribution, and exhibition infrastructure, and its social life. What is notable in many of these mutations is what might be named the '*Sholay* effect' in which even micro film movements such as from Malegaon trace their genealogy to the blockbusters of the 1970s.

In a volume on the legacies of 1970s cinema, the Malegaon film exemplifies how the new forms currently assumed by Hindi cinema refer repeatedly to the transformations that occurred during the 1970s, that critical decade in Bombay film history when the industry first began to be referred to as Bollywood. Like most thoughtful parody, Malegaon films are simultaneously an imitation and critique of Bollywood blockbusters. What *Malegaon ke Sholay* retains from the original film at the remove of almost three decades enables us to grasp what the landmark film signifies for particular audiences today, and the parody provides a particular kind of 'reception' history of the 1975 classic. Some of the differences between original and spoof draw attention to ways in which a local viewing constituency engages and supplements their memories of a classic. As a parodic remake, the Malegaon film brings the narrative protocols and performance codes of A-List Bollywood films into sharp relief and allows us to archive the continuities and ruptures in film aesthetics and sociology between the 1970s and the present. In persistently localizing the 'originals' to make them relevant to Malegaon and its problems that include communal strife, crumbling infrastructure, sporadic development and entrenched poverty, the remakes also remind us that mainstream cinema today appears to have lost its links with the popular that the cinema of the 1970s so confidently claimed. Under these circumstances, 'the people' (outside urban middle classes) must now remake Bollywood classics to suit their own needs at a moment when the cinema of the day ignores them.

Certain key tropes from the 1970s repeat in a survey that includes a 'minor' cinema at the Malegaon end of the spectrum or India's 'first' Mumblecore film, *The Untitled Kartik Krishnan Project* (d. Srinivas Sunderrajan, 2010) which in a 'film-within-a-film' format charts the travails of a Mumbai-based web designer by weekday and a would-be filmmaker by weekend whose attempts to make a new kind of cinema is haunted by the ghosts of cinemas past and present. These tropes include a dissatisfaction with the mainstream cinema that is no longer 'of/by/or for the people' (if it ever was), a creativity spurred by new media technologies, and a resourcefulness and flexibility that spurs all innovators in a zero-capital environment.[2] Thus the film-makers of Malegaon use bullock carts as cranes and bicycles for tracking shots while Sunderrajan shot his Mumblecore film in HDV, edited it on a borrowed MacBook, worked with a cast that all had day jobs, and bribed waiters at coffee shops so he could shoot on location without permission. His budget was $ 800 (Joshi 2010). Also on view in this indie extreme cinema is a mode of social engagement that takes the form of a critique of the cinema itself as a technology for representing the social. Thus in the Malegaon films, the critique of gangster capitalism, structural inequality, state-sponsored communalism is given to us through spoofs of *Sholay*, *Shaan* et al. The same strategy produces the comic tone in *The Untitled Kartik Krishnan Project* whose Tarantino-addled protagonist film-maker is thwarted by the 'system' but also by his own muddled motivations and obsessive cinephilia.

Both tendencies share a reflexive relation to cinema, in particular to the forms it assumed in the 1970s. The 1970s, as this volume has shown, described an industrial terrain, genres, styles, narratives, patterns of production and consumption, audience stratifications that the contemporary cinema both inherits and is attempting to overcome in its indie forms, as well as in the A-list versions put out by top Bollywood producers such Karan Johar and Ekta Kapoor who have engaged in their own projects of self-reflection in films such as *Agneepath* (d. Karan Malhotra, 2012) and *Once Upon a Time in Mumbai* (d. Milan Luthria, 2010). Where the Malegaon films reflect on the blockbuster form, *The Untitled Kartik Krishnan Project,* references the so-called 'parallel cinema' of the same period and its desire to institute an alternative to the mainstream film. The figure of the shadowy bureaucrat who hounds the protagonist might be seen as veiled reference to the state sponsorship (and regulation) of the parallel cinema in the 1970s and 1980s through agencies like the Film Finance Corporation (hence FFC) and the National Film Development Corporation (hence NFDC). If a diversification of the film product and market as shown by Poduval's and Pillai's contributions to this volume might be one of the key achievements of the 1970s, today's Hindi cinema intensifies and takes in new directions this legacy. References to and reflections on the 1970s, ubiquitous in what I have called 'New Bollywood' cinema,[3] are the many iterations through which a 'different' cinema begins to take shape.

In what follows, I show how some of the central debates surrounding Hindi cinema in the 1970s with regard to questions of audience, genre, and self-reflexivity continue to resonate in the present, especially in the indie scene. I use programming at two relatively recent film festivals in the United States focused on the Indian New Wave to draw out some salient features of this indie film scene. I then turn to the 1970s and early 1980s to chart a brief genealogy of these transformations with attention to the discussions and debates in the English language press at the time to show how the film product, its audience, modes of production and exhibition were being conceptualized as increasingly diverse. There was, as we shall see, a growing concern already in the 1970s that the industry needed to reflect on and reform its practices in order to promote different types of films (in today's terms blockbusters and indies) in order to cater to – as well as cultivate – multiple audiences and revenue models. Critique and self-reflection emerged as crucial components in this project of making the industry more flexible and capacious. If the state had been viewed through the 1960s and early 1970s as an agent who might assist in the emergence of a new and reformed Hindi cinema, this hope receded in the latter part of the decade. During the Emergency, the industry not only experienced punitive and capricious forms of state power but post-Emergency the state itself lost interest in cinema and turned towards television as the medium through which it would shape culture. Therefore, the industry began to imagine reform and diversity as commercially-motivated, i.e. the market desires difference so to speak. Here, as I will show, the audience and its changing tastes emerge as very important factors in necessitating new types of products including 'art' and genre films. I conclude by sampling views expressed by key figures of contemporary indie cinema to see how certain tropes and preoccupations of the 1970s persist in New Bollywood cinema that may perhaps explain the urge to remake and refer back to films from that decade that we see everywhere from Malegaon to Mumblecore.

Cinema in search of an audience

As we try to chart the contours of a new cinema, festival programming can be quite a useful resource. In their drive to represent emerging film trends of a region to outsiders, curators try to include a cross-section of work from any given year. With this in mind, let us consider the Indian entries at two film festivals held in New York City in October, 2010 – the South Asian International Film Festival (SAIFF) and Mahindra Indo-American Arts Council Festival (MIACC). These festivals were meant to showcase the 'rise' of independent cinema in South Asia and the offerings from India spanned a wide spectrum. All made in 2010, they included Mani Ratnam's *Raavanan* (one of the most expensive films ever made starring Aishwarya Rai, with a Hindi version called *Raavan* with Abhishek Bachchan playing the title character in lush locales, with song-dance sequences and wire-fu), and Anurag – the 'indie guru' – Kashyap's *Girl in Yellow Boots,* (dirty-realism is the predominant aesthetic). Then there was a trifecta of films that are best described as Ray Redux. While Srijit Mukherjee's Bengali film *Autograph* represents a glossy, slick instance of the 'new Bhadralok' cinema where the central character – a movie star – is attempting a remake of Satyajit Ray's *Nayak*; Sangeeta Padmanabhan's *Charulathayude Bakki* ('Charulata: Sequel of the Untold Story') is a 22-minute Malayalam short where the central characters – an actress and her film-maker lover – are obsessed with Ray's *Charulata.* Rounding out this set is Q's (the artist formerly known as Qashik Mukherjee) *Gandu* (rather coyly translated as 'Loser/Jerk') a film that the filmmaker and his many admirers call India's first sex film and whose ending lives up to that promise. It is best described as 'anti-Bhadralok' cinema, using sex to shock middle-class Bengal out of its genteel preoccupations. Then come genre films in Hindi such as *Paan Singh Tomar* (Tigmanshu Dhulia, the 'dacoit' biopic), *Phas Gaye Re Obama* ('With Love to Obama,' Subhash Kapoor, low budget comedy), and the Tamil-language *Aaranya Kaandam* ('Anima Persona,' Thiagarajan Kumararaja, gangster romance). Rounding out the program is the aforementioned *Untitled Kartik Krishnan Project* and its diasporic double, Rohit Gupat's *'Life! Camera, Action…,'* (about the struggles of becoming a filmmaker in an Indian-American immigrant family that wants a stable career for you) whose budget – $4000 – neatly mirrors *UKKP's* $ 400 (accounting for the exchange rate). This mix of auteurist blockbuster to genre-films to indie and indie extreme from a variety of regional film-making centers and in different languages that nonetheless share certain affinities and dispositions seems to support the scholarly contention that Indian cinema is undergoing an upheaval at the moment.

Yet it is hard to map these multiple becomings as mainstream versus alternative, commercial versus indie, national versus transnational versus regional.[4] For one, these shifts are still ongoing, so any description or taxonomy remains highly contingent and new categories are being proposed all the time. For instance, it has become common in recent years to classify blockbusters in terms of whether they belong (or not) to the '100 crore-club'[5] (big to medium-budget star vehicles that open wide). For another, all these films – from 100-crore to indie – are so self-conscious and citational that it is tricky to categorize what is *new* about them if not this very tendency towards reflexivity that serves various and intersecting ends, some critical and historiographic, others commercial. Hindi independent cinema is a crucial component of what is new about Bollywood cinema and as such it dwells inside New Bollywood, even though its relationship to it might be oppositional and self-reflexive. As such, it is analogous to what has been called 'indiewood,' which Geoff King characterizes as a 'distinct region' where Hollywood meets independent cinema (King 2).

While there is consensus that there is an alternative cinema in India, one is hard-pressed to define what comprises it and whom it is for. It is easier to surmise, on the other hand, what the audience *no longer is.* It is not the 'people' understood as an All India audience. One may safely say that the 'multiplex effect' has truly taken hold in Indian cinema, namely the widespread belief that one does not need all of the people all of the time to make a film profitable – a commercial logic that was developed and demonstrated by the multiplexes. A film may be targeted towards middle-class urban audiences who frequent multiplexes or working-class audiences who go to single screen theaters, and it is possible for both sectors to yield high returns. A multiplex film might span the gamut from the star-driven blockbuster to the genre film to small-budget films with what are characterized as an 'indie' vibe. These segments appear to exist with variations in non-Hindi language cinemas as well, including the markets in the South and to the East. Further, all films to a lesser or greater extent circulate globally: while the big productions receive theatrical release the world over, others are viewed on new media platforms. This notion that there is an audience for all types of cinema and thus it is possible for all manner of films to be potentially profitable makes the categories 'mainstream' or 'alternative' hard to sustain as Indian cinema attempts to reinvent itself.

Galen Rosenthal, curator of the SAIFF festival described above, refers to an Indian New Wave, and this term seems to have gained some currency among contemporary filmmakers. Most recently, a petition to the Indian government demanding reform in the exhibition sector referred to this new cinema as New Wave *Independent* cinema, or New Wave Indie for short. Crafted by Onirban Dhar, the petition entitled 'Save Indie Cinema' was authored by 65 film professionals working in eleven languages. While the term 'indie' is indeed of more recent provenance, this is the New Wave's second outing in India, the first having flashed by in the early 1970s. As we shall see below, the 1970s discourse on the New Wave was more focused on defining the object and specifying its audience, but contemporary 'indie' is less concerned with questions of aesthetics and address. It assumes that there is both a product and a viewer but what is lacking is an exhibition platform. Claiming that there is now an audience for every kind of film and no dearth of new content, the petition states that the biggest threat to indie cinema comes from the exhibition sector where a '150 crore film and a 1.5 crore film has the same ticket price at the multiplex' though the viewer for these films is likely to be from different economic strata. The state had given multiplexes tax exemptions to promote 'small budget content' but the pricing has kept audiences away. In order for indie cinema to survive, it needs to find alternate exhibition venues including television (especially state-owned) and small art theatres.

In contrast, in the many discussions of the Indian New Wave[6] in its first coming in the early 1970s, the question of audience and address was front and center. One of the main reasons that Satyajit Ray attacked the Indian 'New Wave' was on the grounds of its 'minority audience syndrome,' its inability to deal with the 'collective mind' and the 'collective response' (Ray 81, 99). As Ray stressed, an Indian cinema needs to resonate with the Indian people, understood both as sociology and totality. The many defenders of the New Wave, however, claimed that cinema could not be truly reformed without this aesthetic vanguard. Thus in an interview in 1972, when asked whether it bothers him that despite critical adulation, *Uski Roti* has not yet received a theatrical release or been seen by a general audience, Mani Kaul states, "If I start simplifying for the audience, it means I am falsifying the progress of life around me. … A higher experience in life as in cinema is achieved by starting to work against the natural tendencies." He concludes by saying that he would never make a film in the hopes that it may succeed at the box office (Rao 33–34).

From the early 1970s, with the rise of new kinds of Indian cinema, there were concerted attempts to reconceptualize the audience, although the need for cinema to have a 'broad' (or 'public' or 'popular') address was not really at issue. Those who defended mainstream cinema did so on the grounds that it appealed to a lot of people and those who defended the new cinema (some FFC-sponsored – *Dastak*, *Bhuvan Shome*, some not, *Anand*) did so on the grounds that the commercial success of these films attest to the changing desires and tastes of this 'collective' audience.[7] Thus New Hollywood – rather than the more experimental French New Wave – is held up as a model by the reformist film press for the aesthetically-innovative, commercially-viable future of *popular* cinema in India. Thus a journalist notes, "Bombay may very well learn some lessons from its American prototype. Hollywood with most of its studios on the brink of bankruptcy is dead. The films that have been smash hits have not been the spectacular extravaganzas but low-budget films like *Bonnie and Clyde, Easy Rider, Five Easy Pieces* comprising new directors, writers, stars and technicians." The writer however goes on to stress the need for economy, understood not only in fiscal but also narrative and stylistic terms (Bhaneja 27). The very next year, Firoze Rangoonwala, the editor of *Star and Style*, notes that while 1973 will be remembered as the year of Raj Kapoor's *Bobby*, it was also golden for 'minority cinema' (his term) citing as examples *Garam Hawa* (lit. The Scorching Winds, M.S. Sathyu) *Charitraheen* (lit. The Depraved, Shakti Samanta), *Saudagar* (lit. Salesman, Sudhendu Roy) and *Koshish* (lit. Effort, Gulzar) [Rangoonwala 15]. However, certain shifts in the conceptualization of the audience are afoot. As the government's interest in bankrolling a 'good cinema' intensifies, the industry responds by suggesting that such a cinema need not be a state-based pedagogic project to educate the few in the art of cinema, imposed from the above but rather, the commercial product itself might solicit different segments of the audience. For this, cinema would not only diversify into 'genres,'[8] but also into a mainstream and a middle cinema (though this category is not consistently used until the 1980s). Though this is not explicitly stated, the middle cinema was imagined as appealing to a urban middle-class viewer during an era when there was a considerable expansion of this demographic.

With the success of both genre films and small-budget actor-based films, the first glimmerings of the 'two-audience' paradigm that dominates discourse of Hindi cinema in the 1970s and 1980s emerges. Thus one encounters claims that "even while the masses need their entertainment, the classes need it too," and the film journalist Firoze Rangoonwala goes on to remark that the most promising development in 1973 was Dena Bank agreeing to fund Mrinal Sen's *Padatik* to the tune of Rs. 75000. Sen's ability to secure financing from a non-governmental agency implies that film has a future as a credit-worthy commercial good – a big shift in an industry largely funded by rogue speculators and loan sharks (Rangoonwala 5). Thus it would seem that even before the declaration of Emergency by the Indira Gandhi government in 1975, an event that severely curtailed freedom of expression and punished the film industry with brutal and arbitrary censorship, the industry was reacting against the interventionist stance taken by the state towards the establishment of a 'good cinema.' It was proposing, instead, a process of internal reform analogous to what was occurring in Hollywood. The discussions seemed focused on concrete steps like new models of exhibition (art theatres with fewer seats) and financing (banks rather state agencies) that would allow smaller films to reach paying audiences, and thus become commercially-viable.

It is interesting to note that while the reformist discourse emanating from the state sought to *create* an audience for a new cinema, the industry emphasized that such a viewership already existed but was not being adequately catered to. The calls to re-calibrate the audience and promote the small films that are succeeding at the box-office is propelled no doubt by an anxiety that unless the industry reorganizes itself, it will be imposed upon by a national film policy and perhaps, even nationalized. The FFC had been set up in 1960 with the goal of 'providing, affording or procuring finance or other facilities for the production of films of good standard'[9] and had in the course of the decade funded dozens of films including Ray's *Charulata* (The Lonely Wife, 1964), Ritwik Ghatak's *Subarnarekha* (The Golden River, 1964) and Ramu Kariat's *Chemeen* (1967). Film historians note that in the early 1970s the FFC seemed to throw its weight behind films of a distinctly avant-garde nature – Mrinal Sen's Kolkata films, the late Ritwik Ghatak and the early Mani Kaul.[10] Thus in the interview cited above, Mani Kaul approvingly notes that he is very hopeful for the future of Indian cinema, if "the government does not abandon its recently found low budget policy" (Rao 35).

While this support for a more experimental film language seems odd emanating as it does from an increasingly totalitarian state, what remains of scholarly interest is how the industry identified product diversification and audience segmentation as the way forward for commercial cinema, such that films both big and small would occupy different vectors of the value chain. With this in mind, it incited a project of reform from within that prioritized a middle cinema that would be small-scale, realist, innovative and commercial and that would therefore respond to an audience ready for such fare. Thus, in contrast to the paternalist attitude of the state, reformists repeatedly make claims for the intelligence and discernment of the viewing public. Though the film industry had long solicited the government's attention, the Emergency had revealed the relation between a state-supported 'parallel' cinema and a random policing of the mainstream cinema. As the introduction to this volume notes, the Indira Gandhi government was really interested in the cinema and had keenly grasped its mobilizing power. By the middle of the decade, as the state unleashed its force on the industry by increasing levies, restricting licenses for importing raw stock and equipment, and quarantining hundreds of films in the Censor lockbox, the industry realized that appealing to the state for help at the production end could be very dangerous indeed.[11] Thus when the Emergency lifts we notice a flurry of reflections on the lessons learnt from this brush with the state. It was agreed that rather than becoming dependent on the government, the industry was better off seeking the patronage of viewers. There were many calls to clean house and become alert to changing tastes, so that films could potentialize existing markets.

Veteran journalist and filmmaker K.A. Abbas characterizes the capricious actions of the state vis-à-vis the film industry as "a see-saw balance, going up and coming down" and proposes self-management, auto-regulation but especially reform in the exhibition sector as the only answers (The Sword of Censorship n.p.).[12] Janki Dass emphatically concurs, "The answer to my mind comes in two simple words – SELF DISCIPLINE. These two words should shape every aspect of our filmmaking, whether it is the star system, economy of film-making, codes and criteria of the production sector" (High Time for Film Revolution in India). Further, the industry-generated discourse on the need for a commercially-viable popular cinema successfully solicited the FFC's attention away from the nascent avant garde. From Satyajit Ray's celebrated and oft-quoted attack on the Indian New Wave and its inability to address a collective to Kumar Shahani's contention that cinema should not be classified as a mass media and should not attempt, via realism or otherwise to reach the masses at any cost, (cited in Rajyadaksha 243) what we witness during the 1970s is a repeated attempt to clarify cinema's address and to align the question of aesthetics to that of address.

This project of reform takes the form of a sustained attempt to codify and archive the excesses and irrationalities of the mainstream, big-budget Hindi cinema alongside a focus on new practices and processes that can re-orient the industry at a molecular level. In the post-Emergency period we notice an increasing appearance of the term Bollywood. When it first begins to be used in the late 1970s, it is a derisive term applied to a cinema that is somehow viewed as 'fallen' and in need of reform. The term was allegedly coined as an afterthought by a film journalist commissioned to write a news column about the Hindi film industry. As Bevinda Collaco recalls:

> I was given a studio beat to do. I was not happy with the name of the column Studio Roundup and thought of "Flipping around Follywood," but it sounded too harsh. I settled for 'On the Bollywood Beat' instead. From a studio roundup column I began commenting on what was happening off the sets too and it turned into a gossip column. In no time at all the stars were calling up to find out why they were mentioned in Bollywood and others to find out why they were not mentioned in Bollywood. I guess they were responsible for giving my word longevity.
>
> While I worked at Cine Blitz in 1978, 79 and 80, I used the word prolifically, but I never thought it would get official international usage. Actually I don't know whether to laugh or to cry when I see my word become common usage… (qtd in Anand, n.p.).

Collaco's playful coinage was probably inspired by the then current mode of Bombay filmmaking.[13]

> giant-size, multi-star cast extravaganzas are becoming fashionable and profitable, just like multi-nationals minting money. So all the BIG banners fancy for giant-size outfit, starring giant-size talents and giant-size make-believe technicians (sic). Since they believe the best technicians are only born overseas, there is a spree for hiring super technicians from abroad. The foren-touch and foren-feel make the difference … [and] … many are joining the giant-size foren-brain bandwagon (Anon. 1977)

> To provide something for everybody and everything for somebody, the producers of Hindi cinema have cooked movies about people from a never-never land. This has resulted in the prosperity of regional movies that have definite people, of a definite region, with realistic habits, hearths and homes. Hindi film producers have surely to own the blame for creating a faceless cinema (Anon, 1976).

> Today, most Hindi filmwallahs seem least interested in holding up the mirror either to nature or authentic environmental problems. With a sudden and convenient love for amnesia, they hold this mirror up to other mirrors. Mostly phoren-made (Lahiri, 1974).

The common concern in the descriptions above is that the industry had lost touch with the 'real,' exhausted its creativity, and was merely reproducing tested formulas to hedge the risks of rising production and exhibition costs. Many also felt that the malaise in Hindi cinema could be attributed to its predilection for copying Hollywood. Indeed, the word Bollywood begins to connote this mimic-mode. The misgivings and anxieties displayed by these writers, condensed around the increasing use of 'Bollywood' as the name for Hindi cinema, points to a very real process that is alluded to here. But what is also clear from the discourses surrounding the popular cinema in the popular press, is that the will to reform is internal to the industry and not just a project dreamed up by India's non-Hindi film watching elite. Thus film critic Vikram Vohra writes, "If our film people are serious about change, they must dedicate themselves to be their own critics ... encourage experimentation and newcomers, declare assets and clear up finances" (1977).[14] This call to change becomes quite strident in 1977 and a slew of articles propose different modes and sectors through which such changes can occur.

If we noted above that one of the decisive legacies of the 1970s was a reimagination of the audience of the popular cinema as diverse, intelligent and ready for innovative fare, we notice that by the mid to late 1970s the call for reform of industrial practices correlates with an undoing of the masses/classes divide which Tejaswani Ganti has called one of the enduring 'audience fictions' of the industry (16). There is a repeated effort to disarticulate the Bollywood 'masala' film from its so-called intended audience, the masses. As though to counter the repeated claim, most often found in elite discourse, that mainstream film is underdeveloped because the masses seek escapist fare is an effort to dispel the notion of the mainstream film as a 'mass film.' By 1976–77, other names are proposed for the mainstream formula cinema including 'Big Cinema' (Mehra 18) 'Mob Cinema' (Hardikar 29) and 'Gross Cinema' (Valecha 32). 1977, the year the Emergency ended, is hailed as a year of tremendous contradictions. It is the year of the multi-starrer and the year of the small film, or in film parlance, the multi-starrer and the miniatures where the return on investment of a small film like *Gharonda* (d. Bhim Sain, 1977) matched in percentage terms that of mega-hit like *Amar, Akbar, Anthony* (d. Manmohan Desai, 1977). The additional levy imposed on prints especially impacted 'big' films since the first 12 prints of film did not have to pay the levy. The *Stardust* annual of 1977 writes, "The popularity of light, moderately-priced features like *Chit Chor, Chhoti Si Baat* and *Rajnigandha* and the work of a director like Shyam Benegal in *Ankur* and *Nishant* augurs well. This might well be the genre of the Indian film of tomorrow! However to encourage this, the FFC has to move beyond a 5-lakh/16mm film formula, and get into distribution in a very big way!" (Reuben 1977).

Let us conclude this section, by turning briefly to early 1980s when we witness a certain consensus emerging out of the debates of the 1970s. There is now a concerted effort to reclassify the masses/classes, commercial/cinema art cinema divide, and to unify the terrain so to speak using as a rationale an audience that will not longer be placated by escapist fare. 1980 is viewed as inaugurating a 'Great Film Recession' – sometimes also referred to as a 'low tide' or a 'purge' after the glorious decade of the 1970s when all one had to do was "enter the film world, make a commercial film, and make crores" or "make an art film, go to festivals and see the world." (Mehra, 1981, 54) From the vantage of 1982, the 'golden decade' of the 1970s is thus chronicled: "sign Amitabh Bachchan. Failing that there was the second best formula, sign a horde of stars, add Kamal the dance director, add fights by Veeru Devgan or Ravi Khanna, throw in a 100 horses and a 100 dancing girls, do a spell of shooting in Kashmir or Switzerland, build a couple of big sets, build in a revenge theme and some lost and found elements and you just cannot go wrong" (Mehra, 1981, 56). But the advent of new technologies, TV and video, the crashing overseas market, a vibrant regional cinema (in Bangalore there is a move to ban Hindi films, in UP people want films made in Brij Bhasha), means that the "Bollywood era is over" and the too many people have "in the name of mass entertainment, taken the masses for a ride" (Singh 42). So what is likely to work now are "well made, small budget films" for in the last ten years, "a new generation of film audiences has grown up, a generation that rejects mediocrity, hypocrisy, hyperbole and repetitiveness." At the same time, these films are in no danger of being called 'art' or 'experimental' insofar as, in the words of Bikram Singh they reject the chic taboos of the avant garde and achieve, "coherent narrative, naturalistic acting, the spoken words as a means of expression complementary to the visual, tight editing to achieve a fast pace valued in commercial cinema" (41). The list includes film as different as *Shodh* (Return, Biplab Roy Chowdhury, 1979, a satirical ghost story), *Grihapravesh* (Homecoming, Basu Bhattacharya, 1979, extra-marital romance), *Sazaye Maut* (Death Penalty, Vidhu Vinod Chopra, 1981, murder mystery), *Jeena Yahan* (This Life, Basu Chatterjee, 1980, domestic drama), *Aakrosh* (Rage, Govind Nihalini, 1980, urban crime), *Albert Pinto Ka Gussa Kyon Aata Hain* (Why is Albert Pinto Angry? Saaed Mirza, 1980), *Geherayee* (Depth, Aruna Raje, 1980, horror), *Pehla Kadam* (First Step, Kidar Sharma, 1980, Social, offbeat).

In 1981, a *Filmfare* reader asks, "Have the filmfare awards really gone 'arty, arty' this year?" If this view is held by some it is because films like *Kalyug* (d. *Shyam Benegal)*, *Chakra* (d. Rabindra Dharamraj*)* and *Umrao Jaan* (d. Muzaffar Ali) feature in the awards. He goes on to say, "none of the three films mentioned is noteworthy for an extremely subjective and therefore difficult directorial style, and all were made for a mass audience" (Subramanyum 33). The coverage this year of the Filmfare Awards go on to discuss at length the acting prizes – won by Smita Patil, Naseeruddin Shah, Supriya Pathak, and Amjad Khan respectively, noting how thoughtful and natural performances can indeed anchor a film and rubbish the distinction between 'art' and 'commerce,' thus effectively recoding the star system. Remarking that all these actors have made their name in or taken on commercial projects, the film press suggests that new performance norms can change at a molecular level how 'big' cinema works. Further, these performance idioms are theorized as grounded in a new sociology rather than forms of desire (Mullick, 1982). Thus 'the new Devil-May-Care Image of the "In" heroine' is merely the reflection of modern life and modern experience, "a new type of filmmaker has come into prominence propagating this new type of heroine, because there is already a new type of cinemagoer in existence, clamoring for a new, more vivid, more closely-tuned urban cinema" (Vijaykar 56).

This 'molecular' approach is taken by Raman Kumar, FTII graduate and first-time filmmaker, of the box office hit *Saath Saath* produced by Bollywood insider Dilip Dhawan with help from the NFDC. Kumar stresses that this hybrid financing structure is the way forward for popular cinema. He emphasizes that they way the film got made –actors and technicians worked below market value, friends homes were used as locations, post production costs were limited by working in labs during off-peak hours, – was an amalgam of the 'indie' spirit and a toleration for chaos the reigns in the mainstream industry. Kumar suggests that the 'artisanal' mode of production can be channeled towards indie ends precisely because of the lack of structure and rationalities that govern filmmaking in the West. Asked if this film has alienated him from the makers of the 'other' cinema, he responds, "it is not necessary now to have the other cinema ...

the effort is to take two steps towards the commercial cinema and force them to take the other steps towards you." He is hopeful that since there is now an "audience looking for good films," this change is bound to happen (Kumar, 1982). It is interesting to note how the discourse of the audience seems to have come a full circle here – from a new cinema in search of spectators to a young audience in search of a cinema.

Let them have all of it …

The persistence of narrative tropes and production preoccupations from the 1970s in the present in the face of a completely altered media ecology that includes multiplexes, television and new media deserves further study. While first the mass and then the mass/class categorization of the audience may have now yielded place from Malegaon to Mumblecore to the concept of the 'niche' viewer, the will to self-reflection as a key component of reform remains intact. Perhaps this is the most decisive legacy of the Emergency. This event brought home to the industry the dangers of any reformist project activated and managed by the state and its institutions. It also intensified the need for scrutiny, critique and classification that must necessarily accompany the emergence of the new. That so much of contemporary cinema is about *the cinema* might be viewed as symptom of such autonomous drives.

A sample of views expressed by key figures of the New Wave Independent cinema at two recent seminars at the annual THiNK Summit in Goa, 2011 launches the conclusion. One seminar entitled "The Difficulty of Selling Excellence: Movies Bollywood is too Scared to Make"[15] featured Dibakar Banerjee, Abhay Deol and Imran Khan. The other was called "Cinematic Misadventures"[16] and featured Anurag Kashyap, Prakash Jha, Prasoon Joshi and the aforesaid Q. Both panels concurred that audiences now are so varied that all kinds of films will now work in India. "Let them have it all," says Q whose film *Gandu* though screened at festivals worldwide, only had a bit-torrent release online. Knowing that the censors would never clear its color-drenched pornographic finale, Q opted-out by choosing the free download option. When Dibakar Banerjee, notorious for his film *Love, Sex and Dhoka* (Love, Sex and Betrayal, 2011, a film not that sexy per se but a really smart reflection on spectation in a post-celluloid era), was asked what kinds of films is Bollywood afraid to make, he responded "that the kind of cinema Bollywood is afraid to make is the kind of films that India is afraid to see," returning the power as always to the audience. Banerjee went on to say that while the censor was happy to leave the sex in, they made him cut out most of the film's searing depiction of caste violence on the grounds that it might "incite a riot" – a statist characterization of the audience as incapable of handling mediation that has persisted since the colonial era.[17]

Kashyap too alludes to the difficulty of making films with political content (caste and religion primarily), which seems to be the only 'obscenity' in post-liberalization India. The rest of the almost hour-long discussion did not allude to the state at all but rather to the take-over of the film industry by corporates, referred to as 'suits' which Banerjee claimed had actually aided the aesthetically-adventurous filmmaker since the promise of a low-budget film that would be critically acclaimed and give some return on a (small investment) actually appealed to suits. It helps improve the 'image' of the company and garners both social, cultural, and perhaps even monetary capital on a very small outlay. In other words, only the capital-intensive media conglomerate (and not the independent producer who has mortgaged his house and sold his wife's jewels) can afford the risk represented by these *hat-ke* projects. A similar commercial environment is described by Anurag Kashyap and Q, who both promise a brand of cinema that will (and has) at least 'broken even' and even generated some profits. Both panels suggest that 'big' and 'small' films are both inside the 'system' and therefore do not comprise an *avant-garde.* While Prakash Jha and Prasoon Joshi recall an era when state-funding momentarily offered the glimpse of such an *avant-garde*, Kashyap demurs that the state may not be a solution to or a shelter from the market. He is certainly not far off the mark for when we turn to the state-owned NFDC's new website, we notice the emphasis on public-private sponsorships as well as goals that are not much at odds with that of the 'indie' wing of Bollywood conglomerates such as Ronnie Screwvala's UTV. It states that the NFDC's vision is to create, "domestic and global appreciation and celebration of the independent Indian cinema."[18] Thus Kashyap proposes that to be outside the system is not to turn to the state but to opt out of the current film-financing models altogether. He gives as an example the sixty-lakhs he raised for a project through small donations on the internet. Yet Kashyap is hardly a pioneer in this regard. One recalls John Abraham and his Odessa Collective, traveling through rural Kerala in the early 1980s, exhibiting Charles Chaplin's *Kid* to villagers and collecting money that was then used to produce *Amma Ariyan* (Information to my Mother, 1986), a film that went on to receive a non-commercial distribution. Indebted neither to the state nor the market, the Odessa collective represents a rare instance of a truly outsider cinema. Clearly, as both seminars demonstrate, New Wave indie even at its extreme edges prefers to dwell inside. The self-reflexive mode – especially with regard to the cinema of 1970s – therefore signals both an ontology (what cinema is) and a genealogy (where it comes from).

To sum up, the most significant development in Indian cinema in the past decade has been the emergence of this so-called New Wave indie cinema in a variety of languages and across different regional sites. At least in the context of Hindi cinema, the indie resides within and not outside the Bombay-based commercial film industry and, as we have seen above, the relation between the two is sometimes cordial but often uneasy. Moreover, the emergence of this indie scene is a central component in the transformation of Bollywood into New Bollywood, which also corresponds to a transformation of Hindi popular cinema from public culture to a culture industry. As Kashyap and Banerjee describe an industry powered by 'suits,' we begin to realize how decisively cinema has now come under the sway of capital so that 'indie' refers less to a mode of production or means of financing and more to issues of aesthetics and address. This conceptualization of an other cinema and its potential audience as occupying a space continuous with that of the dominant cinema is perhaps an index of Hindi cinema's emergence in recent years as middle-class entertainment. While exhibition, as the 'savetheindie' petition demonstrates, remains a thorny problem, it might only be a matter of time before new media technologies can be efficiently harnessed to create different channels of exhibition. The masala film of the 1970s casts a shadow, no doubt, on mainstream cinema in the present, but the most decisive legacy of this decade might indeed be the New Wave indie as it moves from Malegaon to Mumblecore via New Bollywood.

Notes

1 The production and exhibition history of this documentary is itself quite illuminating of the processes that comprise New Bollywood. Made in 2008 for a Singapore TV channel, *Supermen of Malegaon* was theatrically released by distributor PVR in June of 2012. It had already spent four years on the festival circuits and garnered many awards. The reviews were uniformly positive.
2 These same tropes animate the biopic on Dadasaheb Phalke entitled *Harishchandrachachi Factory* (Paresh Mokashi, 2009), India's official entry to the Oscar's in the foreign language category and available for streaming just a click away at Netflix
3 In a previous work, I have argued that while the 1970s bring "Bollywood" into being, post-liberalization cinema is more properly referred to as "New Bollywood." See Sangita Gopal, *Conjugation: Marriage and Form in New Bollywood Cinema*, Chicago: Chicago University Press, 2011.
4 A number of recent works testify to this including Tejaswani Ganti, *Producing Bollywood* (Durham: Duke University Press, 2012), Sangita Gopal, *Conjugations: Marriage and Form in New Bollywood Cinema* (Chicago: Chicago University Press, 2011), Ashish Rajyadaksha, *Indian Cinema in The Age of Celluloid* (Bloomington: Indiana University Press, 2009), Ravi Vasudevan, *The Melodramatic Public: Film Form and Spectatorship* (London: Palgrave Macmillan, 2011).
5 Approximately revenues of USD 15 million + after taxes that are about 30%.
6 Whether the term NewWave can be applied to Indian cinema in the 1970s or in the present has been, then and now, the subject of great debate. That the elliptical, non-narrative films of figures like Mani Kaul and Kumar Shahani are not the future of a "reformed" Indian cinema was accepted, even by their most ardent defenders, in the 1970s. However, that films such as these should continue to be made (and more importantly funded by FFC/NFDC) even if they comprise a minority cinema seemed to be the issue for the defenders of the Indian New Wave. For others, like Satyajit Ray, these films were simply too eclectic to merit the investment.
7 I trace these debates as they appear in the pages of English language film magazines and trade publications such as *Filmfare, Star and Style, Super, Movie Bazaar*. I consulted interviews with directors, scriptwriters, and stars; editorials by influential film critics and popular historians such as B.K. Karanjia and Firoze Rangoonwala, as well as journalists such as Bunny Reuben and N.N. Sachitanand and would-be filmmakers such as Sriram Raghavan. Representative articles include: Mohan Rakesh, "Let's Decide at the Script Stage." *Filmfare,* Dec 1, 1972, 44-47; B.K. Karanjia, "Art Theatres, at Last!" *Filmfare*, Nov 3, 1972, edit.; N. N. Sachitanand, "The Corn is Entertaining Anyway." *Filmfare*, July 28, 1972, n.p.; Ramesh Saigal, "Stop Underestimating the Filmgoers." *Filmfare,* May 5, 1972, 41-43.
8 Valentina Vitali's work on the "action ingredient" predominant in films targeted towards working class audiences provides a "generic" prehistory of the "angry young man" figure already in the 1960s.
9 Mission Statement of FFC, can be viewed at NFDC: Cinemas of India, www.nfdcindia.com
10 See Ashish Rajyadaksha, *Indian Cinema in the Time of Celluloid*, 231-254.
11 The film press remains relatively muted during the years 1975-76 in terms of direct critiques of the state's actions but constant discussions around what should or should not be censored and references to what films are stuck with the Censor Board alerts us to state's power. Even so occasional articles bring home the Emergency's effects on the film industry. For eg., "So the Censor War is on with Indian Films: 200 full-length Features Stuck in Censors in the Year 1976." *Film Blaze*, Oct 16, 1976.
12 Abbas is not the only one to repeatedly focus on exhibition as the one area where serious reform is needed in order for the smaller film to deliver its box office promise. In 1976, the Samachar Report had proposed a Janata Cinemas Scheme whereby 25000 smaller cinema halls would be built to break the exhibition
13 The term Follywood (that Collaco above rejects) was also used to pejoratively refer to the Hindi film industry. I have found frequent references, the first as early as 1974 in the fanzine *Star and Style.* See Bunny Reuben, "Sharmila Tagore Discusses Women," *Star and Style* (June 21, 1974), 30.
14 See also Naveen, "G.N. Shah: The Money Mogul," *Super*, Feb 28, 1977

15 Can be viewed at http://www.youtube.com/watch?v=KnFhjJ-HhA4
16 Can be viewed at http://www.youtube.com/watch?v=gu8YFsEmzoU
17 See William Mazzarella, *Censorium: Cinema and the Open Edge of Mass Publicity* (Durham: Duke University Press, 2013).
18 www.nfdcindia.com

References

Abbas, K. A. 'The Sword of Censorship Hung Low: Farewell 1976, Welcome 1977', *Film Blaze,* (Jan–Mar, 1977): n.p.

Anand. 'On the Bollywood Beat', *Hindu* (Mar 7, 2004).
http://www.hindu.com/lr/2004/03/07/stories/2004030700390600.htm

Anon. 'Goings On', *Film Blaze* (October 16, 1976): n.p.

Anon. 'Round-Up', *Film Blaze* (July 23, 1977): n.p.

Athique Adrian and Douglas Hill. *The Multiplex in India: The Cultural Economy of Urban Leisure.* London: Routledge, 2010

Bhaneja, Balwant. 'Indian Cinema: Illusion and Reality', *Filmfare* (June 30, 1972): 27–30.

Dass, Janki. 'High Time for Film Revolution in India', *Film Blaze* (Jan–Mar, 1977): n.p.

Dhar, Onirban, et al. 'Save Indie Cinema', http://www.change.org/saveindiecinema, Published September, 2013.

Ganti, Tejaswani. *Producing Bollywood: Inside the Contemporary Hindi Film Industry.* Durham: Duke University Press, 2012.

Gopal, Sangita. *Conjugations: Marriage and Form in New Bollywood Cinema.* Chicago: University of Chicago Press, 2011.

Hardikar, Shyam. 'Multistarrer's Use Music Like Salt and Pepper', *Filmfare* (Jan 16–31, 1980): 29–31.

Joshi, Namrata. 'A Little Thrift', *Outlook* (Mar 8, 2010). http://www.outlookindia.com/article.aspx?264467

—. 'Sirens of Malewood', *Outlook* (May 11, 2009). http://www.outlookindia.com/article.aspx?240414

Karanjia, B. K. 'Art Theatres, at Last!' *Filmfare* (Nov 3, 1972): 1–2.

King, Geoff. *Indiewood Inc: Where Hollywood Meets Independent Cinema.* I.B Tauris: 2009.

Karanjia, B.K. "Art Theatres, at Last!" *Filmfare* (Nov 3, 1972), editorial (np).

Kumar, Raman. 'Two Steps Towards Commercial Cinema', *Filmfare* (July 1–15 1982): n.p.

Lahiri, Monojit. 'The 'Second' Game', *Star and Style* (June 7, 1974): n.p.

Mazzarella, William. *Censorium: Cinema and the Open Edge of Mass Publicity.* Durham: Duke University Press, 2013.

Mehra, Harish. 'The Great Film Recession: Indian Cinema in a Soup', *Filmfare* (July 1–15, 1981): 55–57.

—. 'Two Hours a Day, Five Days in the Year', *Filmfare* (Jan 1–15, 1980): 17–21.

Mullick, Swapan. 'The Heart of a New Indian Cinema', *Filmfare* (March 1–15, 1982): n.p.

Naveen, 'G.N. Shah: The Money Mogul', *Super* (Feb 28, 1977): n.p.

Rajyadaksha, Ashish. *Indian Cinema in the Time of Celluloid: From Bollywood to the Emergency.* Bloomington: Indiana University Press, 2009.

Rakesh, Mohan. 'Let's Decide at the Script Stage', *Filmfare* (Dec 1, 1972): 44–47.

Rangoonwala, Firoze. '1973: The Year in Retrospect', *Star and Style* (Jan 4, 1974): 5.

—. 'Are the Big Films Wiping out the Small Stars', *Star and Style* (Oct 11, 1974): n.p.

Rao, J. S. 'To Reach the Static: An Interview with Mani Kaul', *Filmfare* (Sept 8, 1972): 33–35.

Ray, Satyajit. *Our Films, Their Films.* New Delhi: Orient Longman, 1976.

Reuben, Bunny. 'At The End of Another Year', *Stardust Annual* (Dec 1, 1977): n.p.

—. 'Sharmila Tagore Discusses Women', *Star and Style* (June 21, 1974): 30.

Sachitanand, N. N. 'The Corn is Entertaining Anyway', *Filmfare* (July 28, 1972): n.p.

Saigal, Ramesh. 'Stop Underestimating the Filmgoers', *Filmfare* (May 5, 1972): 41–43
Singh, Bikram. 'Odd Films Out', *Filmfare* (Dec 16-31, 1980): 42–43.
Subramanyam, K. N. 'Filmfare Awards: All the Films were Made for a Mass Audience', *Filmfare (*July 1-15, 1980): 32–36.
Valecha, Vijay. 'The Promise of Gross Cinema', *Filmfare* (July 1-15, 1982): 31–33
Vasudevan, Ravi. *The Melodramatic Public: Film Form and Spectatorship*. London: Palgrave Macmillan, 2011.
Vijaykar, R. M. 'A New Leading Man, A New Leading Lady and a Formula Story', *Filmfare* (Oct 1–15, 1981): 56.
Vitali, Valentina. *Hindi Action Cinema: Industries, Narratives, Bodies*. New Delhi: Oxford University Press, 2009.
Vohra, Vikram. 'Ab Kya Hoga: What Now?' *Film Blaze* (Mar 25, 1977): n.p.

Filmography

Aakrosh. Dir. Govind Nihalini, 1980. Krsna Movie Enterprises. Film.
Aaaranya Kaandam. Dir. Thiagarajan Kumararaja, 2010. Capital Works. Film
Agneepath. Dir. Karan Malhotra, 2012. Dharma Productions. Film.
Albert Pinto Ka Gussa Kyon Aata Hain. Dir. Saeed Mirza, 1980. Saeed Mirza Productions. Film.
Amar, Akbar, Anthony. Dir. Manmohan Desai, 1977. Hirawat Jain and Company. Film.
Amma Ariyan. Dir. John Abraham, 1986. Odessa. Film
Autograph. Dir. Srijit Mukherjee, 2010. Shree Venkatesh Films. Film.
Chakra. Dir. Rabindra Dharamraj, 1981. Neo Films. Film.
Charitraheen. Dir. Shakti Samanta, 1973. Debesh Ghosh Films. Film.
Charulata. Dir. Satyajit Ray,1964. R. D. Bansal Films. Film.
Charulathayude Bakki. Dir. Sangeeta Padmanabhan, 2010.
Chemeen. Dir. Ramu Kariat, 1967. Kanmani Films. Film.
Don. Dir. Chandra Barot, 1978. Nariman Films. Film.
Gandu. Dir. Q, 2010. Kaushik Mukherjee. Film.
Garam Hawa. Dir. M.S. Sathyu, 1973. Film Finance Corporation. Film.
Geherayee. Dir. Aruna Raje, 1980. Arikam. Film
Ghajini. Dir. A.R. Murugadoss, 2008. Geetha Arts. Film.
Gharonda. Dir. Bhim Sain, 1977. Climb Media. Film.
Girl in Yellow Boots. Dir. Anurag Kashyap, 2010. Anurag Kashyap Films/NFDC. Film.
Grihapravesh. Dir. Basu Bhattacharya, 1979. Aarohi Films. Film.
Kalyug. Dir. Shyam Benegal, 1981. Filmwallahs. Film.
Koshish. Dir. Gulzar, 1973. Sippy Films. Films.
Lagaan Dir. Ashutosh Gowarikar, 2001. Aamir Khan Productions. Film.
"Life! Camera, Action…," Dir. Rohit Gupta, 2010. Dot Feather Entertainment. Film.
Love, Sex, Aur Dhoka. Dir. Dibakar Banerjee, 2011. ALT Entertainment/Freshwater Films. Film.
Malegaon ke Sholay Dir. Shaikh Nasir, 2000.
Once Upon a Time in Mumbai Dir. Milan Luthria, 2010. Balaji Motion Pictures. Film.
Paan Singh Tomar/ Dir. Tigmangshu Dhulia, 2010. UTV Spotboy. Film.
Padatik. Dir. Mrinal Sen, 1970. Mrinal Sen Productions. Film.
Phas Gaye Re Obama. Dir. Subhash Kapoor, 2010. Revel Films Film.
Rangeela. Dir. Ram Gopal Verma, 1995. Jhanu Sughand Films. Film.
Raavanan. Dir. Mani Ratnam, 2010. Madras Talkies. Film
Saath Saath. Dir. Raman Kumar, 1982. Film Company. Film.
Saudagar. Dir. Sudhendu Roy, 1973. Rajshri Productions. Film.
Sazaye Maut. Dir. Vidhu Vinod Chopra, 1981. Vinod Chopra Films. Film.

Shodh. Dir. Biplab Roy Chowdhury, 1979. Kalinga Films. Film.
Sholay. Dir. Ramesh Sippy, 1975. United Producers/Sippy Films. Film.
Subarnarekha. Dir. Ritwik Ghatak, 1964. Film Finance Corporation. Film
Supermen of Malegaon. Dir. Faiza Ahmad Khan, 2008. KBS Productions. Film.
The Untitled Kartik Krishnan Project. Dir. Srinivas Sunderrajan, 2010. Enterguerilla Films. Film.
Umrao Jaan. Dir. Muzaffar Ali, 1981. Integrated Films. Film.
Uski Roti. Dir. Mani Kaul, 1970. Film Finance Corporation. Film.

WORKING NOTE

From ceiling fans to A/C and juice: Javed Akhtar in conversation with Priya Joshi

Priya Joshi

Temple University, Philadelphia, USA

Javed Akhtar attended an international workshop on the 1970s and its legacies hosted at Temple University in April 2011, where he held a public conversation with Priya Joshi before an audience of roughly 300 people. A selection of Mr. Akhtar's remarks appears below.

As co-writer of some of the biggest blockbusters of Hindi cinema in the 1970s, Javed Akhtar is also a renowned poet and lyricist whose words have captured the exhilaration and ennui of modern India. His dialogues—*Mere pas Maa hain* and *Kitne admi the?*—have stepped out of the screen and are today the stuff of modern folklore. It is no wonder that he has won every major film award in India numerous times, including 14 Filmfare awards. In addition to his work as a writer, Akhtar is an outspoken figure on matters of social justice and secularism. His efforts have been recognized by appointment as Member of Parliament to the Rajya Sabha as well as the Padma Shree and Padma Bhushan, awarded by the President of India for exemplary citizenship.

At Temple, Akhtar spoke on the 1970s and his start in Hindi cinema, his career as poet and lyricist, and Hindi cinema today, an industry he characterized as devoted to the 'A/C and juice generation.' Akhtar's remarks capture the dramatic changes India is currently undergoing. He describes lining up as a boy in the 1950s to see his first television set at the US Pavilion in New Delhi, when a Murphy radio and a ceiling fan were his family's only 'technology.' Today, he regularly issues Tweets to a quarter of a million followers and composes ghazals on his laptop.

Akhtar outlines the changes undergone by India's middle classes from the 1960s when a humanities education was a passport to advancement to today, when professional credentials have replaced education in the humanities. Culture takes generations to acquire, he avers; but it also takes many generations to lose. As a confirmed secularist, he remains confident that the communal threat is a thing of the past, even as he insists that communalism for *any* side is communalism for *all* sides.

During the public conversation, Akhtar describes his insomniac working habits and, relatedly, the dream-language of popular cinema that requires a special vocabulary to fully uncover. He remains optimistic that the cinema of India's Golden Ages (the 1950s and 1970s) is not a thing of the past: that eventually, today's A/C and juice generation of filmmakers will speak more fully to the many Indias that are currently ignored in their drive to capture the well-heeled multiplex audience.

A selection of Mr Akhtar's remarks addressing the themes of this special issue appears here. A streaming video of the full conversation is archived at http://www.templetv.net/shows/university-lecture-series/javed-akhtar-2011.

Priya Joshi:

When one hears of India today, many of the following terms come to mind: an economic powerhouse, a keen global player, a thriving democracy with an outspoken press and an independent judiciary, and so on. Yet the cinema of this last decade seems somewhat light and fluffy. One almost has to ask, what happened to the 1970s?

Let's begin our conversation today with the 1970s and wind our way eventually to India today, 'India Shining,' or 'India Rising' as some of its boosters call it. Take us back to your early days in the film industry.

Javed Akhtar:

There is a hypnotic quality about cinema, and that is why so many people go to make their fortune there. They are mad enough to take the plunge. I was born in a family where almost everybody was a writer, and a known writer. Books were widely available. I started reading literature at a very young age. At the same time, I was fascinated by cinema. If you read fiction and watch film, there comes a point when you think this book could have been a film, or this short story, or this play, or this novel. And that was how by the time I was in my early teens I had decided that after I completed my formal education, I would one day work as an assistant to some director for a while, and then I would make my own films. I had no idea that I would become a writer. After graduating, I went to Bombay, and somehow I found a job with Mr Kamal Amrohi. My first salary in the film industry was 50 rupees per month. What more can you ask for as a beginner?

I was working under a director, Mr Madhusudhan, and I had to ask him because I had no idea what a screenplay is. So he asked me, 'Do you know what a novel is?' I said 'yes.' 'Or a play or a short story or a poem?' I said, 'Yes of course.' He said 'Have you read a book that tells you what a novel or a short story is, or how to write a short story, or a novel?' I said no. 'Then how do you recognize it as a novel?' I said, 'because I've read novels.' 'Alright then: why don't you read a screenplay?' That made sense to me. The first book I could get hold of was *20 Best Screenplays of Hollywood— All That Money Can Buy* (1941) and *Little Caesar* (1931) and *The Women* (1939) and *The Good Earth* (1937). That is how I came to know about screenplays.

When we [Salim Khan and Javed Akhtar] wrote screenplays, we never thought that these were changing times with a kind of turmoil on a social and political level: we were blissfully unaware of everything. We were just writing screenplays. For us, these were stories, and I'm happy that we were unaware of the social, political, and economic relevance of these stories. Because if we would have been aware of it, it would have meant that we were seeing all of this from the outside as observers.

But we were not observers; we were part of that situation, and that is why we were unaware of it consciously. Somehow in our feeling, our understanding, our aesthetics of priorities, we were in sync with society, and that is how this character came into existence called the Angry Young Man, as it was described later.

We were going around with a script [for *Zanjeer*] where the hero wouldn't sing a song, wouldn't have a romantic scene, wouldn't have any comedy scenes, wouldn't smile. What kind of a hero is this? Most of the directors rejected the script automatically. God bless his soul if there is a God or a soul, Mr Prakash Mehra bought it, and he stuck to this script; somehow he liked it. He stuck to the script even when one after another all the viable actors rejected it. There is a long list, and I don't want to mention all the names because it might be embarrassing for them. They couldn't see that the script would work.

Meanwhile I had seen a couple of films which did not do well at the box office with a tremendously talented actor called Amitabh Bachchan. I kept on suggesting to Prakash Mehra that he should take Bachchan for this role—he would be the best choice. But Prakash Mehra obviously had to sell the film—as a producer he had certain responsibilities—so he kept trying different stars who were saleable at that time. Ultimately, since he had no choice, he opted for Amitabh, and I respect him for that because most of the producers would have dropped the script. That was how *Zanjeer* was made. Then came *Deewaar* and *Sholay*, and *Trishul*, but this was the breakthrough. Selling *Deewaar* was perhaps equally difficult but not as difficult as *Zanjeer* was.

When people write about these films [*Deewaar*, *Trishul*, *Zanjeer*], everybody has 20/20 vision in retrospect. Now we can see that, yes, those were the times where extra-constitutional forces were arising on the horizon, those were the times where the judgments of high courts were being overruled, those were the times when for the first time after Independence the average Indian was losing faith in institutions. A cynicism had set in. It is not a surprise that in such an atmosphere, a character of a vigilante was given a warm reception and was accepted. Because ultimately, who is a hero? A hero is the personification of contemporary morality and contemporary aspirations. That is why at a time where morality changes and aspirations change, heroes change. So perhaps that was the contemporary morality and aspiration that gave birth to the Angry Young Man.

Priya Joshi:

India has changed since the 1940s and 1950s, and certainly since the 1970s. It is different, it is wealthier, and that wealth is allegedly reaching more people. But your work as an activist and in Parliament has drawn attention to inequalities in Indian society. 'India Rising' and 'India Shining' are chapters of a story that exist on one plane but not on many others. The cinema of the twenty-first century seems to have largely forgotten this other India. Why has Hindi cinema turned away from the stories of this India?

Javed Akhtar:

In the last 30 years, India has progressed by leaps and bounds. When I was young, the only kind of gadget we had at home was one electric iron, one Murphy radio, which no child was allowed to touch, and one ceiling fan. That's about all. When I was 12 years old, we went to Delhi on a school tour, and we stood in a 2-mile-long line in front of the American Pavilion, and it took us almost an hour to reach the television because there used to be a queue to see the television at that time in India. We were not supposed to stop in front of it: after an hour of standing in the queue, we just had to pass and say, 'Oh, that's a television!' And that is how I saw my first television.

When my granddaughter was 5 years old, I decided to take her around in my car, so she came with her nanny, and the nanny sat next to the driver, and she sat with me like a young lady, and as the car started she looks toward the driver—as a 5-year-old kid—and says

'A/C' so he put the A/C on and then she looks toward her nanny and says 'juice.' I was so demoralized and intimidated: when I was 5 years old I had no idea of A/C or juice for that matter.

The standard of living in urban India has changed: in the last 25 years, we have brought some 200 million people, if not more, into the middle-class income bracket. This 200 million is slightly lower than the American population. So this is not ordinary, but when you have 1.2 billion people, you think that the 200 million looks very small. But this number is increasing, and people are getting empowered, but there are still many who are out of this privileged, charmed class, particularly in rural India. There are areas where this prosperity has yet to reach. In a way, society is divided between the privileged and that class that has yet to enjoy the benefit of India's progress. Hopefully, it soon will.

People who are making films today are the children of people who came up, and these are privileged children. They were born in a particular segment of society, and they understand that society. You can't blame them for that. They understand the person who goes to the multiplex because they socialize with him or her, so they are more comfortable making films for this person. Creatively, it is convenient, and economically it is suitable because they'll get more money. It is safer.

They don't understand the man who is living in the hinterland, they have never gone there, they have never lived there, they have never interacted with that person. What is happening is that much the way you have hospitals, and hotels, and colleges for rich and poor, and colonies and buildings and flats for rich and poor, now you have cinema for rich and poor, and this cinema that you're talking about is being made for the privileged. The privileged is having a party, the privileged doesn't want to be disturbed by being told that old people are dying, or the tribals have this problem, or in Benares widows are still being treated like this. They just don't want to see that.

I'm not pessimistic, and I have great hope for the future. I believe that culture is the last thing to come and the last thing to go. It takes almost three generations to acquire culture, and it takes almost three generations to lose it. It's the last thing you lose. This new middle class that has come up will take a little time to acquire that kind of sensitivity which was there in the 1950s and 1960s among the traditional middle class. Many from the middle class of my childhood were educated as teachers, professors, doctors, engineers, or bureaucrats, and so on. But in industrialization, what happened is that any major industry has not many ancillaries, and people who become middle class through these ancillaries need not be very educated people.

But once they are privileged, they start sending their children to a better school, the children grow up in, shall I say, better A/C. After that, there are many other things, so after A/C and juice they move forward and find other things. I think our younger generation is in that process. When I go to different colleges and universities, I realize that there is a revival of interest in poetry among young people. No thanks to us—we did not give it to them because we were busy doing other things.

They are realizing that there is more to life than A/C and juice. I think it will take a little time, but certain changes have already taken place. If you see the cinema of 1990s and the cinema of today, you see that we have acquired sophistication, but that sophistication is still only skin deep. This sophistication should turn into sensitivity and sophisticated thoughts: it will take a little time, but it is inevitable, and again you will have films like *Do Bigha Zameen* or *Sahib Bibi aur Ghulam* or *Pyaasa*. It will take a little time, but it will happen.

Acknowledgements

The editors of this volume offer heartfelt thanks to Nasreen Munni Kabir for her friendship and support. Her foundational books, *Talking Films* (1999) and *Talking Songs* (2005), invaluably archive Hindi cinema and Javed Akhtar's career in it. Akhtar's memoir, 'About Myself' (2001), offers an account of his arrival in Bombay and the combination of grit and good luck that propelled his success in films.

Priya Joshi's public conversation with Javed Akhtar in Philadelphia invited him to elaborate on topics fleetingly mentioned in his books with Kabir and to develop themes of more recent interest to scholars working on India's cinemas. We are deeply grateful to Javed Akhtar for his candor and courtly generosity during his visit. Special thanks to Daniel Ryan Morse for transcribing Mr Akhtar's public remarks; Rajinder Dudrah for his perspective and collaboration in planning the workshop and this volume; and Orfeo Fioretos for his immeasurable support and keen critical eye. Priya Joshi selected and edited the transcript for publication in this volume.

References

Akhtar, Javed. 'About Myself.' *Quiver: Poems and Ghazals*. Trans. David Matthews. New Delhi: HarperCollins, 2001.

Kabir, Nasreen Munni. *Talking Films: Conversations on Hindi Cinema with Javed Akhtar*. New Delhi: Oxford UP, 1999.

Kabir, Nasreen Munni. *Talking Songs: Javed Akhtar in Conversation with Nasreen Munni Kabir*. New Delhi: Oxford UP, 2005.

Filmography

Deewaar. Dir. Yash Chopra. Eros Entertainment. 1975. Film.

Do Bigha Zameen. Dir. Bimal Roy. Yash Raj Films. 1953. Film.

Pyaasa. Dir. Guru Dutt. Yash Raj Films. 1957. Film.

Sahib Bibi aur Ghulam. Dir. Abrar Alvi. Yash Raj Films. 1962. Film.

Sholay. Dir. Ramesh Sippy. Eros Entertainment. 1975. Film.

Trishul. Dir. Yash Chopra. Eros Entertainment. 1978. Film.

Zanjeer. Dir. Prakash Mehra. Eros Entertainment. 1973. Film.

Index

Note:
Page numbers in **bold** type refer to figures
Page numbers followed by 'n' refer to notes

Aaranya Kaandam (2010) 123
Abbas, K.A. 126
Abhimaan (1973) 40–1
Abraham, J. 83, 131; Odessa Collective 131
aesthetic argument 91
aesthetic contract 46n
aesthetic dislocations 89–98
aesthetic of mobilization 44
affability 4, 42, 44
Affable Young Man 4, 36–46; advent 42–4
afterlives: 1970s Hindi cinema 120–35
Agneepath (2012) 121
Agraharathil Kazhudhai (1978) 83
Ahammad, N. 94
Aitraaz (2004) 58
Akhtar, F. 23
Akhtar, J. 5, 8, 10, 21n, 136–9; cinema 137; culture 139; *Deewar* (1975) 14; Hindi cinema 136; India's living standards 139; India's middle classes 136; screenplays 137; Vijay Varma 15–16
Ali, M. 129
Alibabavum Narpathu Thirudargalum (1956) 78
alternative cinema 123
Aman, Z. 50–9; cosmopolitan antecedents 51; femininity 59n; sexual politics 50; sexuality 59n
Amar Akbar Anthony (1977) 27, 28, 44, 106–7; fictive kinship 26–9
Amar Prem (1971) 96
Anand (1971) 40
Anand, D. 51, 52
Ananda Vikatan 83
Angry Young Man 4, 39, 41, 44, 116, 132n
Anjaria, U. 23–33
Antony, P.J. 94
Arriflex camera 5
Athithi (1975) 90, 94, 95
Autograph (2010) 123
Aval Appadiththan (1978) 82
AVM Studios (Madras) 78–9

Babu, R. 83
Bachchan, A. 8, 32, 40, 41, 42; coded values 44
Backer, P.A. 90, 94
Balan (1938) 78
Banerjee, D. 130, 131
Bangladesh War (1971) 1
Barjatya, S. 66–7, 70
Baskaran, T.S. 78
Bawarchi (1972) 41
behavior: mimetic 72; participatory 72
Benegal, S. 129
Bharatan, R. 47n
Bharatha Vilas (1973) 81
Bharathiraja, P. 83, 84
Bharucha, R. 46
Bhattacharya, B. 38
Bhushan, B. 73n
blockbusters 2–6; Hindi cinema 62–73
blood bonds 25–6, 28
Bollywood 127, 128–9, 130; New 3, 122–3, 132–3n; term 117n; 2000s cinema and 1970s Hindi films 101–17
Bombay cinema 62, 66
Bordwell, D.: on Hollywood 77
Bresson, R. 83
BRICS (Brazil, Russia, India, China, South Africa) 111, 117n
brotherhood: and queer kinship 30–2
Buckland, W. 77
buddy films 33n

camera: Arriflex 5
capitalism: world 37–8
censorship 125, 126, 130, 132n
Chakra (1981) 129
Chakravarthy, V. 78
Chandralekha (1948) 79
Charulata (1964) 126
Charulathayude Bakki (2010) 123
Chatterjee, B. 3, 36, 38, 39, 43, 45
Chatterjee, P.: Indian cities governance 47n
Chemeen (1967) 126

Chemmeen (1965) 90
Chhoti Si Baat (1975) 42
Chit Chor (1976) 43
Chithralekha 93
Chopra, Y. 20n, 25, 30
cities governance 47n
civility 39, 41, 47n
class: middle 36, 37, 41, 43, 136; upper 39; working 39
Cold War cinema: US 19
Collaco, B. 127
corruption 1
cricket match ritual 74n
cultic behavior 72
culture: public 3
Cyril, S. 105

Dass, J. 126
DCH (*Dil Chata Hai*) (2001) 23
Deewar (1975) 8, 9, 11–15, 16, 25–6, 62; family 10–11; latent narrative 13–15; 'lost-and-found formula' 25; manifest narrative 11–13
Deleuze, G. 86n
Delhi Belly (2011) 102–3, 109–15; Disco Fighter 111, 113–14, **114**; DVD menu screen **110**; *masala* genre 115–16; retro uses 109
Deo, A. 102, 109
Desai, M. 26, 44, 107
desire: and homosociality 29–30
devotional songs (*bhajans*) 65
Dhandekar, A. 113
Dhar, O. 124
Dharamraj, R. 129
Dhawan, D. 129
Die Hard (1988) 77
Dil Chata Hai (2001) 23
dislocation: aesthetic 89–98
diurnal rites 62
Doordarshan televison 3
Dravida Munnetra Kazhagam/Dravidian Progressive Front 79
Dudrah, R. 5–6, 34n, 101–17; and Joshi, P. 1–7
Dum Maaro Dum (2011) 60n
Dyer, R. 43

Elsaesser, T. 77

family 10–11; broken 24–9; and sexuality 23–33
family romance: cinema as 8–19; as liberation narrative 11
femininity 59n; construction of 50–9; stereotypes 40–1
fictive kinship 26–9
Film Finance Corporation (FFC) 2, 38, 122, 125–6, 128
Film and Television Institute of India (FTII) 1
Filmfare 129
folklore: oral 15
Follywood 132n
food shortages 1
Freud, S. 11
Furgele, J. 109

Gabriel, K. 46n
Gandhi, I. 1, 3, 41; Emergency 14, 24, 69–70, 125–6
Gandu (2010) 123
Ganesan, S. 76, 79–81; career 81
Ganti, T. 128; 'lost-and-found formula' 24
gaze 92–3
gazing: politics 50
Geertz, C. 62
Gehlawat, A. 4–5, 50–9
Gemini Studios (madras) 79
gender: norms 40; social politics 41
genre: *masala* 115–16
Ghatak, R. 83, 126
Girl in Yellow Boots (2010) 123
Golmaal (1979) 44
Gopal, S. 5, 6, 120–35
Gopalan, L. 54
Gopinath, G. 33n
Guddi (1971) 44
Guffey, E. 102
Guffrey, E. 101
Gulzar 38

Haasan, K. 5
HAHK (*Hum Aapke Hain Koun..!*) (1994) 63, 66–8; *JSM* comparison 69–73, **71**
Hare Rama Hare Krishna (1971) 51
Harishchandrachachi (2009) 132n
Hindi cinema 1, 5, 8, 9, 33n, 136; afterlives 120–35, 121–31; blockbusters 62–73; family romances 18; middle-class melodramas 36; scholars 70
Hindi films (1970s) 117n; in 2000s Bollywood 101–17
Hindustan 12
historical forms: in Indian cinema 46–7n
Hollywood 77, 125; melodrama 20n
homosociality: and desire 29–30
HRHK (*Hare Rama Hare Krishna*) (1971) 51
Hum Aapke Hain Koun..! (1994) *see HAHK*
Hum Kisise Kum Naheen (1977) 110
Hussain, N. 25, 53, 110

Ideology of the Hindi Film, The (Prasad) 73n
I'll Die for Mama (1975) *see Deewar* (1975)

Imaginary Signifier, The (Metz) 98
India: corruption 1; food shortages 1; global oil crisis 1; labour stoppages 1; modern mythologies 9; nationalist discourses 38; Oedipal narratives 14–15; political crisis/change 36, 138; political life 37; wars 1
India-Pakistan War (1971) 24
Indian cinema 3; legacies 2; 1970s 1–7
Indian New Wave 124–5, 126, 131, 132n
inner view 50
International Business Overview Standard 20n
Iqbal, M. 12

Jagannathan, P. 113
Jai Santoshi Maa (1975) 63–6; *HAHK* (1994) comparison 69–73, **71**
Jameson, F. 102
Jha, P. 31, 131
Jhunjihunwala, U. 51
Joshi, P. 4, 8–19, 131, 136–9; cinema as family romance 8–19; and Dudrah, R. 1–7
JSM (1975) *see Jai Santoshi Maa* (1975)
Jurmana (1979) 44

Kabaneenadhi Chuvannappol (*Kabanee*) (1975) 94–6
Kaif, K. 58
Kalyug (1981) 129
Kamal Studio (Ludhiana, Punjab) 44
Kambakkht Ishq (2009) 58–9
Kanagal, P. 84
Kapoor, K. 58
Kapoor, R. 29
Karasseri, S. 97
Kariat, R. 90, 126
Karunanidhi, M. 79–80
Kasbekar, A. 60n
Kashyap, A. 130–1
Kaviraj, S. 3
Kazmi, F. 44, 51
Kazmi, N. 45–6
Kerala 95–6; film societies 93
Khan, F. 50, 57, 120
Khan, G. 103
Khan, I. 103
Khan, M. 84
Khan, Sabir 58
Khan, Salim 10
Khan, Salman 67
Khan, Shah R. 102, 103
Kimmel, M. 42
kinship: fictive 26–9; queer 30–2; terms 33n
Klapp, O.E. 47n
Kumar, A. 86
Kumar, M. 50
Kumar, R. 129
Kumaran, K.P. 90, 94

Lal, V. 20n
Lalita, K.: and Tharu, S. 37–8
latent narrative 13–15
legacies 3–4
Life! Camera, Action... (2010) 123
living standards: India 139
lost-and-found formula 24–5
Love, Sex and Dhoka (2011) 130
Lutgendorf, P. 62–73
Luthria, M. 121

Mctiernan, J. 77
Madhya Pradesh: Santoshi Maa 64
madhyavarthi cinema (middle-brow cinema) 98
Madras 5, 77–8; studios and Tamil films 78–9
Madurai Veeran (1956) 79
Mahatma (1982) 3
Mahendran, J. 85
Mahindra Indo-American Arts Council Festival (MIACC) 122
Maine Pyar Kiya (1989) 67, 70
Maintenance of Internal Security Act (1971) 84
Malayalam cinema 5, 89–98; art house 90; independence from Madras 89; parallel cinema 2, 3, 90, 126
Malegaon ke Sholay (2000) 120–1
Malhotra, K. 121
manifest narrative 11–13
marriage 67–9
masala genre 115–16
masculinity 42
maternal power 15
media scholars 45
Mehra, P. 24
melodrama 95; Hollywood 59n; middle-class 36
Menon, N.: and Nigam, A. 46n
Metz, C. 98
MGR (M.G. Ramachangran) 5, 76, 79–81; persona 80; persona as oppressed 81
middle class 41, 136; cinema (1970s) 37, 43, 47n; melodramas 36
middle-brow cinema (*madhyavarthi cinema*) 98
mimetic behavior 72
Mirza, A. 45
Modern Theatres Ltd (Tamil Nadu) 78
Mother India (1957) 84
Motion Pictures Exporters Association of America (MPEAA) 38
Mukherjee, H. 3, 36, 38, 39, 40, 44, 45
Mukherjee, M. 52
multiplex cinema/film 47–8n, 123

Mulvey, L. 9, 59n
Mumblecore 121
Muthu, M.K. 80
mythologies: modern 9

Nagarajan, A.P. 81
Nair, K.B. 97
Nair, K.S. 94
Nair, V.C. 92
Nam Naadu (1969) 80
Namak Haraam (1973) 40, 41
Nandancode, B. 84
Nandy, A. 42; Hindi popular cinema 33n
narrative: latent 13–15; manifest 11–13; mechanisms 24; Oedipal 14–15; rupture 23
Nasir, S. 120
National Film Development Corporation (NFDC) 122
nationalism 16
nationalist discourses 38
Nayak (2010) 123
Nehru, J. 10
Nehruvian consensus 46n
New Bollywood cinema 3, 122, 132–3n
New Indian Cinema 89
New Wave (indie) 124–5, 126, 131, 132n
Nigam, A.: and Menon, N. 46n
Nivas, P. 83
nostalgia 102
Notani, S. 78
noughties films: retro 101–17

Oedipal narratives 14–15
Om Shanti Om (2007) 102, 103–9; DVD menu screen **104**; multi-genre 115; 1970s filmmaking practices 115; Om Makhija 103, 106, **107**, **108**; Pappu Master 106, **108**; Shantipriya 103, 106, **107**
Once Upon a time in Mumbai (2010) 121
oral folklore 15

Padatik (1973) 125
Padukone, D. 102
Palekar, A. 41, 42, 43
parallel cinema 2, 3, 47n, 90, 126
participatory behavior 72
Partition 24–5
personal tension 40
Phalke, D. 132n
Phas Gaye Re Obama (2010) 123
Pillai, S.E. 5, 76–86, 98n
pleasure 6
Poduval, S. 3, 4, 36–46
political crisis/change 36
politics: gazing 50; sexual 50; social 41
popular film (1970s) 23; desire 29–30; homosociality 29–30; rupture narrative 23
post-classical turn 76–86
postmodernism 102
Prakesh Rao, T. 79
Prasad, M.M. 9, 20n, 38–9, 70, 73n, 98n; Indian cinema 44–5; viewing positions 39
Priyadarshi, P. 63
progressive realism 38
psychoanalysis 20n
public culture 3
Punniya Bhoomi (1978) 84

queer kinship: and brotherhood 30–2
Qurbani (1980) 50; Sheela 57–9

Raavanan (2010) 122–3
Radhakrishnan, R. 5, 89–98
Rai, A. 58
Rai, B. 40
Rajadhyaksha, A. 93
Rajaraja Cholan (1973) 81
Rajasthan: Santoshi Maa 64
Rajnigandha (1974) 38, 42, 44, 47n
Rajshri Productions 46
Ramachandran, M.G. *see* MGR
Ramanujan, A.K. 14, 15; India's oral folklore 15
Rangoonwala, F. 125
Rao, K. 109
Ratnam, M. 5
Ray, M. 52
Ray, S. 124, 126
re-take 94–7
realism 90, 92–3, 97–8; progressive 38
Red Chillies Entertainment 103
Rekha (Bhanurekha Ganesan) 32
Retro: The Culture of Revival (Guffey) 101
retro: as cultural device 102; noughties films 101–17; uses of 1970s 109
ritual/rites 62–73
RKM (1974) *see Roti Kapada aur Makaan* (1974)
Rogin, M. 9
romance: family 8–19
Rosenthal, G. 124
Roti Kapada aur Makaan (1974) 50; Rajesh 57; Sheetal 53–6
Row Kavi, A. 34n
Roy, B. 38
Rudraiah, C. 82
Rukh Khan, S. 45
rupture narrative 23

Saath Saath (1982) 129
Salim-Javed 20n
Samachar Report (1976) 132n
Samanta, S. 96
Sangam (1964) 29

Sankara Pillai, G. 92
Santoshi Maa: origins 64
Sanyal, K. 37
scholars 70; media 45
Screen 72
screenplays 63–4, 137
Screwvala, R. 45, 131
Sen, J. 39n, 47n
Sen, M. 125
Sengupta, R. 38
Seth, S. 37
sexual politics 50
sexuality 50–9, 59n; and family 23–33
Shakti (1982) 8
ShantRaj Enterprises (Jaipur) 17
Sharma, V. 64
Sheela 94
Sheikh, M. 104; *Om Shanti Om* (2007) 105–6, 107
Sholay (1975) 8, 29, 107
Shri 420 (1955) 59n
Silsila (1981): brotherhood and queer kinship 30–2; transgression 32
Singh Bedi, R. 38
Sippy, R. 17, 29, 107
16 Vayathiniley (1977) 83, 84
social politics: of gender 41
social types (Klapp) 47n
song 30, 65; devotional (*bhajans*) 65; sequences 50–9, 59n, 63
South Asian International Film Festival (SAIFF) 122–4
spectator 90–4
Srinivas, S.V. 47n
Star and Style 125
state conflict 16
stereotypes: femininity 40–1
Subarnarekha (1964) 126
Sundaram, T.R. 78
Sunderrajan, S. 121
Supermen of Malegaon (2008) 120
Sussman, H. 46n
Swayamvaram (1972) 90–1

Tamil cinema 1, 5; classical period 77; Madras studios 78–9; 1970s 76–86
technicians 81–6
television: serials 45
Tharu, S.: and Lalita, K. 37–8
THiNK Summit (2011) 130
Thomas, R. 33n
Tirulokachandar, A.C. 81
Tomkins, J. 20n
transgression 32
Trishul (1978) 8, 10, 16, 20n

Umrao Jaan (1981) 129
Untitled Kartik Krishnan Project (2010) 121, 123
upper class 39
US (United States): cinema 9; Cold War cinema 19
Uthamaputhiran (1958) 79
Uthirippookkal (1979) 85
UTV 131; Motion Pictures 109

vamp 60n
Vasan, S.S. 79
Vasudevan, R.: historical forms in Indian cinema 46–7n; narrative mechanisms 24
Venkiteshwaran 98
Verma, A. 109
Vijaya-Vauhimi Studios 79
Vijayan, K. 84
violence: India 9
Virdi, J. 20n
Vitali, V. 47n, 132n
Vohra, V. 128

weddings 67–9
Willemen, P. 93
Wood, J.W. 98
working class 39
world capitalism 37–8

Yaadhaarthyathinte Naalu Mukahangal 94
Yaadon (ki Baaraat) (1973) 25, 28, 53
Yoganand, D. 79

Zanjeer (1973) 24

